Peter Fenton was born in Boggabri, NSW, in 1936.

He has written and co-produced documentary films, and has established a stellar career as a sound mixer on around 150 films. Film and television credits include: *Sunday Too Far Away, Newsfront, Picnic at Hanging Rock, My Brilliant Career, The Devil's Playground, The Year of Living Dangerously, Gallipoli,* 'The Harp in the South', 'A Fortunate Life', *Six Degrees of Separation* and *Paradise Road.*

He is the author of six books: *Sport the Way I Speak It*; *Syringes in the Locker*; and *I'll Meet You Down The Pub,* all consisting of sporting anecdotes and poetry on sport; *Les Darcy the Legend of the Fighting Man,* a biography on the famous boxer; *For the Sake of the Game,* the story of the 1928 NSW Rugby team's tour of the UK, France and Canada; and *Riding on Courage,* a biography of jockey Wayne Harris.

Somehow while working and writing, Peter has also found the time to coach first grade and representative rugby. He was awarded the Australian Sports Medal for services to Rugby in 2000.

He is a columnist for ACP's *Inside Rugby Magazine* as well as for test match and Super 12 programs. He is also a regular speaker at corporate and charity functions.

Olive Weston: The heroic life of a World War II nurse is his seventh book.

To Dinkie, + Brian
from Sally's next door
neighbour who loves
our Ollie,

Regards

Ollie

1/1/2012.

OLIVE WESTON
The heroic life of a World War II nurse

PETER FENTON

Foreword by Nancy Wake

HarperCollins*Publishers*

HarperCollins*Publishers*

First published in Australia in 2003
This edition published in 2004
by HarperCollins*Publishers* Pty Limited
ABN 36 009 913 517
A member of the HarperCollins*Publishers* (Australia) Pty Limited Group
www.harpercollins.com.au

Copyright © Peter Fenton and Olive Weston 2003

The right of Peter Fenton to be identified as the moral rights
author of this work has been asserted by him in accordance with
the *Copyright Amendment (Moral Rights) Act 2000* (Cth).

This book is copyright.
Apart from any fair dealing for the purposes of private study, research,
criticism or review, as permitted under the Copyright Act, no part may
be reproduced by any process without written permission.
Inquiries should be addressed to the publishers.

HarperCollins*Publishers*
25 Ryde Road, Pymble, Sydney NSW 2073, Australia
31 View Road, Glenfield, Auckland 10, New Zealand
77–85 Fulham Palace Road, London W6 8JB, United Kingdom
2 Bloor Street East, 20th floor, Toronto, Ontario M4W 1A8, Canada
10 East 53rd Street, New York NY 10022, USA

National Library of Australia Cataloguing-in-publication data:

Fenton, Peter.
   Olive Weston: the heroic life of a World War II nurse.
   Includes index.
   ISBN 0 7322 7644 6.
   1. Weston, Olive. 2. Military nursing – Australia –
   Biography. 3. World War, 1939–1945 – Medical care –
   Australia. 4. Nurses – Australia – Biography. I. Title.
610.73092

Cover designed by Louise McGeachie, HarperCollins Design Studio
Typeset by HarperCollins in Minion
Printed and bound in Australia by Griffin Press on 50gsm Bulky News

5 4 3 2 1   04 05 06 07

This book is dedicated (at Olive's request) to Australian missionary MAVIS PARKINSON and Australian missionary nursing sister MAY HAYMAN, bayoneted to death by Japanese soldiers at Popondetta, New Guinea, 1942, and to the following brave souls beheaded on Buna Beach.

CAPTAIN LOUIS AUSTEN,
Australian Armed Forces

REVEREND FATHER REDLICH,
Australian missionary

MARGERY BRENCHLEY,
Australian missionary nursing sister

LILLA ASHMAR,
Australian missionary schoolteacher

REVEREND FATHER HENRY HOLLAND,
Australian priest

JOHN DUFFIELD,
Australian builder

TONY CORS,
native aide to Captain Austen

TONY CORS' WIFE AND SIX-YEAR-OLD SON

May they rest in peace.

Contents

Foreword

BY NANCY WAKE

In September 2001 I was privileged to attend the week-long celebration of the centenary of the historic South Australian town of Kapunda. The invitation came from the Festival Director, the late Charles Smythe, who, along with his energetic committee, left no stone unturned to make sure I was made extremely welcome.

It was a chance to renew acquaintances with Olive Weston, with whom I'd had many meetings over the years. Ollie had been a key player in the restoration of the War Memorial Gardens, the official opening and dedication being a major part of the celebrations. Of course it was also wonderful to meet up with the likes of Major Vivienne Holmes, who had been personal assistant to General William Slim in Burma, and famous nurses Jean Ashton and Betty Bradwell. Here was a gathering of wonderful women who had given so much during the war against Japan while I was engaged across the world with the French Resistance. We represented three theatres of war. We traded stories, laughed and joked but also remembered personal things like the bitterness and sorrow I felt when I first learnt how the Japanese had mistreated my brother Stan, at the Changi prisoner-of-war camp.

About this time my biography was doing nicely, thank you very much. Quite often the possibility of a biography of Olive Weston was raised. Ollie's own story was quite remarkable, one that began with her wartime nursing and continued long after the war. Considering the success of my book it was not surprising that her story came to be of interest to authors and publishers. It was not long before Ollie's exploits caught the attention of Peter Fenton, who, but for a previous commitment, would probably have written my story. Peter took the opportunity to study Olive's diaries and was overwhelmed by their detail. He was reading history that was unknown to most Australians. In his hands was the basis of a truly inspiring story.

The exploits of Australia's women at war have been sadly neglected for years. The magnificent Memorial Gardens might help address this, as I'm sure this book will. The story of Olive's childhood in northern Queensland, her ambition and study to be a medical missionary in New Guinea, interrupted by the war, her work for General MacArthur and the devotion to her intellectually disadvantaged son Steven are an inspiration. Ollie's story is a wonderful revelation of the life of a beautiful person, full of courage and compassion, someone of whom all Australians should be proud.

Nancy Wake, 2003

Preface

I met Olive Weston through an old friend, Jim Cowley. Jim, a pharmacist from northern New South Wales, is a great talker and, in fairness, a great listener. He has some very special friends not the least of whom is the famous World War II hero Nancy Wake. He assured me he had others just as interesting. There was one in particular he wanted me to meet, a friend whose life story is quite remarkable. My previous books had all been to do with sport and I recall Jim saying, 'You have always written about champions, it's time you wrote about a hero.'

At Jim's suggestion I rang Olive at her home in Christie Downs, on the southern outskirts of Adelaide. It's not ever easy talking to someone on the phone when you have never met them, but she was expecting my call and had just read, at Jim's suggestion, a poem that I had written many years earlier about our great cricketer Don Bradman. Whether the poem impressed her or not I don't know but she came straight to the point. 'If you want to discuss a book you'd better get yourself down here to Adelaide. You might find my story interesting. I'll leave that to you. Do you enjoy a glass of red? Good. Don't bother bringing any with you, we've got plenty here. You've heard of the Barossa Valley no doubt. And the McLaren Vale. Here's my address. I don't go out that much' — this proved to be slightly inaccurate — 'so just give me a day's notice. We'll have a lot to talk about so you should allow time to stay a day or two. No, you won't be booking into any hotel in Adelaide, you will stay here, there's just Steven and myself and there are three bedrooms so that's no problem. Just let me know when you're coming.'

So I went. And she was right about the red wine. It was good and there was plenty of it. Given there were just the two of us, we made a reasonable contribution to the Barossa's monthly income. When I replayed my tapes later the words seemed to come out more slowly in the sixth hour than the first and I was inclined to put this down to the recorder's batteries. Subsequent tape sessions where we curtailed our wine intake showed the batteries were fine.

I wasn't presumptuous enough to assume she would trust me with her story but as it turned out she did. Olive scoffs at the thought of being a hero. 'Just call me a humanitarian,' she says. Humanitarian she certainly is. The decision as to whether she is more than that I will leave to you.

Olive spent her teenage years working as a nurse in a large US military hospital in Townsville, her home town, tending to American GIs suffering from tropical fevers or casualties from the fierce fighting in New Guinea. She enjoyed the rank of a commissioned officer when most girls her age were concerned with what to wear to the next party, or perhaps whether to go south to avoid the impending Japanese invasion. Some of her nursing memories are still very painful but she has been totally open about them with me as she feels a need to tell them. For 60 years she has longed to free herself of a burden she was forced to keep because of her vows of secrecy, military vows taken when secrecy was not only essential but also compulsory. This was wartime and things were different, especially for an innocent teenager like Olive.

Having heard her story I was motivated to take a trip around Queensland's north to visit the areas that played such an important role in the Allies' defence of the Pacific. Many of these places on the coast and in the hinterlands have now become famous as tourist attractions. Cairns, Mossman Gorge, Magnetic Island, Mareeba and Kuranda, where the sky-rail makes its way above the jungle tops to its lush destination, then accessible only by a primitive railway track or a winding, tortuous gravel road, were known to few but the locals. There was no village at Port Douglas, an occasional fishing hut perhaps, but more importantly a flat four-mile beach that was ideal for emergency landings for stricken aircraft. I was at primary school when such drama was unfolding and came away knowing plenty about the Magna Carta, the Pilgrim Fathers, Captain Cook, and Burke and Wills but took for granted what was happening in my own lifetime. Yes, I knew Darwin had been bombed, but not 64 times! Olive's personal account of this stage in Australia's history will almost certainly surprise you whether you are young or not so young.

I was also motivated to find soldiers, boys at the time, now men in their eighties, who retain vivid memories of Townsville in wartime. My old friend from Maitland, Harry Boyle, who was a member of Z Force, and Arch Fraley, an American GI who came to stay, had happy, and even humorous memories. Others were not so lucky. They gave extraordinary accounts of voluntarily undergoing mustard gas experiments from which they have suffered ever since. And others who unwittingly, and therefore unwillingly, were subjected to massive insulin injections. The untold stories of war are innumerable.

Olive is elated that there seems to be a 'rediscovery' by young people of the history of Australia in both world wars and the efforts of valiant men and women, without whom we would all be living so differently, if at all. The number of youngsters who have recently embraced the story of Gallipoli, their desire to visit Anzac Cove and to march on Anzac Day, gives her great heart. Yet she is disappointed that so many are generally unaware of the great drama that unfolded in the north of our own country during the Second World War as the threat of invasion tore people's lives apart. Now that the last of the Anzacs has died, perhaps those epic battles at Kokoda, Milne Bay, Buna and the Coral Sea will take their rightful place in our history.

In fairness to the youngsters this criticism could apply to many older people as well, particularly those from the southern states who generally felt somewhat removed from the action. Well, removed at least until a miniature Japanese submarine ran amok in Sydney Harbour and sank the ferry *Kuttabul* which was being used for naval accommodation. I for one, inspired by Olive's reminiscences, have read more about the war in Australia in the last few months than I had ever read before. *Curtin's Cowboys*, *Bloody Buna* and Nurse Vivian Bullwinkel's biography, simply titled *Bullwinkel*, made extraordinary reading. Many hours on the internet were rewarded with a host of personal stories and the discovery of a wonderful website called Australians At War that contained pictures of the 12th Station Hospital in Townsville looking exactly as Olive had described it. I had the pleasure of working on Bruce Beresford's excellent film *Paradise Road*, which told the story of Australian nurses captured when Singapore fell in 1942, so I was aware of the courage of these women. Many of these nurses, including Vivian, became friends of Olive many years after the war.

But hers is not simply the tale of a wartime nurse. I found the rest of her life just as interesting, emotional and inspirational. Many people follow a path where circumstances determine which way they travel. Was she destined or determined to become a carer of others? She believes the former, but the real answer is probably the latter. Certainly she was driven by a desire to correct injustice and to care for the underdog. This desire has never waned. Her tenacity is astonishing as friends, and many an antagonist, would verify.

Olive and I have become genuine friends. I know how hard it has been for her going back over some events in her past. As she says, 'I think some people are just asked to do different things. I just did what I had to do. We should just all do what we have to do.' I'll drink to that and to Olive. With a glass of red wine from the Barossa Valley, of course.

Chapter One

THE TOMBOY

I just went to bed one night, without any inclination that there was anything wrong with me, and woke up about one o'clock feeling absolutely terrible. I knew I was in trouble so I rang an ambulance. I hadn't been in hospital — well, not as a patient — since I was three years old when I had my tonsils out and they'd fed me jelly and ice cream. But I knew I had to get there straight away. When the paramedics came they tried to get a cannula into a vein but found they'd all collapsed so they agreed we'd have to go to hospital immediately. They asked which one I'd prefer and I told them Wakefield Private.

I had to wait until they got a cardiac specialist in around about four o'clock in the morning and straight away he said I'd have to be admitted. So then it was a matter of waiting for a bed to become vacant. By half past five they'd found one for me. I had all sorts of tests done with X-rays of course, and a couple of days later I was told I'd have to have a triple bypass. I thought, so be it.

The surgeon came in to explain to me all about the procedure and what might happen. I listened carefully to what he had to say. The one thing I said to him was, 'You better make sure that I come out of this because I've got a lot of work to do yet!' And I meant it. Some people might think they're coming to the end if they need a triple bypass after they've passed 70 but I certainly didn't.

I never actually prepared for the operation, I just went to bed and woke up in the intensive care ward. Obviously I'd been sedated and whisked off to the theatre. The job had been done without my even knowing it. As I was coming to I heard the last rites being read so I was a bit scared to open my eyes in case they were for me. I'd heard them plenty of times before with my soldier boys. Then there was a big kafuffle while they wheeled a man past me and then brought him back towards the surgery. There'd apparently been some minor complication and he had to go back in. He was really going to town, yelling, 'I've spent enough on my insurance and I want to make sure I get my money's worth!' I remember thinking that was a rather unusual request, but of course he was still under the effects of the anaesthetic.

When I finally opened my eyes I saw it was another patient, a man, getting the last rites and I thought, oh, thank God, I'll be able to get on with my work. I got up for a shower the next day; they said that was okay as long as I felt up to it. All up I spent two months in hospital. They moved me after the first month to College Gardens. I don't think they were in any hurry to get rid of me there — they were getting about $300 a day while I recuperated. I felt fine in no time at all as far as my heart was concerned but they had taken veins out of my thighs to repair my heart and one of them took quite a while to get better. I looked back later and guessed I should have known it couldn't have been me receiving the last rites. Your life is supposed to flash past you and I hadn't even seen one glimpse of Townsville.

When Olive was born in Townsville on 4 July 1926, her debut caused something of a surprise. Not that she hadn't been expected; it was just that she arrived slightly before schedule. Her mother, Alda, was entertaining her sister-in-law Eva, also pregnant, at the Pilot Hill lighthouse on the entrance to Ross River. Suddenly labour overtook her. Within minutes Olive was born and placed on the couch. Much panic saw Olive's father William rush from the house to return with the local midwife and order was slowly restored. Believers in omens might have noted that her birthday coincided with American Independence Day.

Olive firmly believes the circumstances of her birth had a profound effect on her character. Much later in life she suffered anxiety attacks, caused through stress, and underwent hypnotherapy. Olive regressed right back to her birth. She clearly remembers lying on that couch, frightened and cold — but most of all, rushed. At the conclusion of the hypnotherapy sessions, her anxiety cured, she declared she would never be rushed again. She realised that throughout her long life she had always resented being rushed.

Olive had come from adventurous stock. Her maternal grandfather Alfred was born in England. At sixteen years of age he ran away from home in Devon and without a word to his parents absconded to Queensland to make his fortune. He never saw either parent again, despite his mother living until the age of 102. Ten years later he met and married a well-educated English girl named Mary Ann Barker and took her to a mining town, Ravenswood, adjacent to Charters Towers. Having decided there was a better and safer future to be had looking after the miners than joining them in their search for a quick fortune, he became a successful merchant, selling supplies and clothing. The couple had three girls, Alda, Ettie and Ellen, known later to Olive as Aunty Nell. When Alfred left for New Guinea in 1901 in pursuit of further riches, he left his gentle English wife and children behind in Townsville. Alda, the youngest child, was eleven years old. Mary Ann died in 1915 but Alfred remained in New Guinea. Unlike many, who found the Antipodes too harshly different from the old country and returned home, he had the fortitude and initiative to make his fortune. When Olive met him on one of his regular trips to Queensland, he was the owner of two major goldmines in Wau and Bulolo and carried a wad of money the likes of which Olive had never seen before or since. Always included were some hundred pound notes. On one occasion he impressed his grand-daughter by showing her a bank note made out for a £1000.

Olive's paternal grandfather, Frederick, whose father had come from Wales to the goldfields of Ballarat in search of his fortune, was born at the Eureka Stockade in 1854. He too learned to cater for the miners rather than compete with them. If any bunch suffered from interminable thirst they did, so he satisfied their needs by becoming a publican with hotels on Thursday Island, Prince of Wales Island and Cooktown. He married Mary Faulkner from Bowen, who cooked at his several hotels. A son, William, was born on Thursday Island. Frederick then leased mining land in the Palmer River district on which he eventually negotiated a considerable profit and came to Townsville where for many years he ran a very successful business with horse-drawn taxis. Photographs of his horse-drawn cabs still adorn the walls of the hotel opposite Townsville railway station.

Townsville, 1350 kilometres north of Queensland's capital Brisbane, was typical of the state's coastal towns, the biggest in the far north, but nevertheless very small by city standards. Isolated simply by virtue of distance, it was hot, dry, dusty and very tropical. A port rising out of the gold rushes of the 1860s and soon after boosted by the massive sugar cane industry, it was the home of tough, practical, resilient and, in the main, hard-working people. Within 20 years of the gold rushes the first railway line in northern Queensland ran from Townsville to Charters Towers, 135 kilometres to the west. The post and telegraph office, which transmitted messages by code as well as sending mail by coach and ship, opened in 1879. By the time of Federation in 1901, Townsville's population was 16000, making it Queensland's fourth biggest city. Adventurers came and went, mining, prospecting, timber and cane cutting, farming, and generally trying their luck in a tough and unforgiving region. The stoic remained. By the time of Olive's childhood, the population was approaching 30000. Only Brisbane was larger.

A large rocky outcrop that jutted into the sea had been broken up to make breakwaters for the substantial harbour in the 1880s. Alongside the harbour entrance was the mouth of Ross Creek. Less than a kilometre south was Ross River, which extended five kilometres inland. Here the two streams met. Those living on Ross Island, formed by the meeting of the two waterways, were known as 'Mudpickers'. The name came from the hundreds of curlews who fed, morning and afternoon, on the mudflats that rimmed the island. Olive was a Mudpicker. The penny ferry, which transported the Mudpickers across the creek to the mainland, was replaced by the first of two bridges at about the time of Olive's birth.

Immediately north of the harbour, a two-kilometre beachfront, the Strand, separated the township from the Pacific Ocean. On the northern end of the Strand rose Kissing Point, providing a perfect view of the harbour to the south, Rowes Bay to the north, and Magnetic Island sitting five kilometres offshore with a rugged shoreline of approximately 75 kilometres. Magnetic Island, erroneously named because Captain Cook believed severe interference to his ship's compass must have been caused by the huge granite rocks that dominated the island, was a haven for fishermen who sailed from the mainland to fish the many idyllic sandy bays on the far side of the island. Inland from Rowes Bay was Garbutt, site of the single strip Townsville airport. Overlooking the entire township stood the hulking red rock figure of Castle Hill. Further inland was Mount Louisa, at the beginning of the mountain ranges, modest in height but heavily timbered.

Locals boasted even then, well before the Townsville area had any pretensions about being a tourist destination, that they expected 300 sunny days each year. They spoke less frequently about the monsoon season. Outside of this wet season water was invariably in short supply and the scrub that surrounded the town became dry and parched. The months of May until September brought beautiful weather with no rain and constant, pleasant temperatures in the mid to high twenties. But approaching the monsoon season, which extended from October to March or April, conditions became very humid. Locals did not appear to notice but visitors from the south were quick to complain. Once the monsoons hit, the area was inundated with persistent tropical downpours. Annual rainfall was amongst the highest in Australia despite long periods with no rain at all. Unlike people from the southern states who related their weather to the four seasons, in Queensland's north it was simply the wet season or the dry. Olive recalls living in Cairns one year when it rained continually for two months:

I was actually able to dive off the back steps of our verandah and start swimming. The water just couldn't get away and so the backyard was a pool. The monsoons didn't worry us. We never ever wore shoes then because they were too expensive and they'd be ruined in no time. We couldn't afford leather shoes anyway so we only ever wore sandshoes. We took the rain in our stride but of course cyclones were a different matter. We used to ride our bikes up to the Esplanade in Cairns where they flew a flag to say a cyclone was imminent. We'd see the warning and home we'd come to let everyone know to 'batten down'. Doors and windows were locked, anything in the yard was placed inside and we took cover in the most secure part of the house. The pets were brought inside and they were usually terrified.

We copped one beauty when I was in bed and the wind ripped the roof off and the rain came streaming in just drenching me. We found the roof up the road in the morning, not that it was any use anymore. Generally they lasted for three or four hours. They were frightening, even to those who had endured them before, but they were simply a part of living in the tropics. The worst thing was that they were so unpredictable. The wind would suddenly change course a few kilometres out to sea and the storm would hit the coast 200 kilometres from where it was expected. So you never knew if you were for it or not, until the last few minutes.

Mind you, my most terrifying experience was not in a cyclone. It was in the monsoon season but on a bright sunny day. Suddenly there was a severe electrical storm with lightning close by and without warning a fireball appeared from nowhere. It struck outside the house, rolled down the hall, right past me and out the back door. It was one of the few moments of my life when I was petrified.

The nearby Burdekin River invariably flooded during the wet season, cutting the rail line and the road from the south. With the bridge and railway line submerged for days, barges ferried supplies across the swollen river. On hot, steamy summer nights the mosquitos were as prevalent and persistent as the huge blowflies had been during the day. The sandflies, millions upon millions of them, were ever present. As with the humidity, southern visitors seemed to notice the flies and mosquitos more than the locals did.

When William and Alda were raising their family of two daughters, Olive and Betty, Townsville was very much working class with large numbers of men employed at the Ross River meatworks, the railway and the waterfront. The town had very strong Labor Party traditions. William, working on the waterfront, was a life member of the Labor Party as was his father before him. Times were tough and families were often forced to move to wherever work took them, or more often because their rent was in arrears. A very strong feeling existed among a lot of residents that North Queensland should be a separate state with Townsville as its capital. Being controlled by 'city slickers a million miles away' made little sense to the working class of the north. The Great Depression and then the war strengthened this belief in many.

The crash of the New York Stock Exchange in October 1929 began a depression that lasted for a decade. It was the greatest financial disaster America and her trading partners would ever see and its effect was felt across the world. Millionaires became paupers overnight. Within weeks dole queues stretching for hundreds of metres were a common sight, not only in the cities of America but in Europe and Australia. England reported two million people unemployed less than twelve months after the crash. In Australia isolated towns had already been struggling, with work opportunities at a minimum. Olive was not yet three when her family moved to Cairns, a much smaller coastal port 350 kilometres further north, where her father found work on the wharves.

Conditions immediately after the Depression became absolutely desperate. Still, with a little female fox terrier called Tiny, destined to spend the next ten years with her, two tortoises, Tim and Tom, who lived in a giant clam shell, a galah that could 'talk like a politician but make more sense' and an orphaned baby kangaroo who slept in a sugarbag which hung on the kitchen door, Olive enjoyed herself most of the time. She has some clear memories of those early Depression years, some humorous, some tragic, but each important in creating the person she was to become:

The waterside workers went on strike while we were in Cairns and the land owners, or 'cockies' as Dad used to call them, were furious they couldn't get their produce through the port. There was talk of them forming a lynch mob and things got so ugly it was not beyond the realm of possibilities. They were roaming around the town looking for the men who had refused to load their produce. We were sharing a house with Mr and Mrs Evans for ten shillings a week. Mr Evans was also a waterside worker and three very angry looking 'cockies' came to the house determined to sort things out, but our men weren't there. Mum armed herself with an axe and Mrs Evans went one better, she had a loaded shotgun. They answered the door and the men asked for Dad and Mr Evans by name.

'They're not here,' Mrs Evans told them.

'Well, we'll wait,' said one of them, taking a step towards the doorway.

'Not here you won't, you're trespassing. Now beat it or I'll shoot you,' Mrs Evans said. Sure enough she cocked the gun. They 'beat it' all right, with me standing there hanging on to Mum's legs. With the departure of the would-be posse Mum and Mrs Evans made a cup of tea. Clearly it wasn't only the men who could look after themselves. That lesson never left me.

Not all childhood experiences were pleasant. One that has stayed in my mind forever was the stillbirth of my baby brother. I saw the sheets soaked in blood put in the laundry sink and the bloody body of that tiny little baby placed on top of them. These incidents occurred well before I turned four.

Times were extremely tough for everyone and people became very frugal. Most of the cats disappeared in time. The Chinese used to nab them. We'd see them skinned, hanging up behind the shops. They looked just like rabbits but we knew they were cats. They made hats from the fur as well. It was common knowledge that if you had a pet cat you looked after it or the Chinese would have it for a meal or sell it back to you.

We often had to move when the rent got beyond our means or work came up for Dad somewhere else. One night I was sitting at the dinner table with my sister Betty, older by two years, eating a lump of cheese and a piece of dry bread. Mum and Dad sat with us having just a cup of tea. When I asked them why they weren't eating too, Mother told me quite simply there was nothing else for that night.

Despite all this we kids saw the place as paradise. It was a beautiful area to grow up in. We were coastal kids so we swam virtually all year round in the creek or the ocean. There were plenty of crocodiles in the creeks and it seems mad now but we didn't care. Little 'salties' they were. I was a tomboy, born and bred. It was instinctive. Later on when my sister had her accident I became her protector and I'd punch the boys who teased her at school but I'd have been a tomboy anyway. I often think it's funny that I was called Olive. It was a very rare name until the first war but then became popular because of the olive branch denoting peace. I've always liked my name but I'm not absolutely certain it ever fitted. It wasn't that I had anything against the idea of peace; I just needed action with it.

We holidayed at Bribie Island outside Brisbane when I was only two and I had to be rescued more than once from the lighthouse stairs. My uncle, James Duce, was a lighthouse keeper and our family stayed with him at several different lighthouses in my early years. I saw a lot of lighthouses as Uncle James moved to different towns. They were very exciting places for a small kid. The one at Bribie Island had two or three hundred steps. One day I got a fair way up towards the top with Betty trying to keep up with me. I could climb up all right but coming down backwards, particularly with my terrified sister behind me, was a bit too difficult and Uncle James had to rescue us. I was in big trouble that day but I was a natural climber. Even before that my family was billeted at the Crown Hotel in Cairns and I climbed up and down the stairs at every chance I got.

I can recall several rescues in my young life, the most exciting being from the floodwaters when I was about six. We were living in a boarding house on top of the hill in Innisfail where Dad had been lucky enough to get a photographer's job. Innisfail, between Townsville and Cairns, had the highest rainfall in the country and I'd been warned not to go anywhere near gullies or culverts in the monsoon season. Unfortunately my nature was such that I just couldn't avoid danger. The floodwaters came up suddenly and I was trapped in a culvert. Luckily council surveyors had left posts over it. I clambered to the top of a post and was rescued by the police in their boat.

Twenty-five years later I told my very proper English gentleman husband, well disciplined through many years of army life, of these escapades and after our first major argument he said, 'Olive, you are nothing but a bloody Australian rebel,' to which I replied, 'That's right and don't forget: you only married me, you don't own me.' Of course I was a rebel. What on earth did he expect from my breeding? After all, one grandfather had run away from home when he was sixteen and never came back while the other was born during the Eureka Stockade to an Irish Catholic mother.

Not all rescues were attributable to Olive's enthusiasm for adventure. Returning to live in Cairns from Innisfail during the same year as her police boat drama, the family was given a lift by friends. Their car became bogged in a remote place called Wars Pocket Swamp. It was after dark so the driver went looking for a farmer to render some assistance and the family found themselves covered in leeches that they had to burn off with matches. It was tricky holding the match close enough to burn off the leech without burning the skin. Some hours passed before the farmer arrived with a tractor to pull them out. Nobody seemed too concerned, particularly Olive.

By the time Olive was five her parents were very pleased to pack her off to St Joseph's Infants School. She was a good girl but extremely strong willed and high spirited and they thought some discipline from the nuns would certainly do her the world of good. Classes were mixed with the boys on one side of the room and the girls on the other. At lunchtime there was also little or no contact between girls and boys. Talking was forbidden in class, unless spoken to by the teacher, and a sharp rap on the knuckles was readily supplied to any boy or girl who infringed this. Olive found this regime very tough indeed. Despite often being in trouble she was very well liked by the nuns, who saw much in her character.

At this time the family rented a house in Bunder Street and William dug up most of the backyard to plant a variety of fruit and vegetables. Being self-sufficient was the only answer to poverty. Families shared their crops of pumpkins, squashes, bananas, chokoes, corn and the like with friends in the street. A batch of Rhode Island Red chooks was penned at the back of the vegetable patch and eggs were placed under the clucky hens to keep the tribe on the increase. There was invariably a spare young rooster ready, if not exactly anxious, to play his part in the celebration of Easter,

Christmas, New Year or birthdays. People made their own jams: cumquat, rosella, fig and marmalade as well as mango, tomato and choko chutney. Alda boiled green pawpaws when vegetables were short and regularly cooked chokoes with white onion sauce. She also made her own ginger beer and sarsaparilla. Money was extremely scarce but, provided a family could scratch up the rent, they knew how to make do by working the soil.

Later on the family moved to a cottage around the corner in Hartley Street where they lived for some years. Next door there was a shack, the home of two old professional fishermen, at the back of which was a creek that ran out into the Pacific Ocean. By now Olive had quite a large group of friends with whom she played after school. The girls invariably joined in all the games, sharing the bumps and bruises that came with football and cricket as Olive's younger cousin Noel recalls:

> We treated the girls no differently really. Sometimes they got tackled a bit hard and got a nick over the eye or a bloody nose but that was all part and parcel of the game. Now and again someone might get a bit upset but they soon made up. Olive was a bit of a tomboy, I suppose, but we didn't think about that then. The girls could stick up for themselves and bait a hook and catch a fish as well as the boys. Sometimes the fishermen would lend us a flattie and the boys would go off for half a day. We always came home with some fish. We had a great childhood, really, even though we were poor. Just down the road was an area we called Malay Town where about 200 Malay and Torres Strait Island people lived. They'd built houses up on bamboo poles on the edge of the creek. It was a very friendly community and we went down there quite often to play.

Olive too has fond memories of Malay Town:

They had a community leader, a very nice man named Mr Pitt, and of a night time they often had dances and they would sing songs in their own languages and play guitars. We used to listen to the music from the verandah outside the hall and Mr Pitt would bring us out soft drinks. He always carried a white table napkin with his tray of drinks. One family had three girls, Sophie, Heather and Dulcie, who sang beautifully. Dulcie went to Brisbane and became a very well-known singer. When I was in London after the war she was the vocalist with a famous dance band called Guy Lombardo and the Royal Canadians. There was also Jap Town a bit further towards town where several Japanese families lived. They were very friendly as well. We never had any trouble with them but they were interned once the war broke out. Both Malay Town and Jap Town disappeared after the war and that area of the creek was filled in and several large oil tanks took their places.

During this time Olive and her cousins Noel and Sid were able to contribute considerably to the dinner table:

We would look around the place and find some old cast iron and take it up to the foundry and sell it. We usually got threepence for a few pieces. Next stop was the butcher where we'd buy a parcel of soup bones. Then it was off to the mangroves and our favourite crabbing spot, Alligator Creek, only a few hundred metres from our back door. We took Dad's traps with us, made of rings of wire and fishing net. We'd bait the traps with the bones and wait for the tide. Once you got the hang of it there was nothing to it. As the crabs came in and out on the tide they were attracted by the bones and became entangled in the mesh. One gave me a hell of a nip on the thumb once but I was very careful after that. We often took home ten or twelve big mud crabs which Mum boiled in a kerosene tin over an open fire. We all had these beautiful crabs supplemented by large jugs of wild lemon juice. Mum always had a jug of lemon juice on the table and if visitors arrived they'd be given a glass. It was lovely to drink on a hot day and was also a vital source of vitamin C.

The other treat was having granadilla pie for dessert. I only ever saw granadillas in North Queensland. They were like a large passionfruit and you could eat them straight off the vine if you liked. But they were beautiful when Mum baked them in a pie, you couldn't believe how sweet they were. We kids found the best way to eat mangoes without getting a mess all over your clothes was to climb the tree, hook your legs over a branch, hang upside down like a bat and eat them that way. We didn't have two pennies to rub together but what with fresh eggs, home grown vegies, mangoes, mud crabs and granadilla pie, boy oh boy we ate well.

Towards the end of her first year at St Joseph's, Olive suffered an even greater tragedy than the stillbirth of her baby brother. Her seven-year-old sister Betty was severely injured when the school bus collided with a train at a level crossing. She was thrown from the bus and was in a coma for several weeks. Though she slowly recovered it was realised she had suffered permanent brain damage. Mentally she would remain a child for the rest of her life. Olive and her parents handled the tragedy in typically stoic fashion. Olive became her carer and looked after her throughout her school years. Though her ability to learn had all but ended, she was allowed to sit next to Olive as the younger sister progressed through the classes.

With Betty an easy mark for cruel taunts, Olive took up the challenge and had no compunction in arguing and even fighting with her fists to protect her sister. Whenever Betty had a problem she came to Olive and the score was settled. This often had Olive in trouble with the nuns. Boy punching boy was not too well accepted but girl punching boy was unthinkable. Nevertheless, Olive saw it as her duty to care for Betty. The benchmark was set. Injustice could not be tolerated. The tomboy would remain a tomboy but was now a carer as well.

In 1933 Olive's family relocated to Cardwell, a small coastal town midway between Townsville and Cairns. William went into business for a few months with his brother-in-law Alex, trapping fish at Cardwell Beach. Olive enjoyed staying with Uncle Alex and Aunt Nell, who had no children of their own and spoiled them accordingly. It was Christmas holidays, so there was no school to interfere with her fun. She swam every day. Behind their property was a sanctuary through which ran a creek infested with crocodiles that could be heard snapping their jaws all night. When the kids swam in the creek during the day, Alex would sit with his .303 rifle to protect them in case any large marauder took a fancy to them. Aunt Nell's beautiful red kelpie dog had already fallen victim to a saltwater crocodile.

The presence of the vicious reptiles made little difference to the kids' fun. Once Olive brought home a baby 'saltie', about as long as her forearm, and was most disappointed that her mum sent her straight back to return it to the creek. Another time she accepted a dare from sister Betty to run up the back of a very large crocodile which was sleeping in the hot sun on the edge of the creek. She was on his tail, up and across his back and had clambered into a tree before the five-metre crocodile knew what had happened. This escapade landed her in more hot water with her anxious mother.

Simple pleasures were greatly appreciated in Cardwell, which was a very isolated place. On one occasion Aunt Nell packed the kids into the back of the truck and took them to the picture theatre in the neighbouring town of Tully to see Walt Disney's cartoon feature *The Three Little Pigs*. To go to the cinema was a rare treat. It was a full day's excursion and Olive and Betty fell asleep in the back of the truck on the way home. All agreed it was one of the best days they'd ever had.

Cardwell was proving too tame for the adventurous Olive so, once the school holidays were over, her parents sent her to stay with her Grandma in Townsville for eight months, to attend St Patrick's Convent, a boarding school renowned for its discipline. It was a far cry from Cardwell but Olive enjoyed the weekends particularly. Her uncle had a fishing boat moored in Ross Creek and she accompanied him to Magnetic Island to fish for flathead. When she tired of fishing she swam in the warm waters of the secluded bays or walked the bush tracks to look at the large colony of koalas that lived in the trees quite close to the shoreline. When her family moved back to Cairns Olive continued her schooling at St Joseph's. Here Sister Mary Joseph taught her a short poem by John Wesley which she never forgot:

> *I shall only pass this way but once*
> *And what good I can do let me do it now*
> *Because I shall not pass this way again.*

She decided to make it a rule to live by.

Soon after her return there was an outbreak of polio that claimed the life of a classmate, a young boy. Alda was encouraging her rebellious daughter to become a nun and the sisters at the convent were doing the same. They saw that the spirited, athletic youngster with the creamy skin, lanky legs, long fair hair and constant good humour had qualities that stood her apart from many of her quieter companions. If her enthusiasm could be bridled then she would make a fine teacher.

One of her classmates suffered from epilepsy and after she had a fit it was Olive who was assigned to sit with her on the verandah until she regained consciousness. The nuns allowed Betty, who depended heavily on her younger sister, to sit with them. Olive had tremendous respect and admiration for her mentors but doubted their disciplined lifestyle would suit her. At this same time her grandfather was encouraging her to become a medical missionary. She found this idea more to her liking. Photographs he had sent her of local tribesmen in their colourful, ornate headdresses and armbands, made from bird of paradise feathers, increased her interest in New Guinea.

Olive enjoyed a three-year involvement in the Girl Guides, a highlight of which were the regular trips to beautiful locations, many in the mountains and forests inland from Cairns. Olive rode her pushbike 25 kilometres north to Smithfield where the hike to the most spectacular region began. It was a tough two-hour climb up the peaks that led to breathtaking views of Barron Falls and the Barron Gorge. Trekking through the coolness of the lush forest under a jungle canopy so thick that it often hid the sky completely for several minutes and then resting under the huge kauri pines was bliss to an outdoor girl. The densely wooded rainforest was home to a variety of colourful tropical birds: kingfishers, egrets, parrots and blue-winged kookaburras.

Occasionally the girls would catch sight of a platypus in one of the dams at the foot of the gorge or a cassowary with its large black body, brightly coloured red, blue and yellow neck and large, bare head topped with a bony crest, picking its way through the undergrowth. They gave these birds, as tall as many of them, a wide berth. Cassowaries are very timid by nature but can be quite vicious if threatened. They were an exhausted but happy troop by the time they had cycled back to Cairns after their all-day adventure. Olive also became a member of the Red Cross, and was barely eleven years old when she received her first certificate for first aid.

Meanwhile, across the globe, a situation was emerging that would shape Olive's life. In Europe, Adolf Hitler, Germany's chancellor, was setting the groundwork for war. The Berlin Olympic Games of 1936 were a platform to show Germany's might and his own megalomania. His vision of a superior Aryan race was pronounced loudly and clearly. He proclaimed to all that other races, particularly blacks, were vastly inferior in every way to his blonde supermen. When the world's best athlete, black American Jesse Owens, won four gold medals, Hitler snubbed him completely. Just two years later Germany's most famous boxer, Max Schmeling, was knocked out in one round by another black American, Joe Louis. Hitler banned film of the contest from being shown in Germany.

He was fanatical, ruthless, power-crazed, bent on revenging Germany's loss in the First World War 20 years previously, and quite mad. While he signed peace agreements with world leaders, he was preparing for war. If it eventuated and Britain became involved then Australia, as part of the British Commonwealth, would certainly be involved as well. Not that Olive would have given any thought to Hitler's ambitions if indeed she had heard of him. She was too busy enjoying growing up.

Towards the end of her schooling Olive lost Tiny, her pet of ten years. When the little terrier suddenly had spasms Olive carried her nine blocks to the chemist in Cairns' main road and nine blocks back home. Tiny had been bitten by a snake and died that night. Olive still retains memories of her standing guard at the front of the house, letting everyone in but no one out. It wasn't until Olive or her mother gave the okay that Tiny would let any stranger leave.

In her latter years at St Joseph's Olive blossomed into a very good swimmer and diver. Swimming was the only sport that interested her, though many of her friends played basketball and took part in athletics. She had been a natural in the water since her father had thrown her in the creek when she was three years of age and told her to 'get a move on before the crocs get you'. Each morning she took herself to the Cairns baths and swam laps in preparation for the Far North Queensland championships. She wasn't coached, nor did she belong to any swimming club, but approached the challenge with a whole-heartedness that was typical of her nature. In 1939, aged thirteen, she won the 50 metres freestyle and diving titles and also the Mareeba diving championship. The newspaper clippings recording these victories are among her possessions to this day. Growing older did nothing to dampen her love of adventure. She recalls holidaying in Bowen in her early teenage years:

We were staying on North Head Island off Bowen near the lighthouse, and were the only ones there. There was a drought and Betty and I sat in a galvanised tub outdoors waiting for rain that never came. It was a very isolated spot and to get supplies was a marathon event. We had to row with my uncle across from the island to the pilot station and then walk four miles to cross a creek at low tide. There we changed clothes in a boatshed and went shopping in town. Uncle would carry two sugarbags of supplies over his shoulder. There were goats on the island so he had fresh meat to supplement his rations for the monsoon season.

Even out there I managed to get into trouble. There was a large beehive in a tree halfway across the pilot's hill. We went walking one day and I lagged behind until Uncle, Aunty, Mum and Betty got far enough ahead. Then I picked up some stones and let the beehive have it. The stings from the bees were accompanied by a good scolding from Mum. I might have been a slow learner — I'd been stung years before by bees, and Uncle had taken tobacco from his pipe to rub on the stings.

There were plenty of taipans and copperhead snakes in North Queensland but I didn't fool around with them. But ants were a different matter. I was playing with Betty, well after her accident, pushing her around in a barrow, when the temptation to leave her, still in the barrow on an ants' nest, proved too strong. Betty yelled her lungs out once the ants got busy and I was severely chastised for that too. Not that I would have deliberately hurt Betty — after all, I was her protector.

During the decade of struggle that followed the Depression, Australians' spirits were lifted by the achievements of special people who had shown they could rise above the pack. The great aviators Bert Hinkler and Charles Kingsford Smith were perfect examples. Hinkler, born in Bundaberg, made the first solo flight from England to Australia in 1928 and the first across the southern Atlantic in 1931. Kingsford Smith made the first solo flight in 1928 from America to Australia, travelling from San Francisco to Brisbane in 83 hours. Then in 1930 he won the 16 000-kilometre air race from England to Australia. Australians thrilled to the deeds of these courageous pioneers, peering through rain-drenched goggles in their open-cockpit planes.

Sporting idols also played their part. When the famous racehorse Phar Lap died in America in 1932 there was national mourning. The champion of the 'two bob' punter was as popular as any human sports hero had ever been. The cricketer Don Bradman, whose career had spanned the Depression years, was another whose exploits were able to lessen the workingman's worries in no small way. The deeds of such champions were invariably accompanied by the acclamation afforded folk heroes.

Olive wasn't one for sporting idols even though she liked her swimming. She now found herself a hero of a very different type, being influenced by a wonderful Australian who became a role model for her. It was his courageous, daring achievements that were the major influence in the most important decision she would ever make. Her hero was the founder of the Royal Flying Doctor Service, John Flynn. His willingness and ability to overcome seemingly impossible conditions as he travelled to remote areas to tend the sick and needy slowly became the most inspiring thing in her young mind. There were no vast admiring crowds to witness Flynn's achievements but his contribution to Australia's way of life was immense.

John Flynn, born on the Victorian goldfields in 1880, began his working life as a schoolteacher, became a lay preacher spreading the gospel in Victorian country towns, and in time a minister with the Presbyterian Church. He was at first fascinated and then obsessed with the difficulties faced by people in remote areas of the continent. With colleagues he wrote a booklet called *The Bushman's Companion*, containing all sorts of advice, particularly on first aid. In 1911 he began preaching at an inland mission several hundred kilometres north of Adelaide. A year later Flynn was instrumental in setting up the Australian Inland Mission. He travelled for days in an old utility to visit settler families, farmers, shearers and stockmen in the most remote areas of South Australia and across the border into Queensland. The minister who arrived with a set of tools and the ability to fix anything from a broken heart to a kitchen clock became an institution.

In 1927, just a year after Olive's birth, he had his proudest moment when the Flying Doctor Service came into operation.

Twelve months later Australia's first flying doctor began visiting patients in outback areas. The tyranny of great distances in the bush was about to be challenged and beaten by Flynn's famous flying doctors. Single-engine planes made their way across the outback to deliver medicine and services to people who contacted them on pedal radios. Even the clever young inventor of this brand new device had been inspired by Flynn to create a way of contacting those living where there were no phones. The Reverend John Flynn was now known throughout Australia as Flynn of the Inland. The more Olive learned of him the surer she was about the path she must take, a path that would carry her to even more remote areas than Australia's outback. The blonde tomboy with the indomitable spirit and great sense of adventure was determined to train as a medical missionary and follow her grandfather Alfred, whom she also admired enormously, to New Guinea.

Chapter Two

THE MISSIONARY NURSE

Olive's inspiration, gained from John Flynn and his Inland Mission, was no passing phase. She read all she could about him and his nurses who were now working in remote areas of inland Australia. Here were women breaking new ground, providing medical assistance in previously inaccessible parts of the country. They were pioneers. She longed to work alongside such women.

The inevitable outbreak of war in Europe in September 1939 meant Australia was immediately involved. Initially it made little difference to Olive's life and none whatever to her ambition. Announcements that Australia intended to draft 20 000 soldiers and train 11 000 airmen were welcomed by the needy as well as the patriotic. It had been a slow climb out of the Depression and the unemployment rate was still around twelve and a half per cent.

There was not much evidence of military movement in Cairns or its surrounds. Most of Australia's fighting men were to be deployed overseas and it was assumed they would not be needed at home. Olive was concentrating on her new career:

Strangely we didn't seem to notice the war that much at first. I certainly didn't. We were very isolated and though the papers obviously had coverage of the fighting overseas, there was not as much as you might imagine. Not all that much was written in our local papers. Even when our boys were fighting in Tobruk and those places in North Africa later on, there wasn't a great deal in the local press. We understood what was happening, of course, but it all seemed too far away to actually involve us. You had to live in the north to really understand its isolation. Another reason we weren't too perturbed was that we didn't know how much censorship was going on. The newsreels always seemed to put a really good light on what was happening overseas. Later on the war became the main thing in all our lives but at the time I was mainly thinking of my nursing.

With my mother's consent I joined the VAD, the Voluntary Aid Detachment, an organisation formed in England by the Red Cross and the order of Saint John of Jerusalem prior to World War I. Originally consisting of upper-class women who volunteered to do work in public hospitals, the organisation had become firmly entrenched in Australia. VADs had gone to war in 1914 to assist fully trained military nurses and at the end of hostilities continued their community work. It was a natural progression from the Red Cross and certain to help me with my ambition. I did menial hospital tasks like scrubbing pans, cleaning bottles, washing soiled linen and so on and often got time off school for this purpose. All the major North Queensland towns had a Voluntary Aid Detachment. Our traditional uniform, which I was very proud of, was blue with a red cross over our heart, and a cape and veil. We were described as wearing the apron of a serving maid, the cape of a gentlewoman and the veil of a nun.

In July 1940 I turned fourteen and was able to officially begin my apprenticeship to become a medical missionary. My family had to lodge a bond of £50, which was a fair amount of money for them to find, but they were very much in favour of what I was doing. Grandfather in New Guinea was delighted of course. Because of the war the nursing course had been reduced from four years to three. I took up residence at the nurses' quarters at Cairns Base Hospital, which was the first time I'd been away from my family. I wasn't worried though; I was very independent. I think looking after Betty all those years had been a big influence. I'd gone from being little sister to big sister in one fell swoop, really, so those responsibilities probably made me a bit tougher and more advanced in certain ways than the average fourteen-year-old. Mind you, I hadn't let it dampen my sense of adventure. I was born with that and never lost it.

The discipline at the quarters was very strict with a curfew at night. We wore bottle green cotton uniforms with white caps, big white aprons and white cuffs. Unfortunately my room was right next to the matron's so whenever she had an emergency she always took a short cut through my room to get to the corridor. She'd say, 'Nurse, Nurse, come on, get up, out of bed quick, we've got an emergency.' The other nurses used to say, 'I wouldn't have that room for all the tea in China.' At times it got a bit much but 'it kept me busy and I was there to learn.

A special part of Olive's nursing course was the study of tropical medicine. This was an important part of her preparation for work in New Guinea. Malaria, dengue fever, tropical ulcers, dysentery, beriberi and scrub typhus were diseases typical of, if not exclusive to, the tropics. New Guinea was similar to northern Queensland in terrain and climate so such ailments were common to both places. Specialised knowledge of tropical medicine would stand her in good stead even if she remained to work in Cairns. Not that she really saw this as an option. She was determined to join her grandfather.

Olive settled down well to a nurse's life, thriving on the work, tough though it was. The nurses worked 126 hours per fortnight as well as studying for exams at night. It was very much 'hands on' learning, with much more practical experience than theory. On a typical day nurses rose at five-thirty, woke and bathed their patients in wards that contained up to 40 people, organised breakfast, attended to patients' dressings, saw to medications and served lunch. During visiting hours they sorted linen and put it in proper order in the large linen cupboards. They then accompanied doctors as they checked their patients before serving dinner in the evening.

Days rarely ever went exactly according to plan. There were always unscheduled events. When a patient died the nurses laid out the body and had it taken down to the morgue. The bed was stripped down to the metal, scrubbed with carbolic acid, and then made up with new linen, including the mattress, ready for the next patient. On lecture nights a nurse who had risen at five-thirty would probably get to bed a little before midnight. Whenever Olive got her one day off per fortnight she hurried home to see her parents. She missed seeing her father, who had invariably been absent when the family had holidayed during her childhood. He had been unable to enjoy those happy occasions, remaining at work on the wharves trying to keep the bank balance in the black. William had always wanted a son, so his tomboy Olive was 'the apple of his eye'. Despite her busy schedule, Olive continued her work with the VADs.

She gained experience in the various wards including casualty and the special isolation ward that housed patients with contagious ailments such as scabies and a number of leprosy victims, mainly Aboriginal or Chinese. Many of them were from the leper colony at Palm Island, 30 kilometres off the coast between Cairns and Townsville. This was one of two colonies that Olive was aware of, the other being in the Gulf of Carpentaria. She was surprised at just how many Aborigines suffered from leprosy. Many were incurable but some who were lucky enough to have had their condition detected early were eventually able to resume normal lives. It was believed the disease had been introduced to the country by Chinese who had come to the goldfields.

Though masks were not needed, nurses had to be very careful to wash their hands thoroughly with disinfectant when entering and leaving the isolation ward. There were strict procedures to follow to ensure that disease did not spread. Dr Moffett, the chief medical officer, used to advise the girls to have a cigarette when they returned to their quarters after working in the isolation ward. He assured them that it helped kill germs in the throat. Sadly Olive took up smoking to follow his advice: 'I cursed the bastard for more than 30 years. That's how long it took me to kick the habit.'

Then there was the morgue. Situated in the far corner of the hospital grounds, separated from the main building by trees and shrubs, it was quite eerie to walk to, especially at night. The only light came from a hurricane lamp that the nurse carried, and it made shadows dance on the trees as she walked. Autopsies were not pleasant, particularly the first few. Seeing a body cut up like a carcase in a butcher's shop was too much for some. Olive noticed how often strapping young probationary police officers, part of whose training involved witnessing autopsies, passed out during this procedure. They would be carried outside and propped up against the wall in the fresh night air. It seemed to Olive that women had a more natural and stronger defence mechanism on such occasions. When a young constable toppled over there was a wry smile at the 'stronger sex'.

Twice a week nurses were allowed late nights to go to the cinema. The night staff signed a book as nurses re-entered the hospital. At ten o'clock sharp a red line was drawn across the page to show who had not yet returned. Matron examined the book next morning. On one rare occasion Olive was returning by bicycle to her quarters at one-thirty in the morning when who should arrive simultaneously by car but the matron. Her superior had obviously had a lot to drink and was quite tipsy, which came as a surprise to Olive. 'Good morning, Nurse,' said Matron, putting strong emphasis on the word 'morning'. 'Good morning, Matron,' she replied most politely. Olive was surely doomed. That morning she waited for the inevitable call to Matron's office. It never came and not a word was ever said.

She was called to Matron's office some weeks later, however, to find her holding a little bundle of misery: a young, full-blood Aboriginal girl who had been abandoned after her parents had died. It was believed that this had occurred following a bone-pointing ceremony where the victims just lay and willed death upon themselves. This was difficult to confirm but was the belief of the police who had found her. She had certainly been left without care for a long period and was suffering from malaria, malnutrition and rickets. Olive, who was assigned to the isolation ward at the time, was directed to take her back to the ward and 'do what you can for her':

To start with I gave her a name, Frances. I don't know how the poor little thing took to me after all the apparently terrible things I did to her. I shaved her head and took blood to start with. She was absolutely terrified. Frances was eight years old but had the physical development of a child of four. She used to follow me everywhere like a shadow. She made good progress and after three months was looking quite fit and healthy, and we bought her a red satin frock. Her 'Sunday frock' we called it. She was so happy she thought all her Christmases had come at once. She was now well enough to be transferred to the children's ward on the top floor, which was at the opposite end to the women's ward. One day she caught sight of me in the women's ward and ran all the way from her ward and threw her arms around my neck. I took her around and introduced my little curly mop to the various patients. One woman asked her, 'Who's got you in her arms then?' She gave this lovely smile and said in a big voice, 'Mummy!' From then on I was known as Frances's mummy. I was thrilled to bits. It was one of those occasions when you knew all the effort and tough jobs in nursing were worthwhile.

As time went on Olive believed Frances might be better off if she was returned to her tribe, but the elders did not want her back. As an outcast they had no interest in her. She would certainly have starved if she had not been found. It was decided the hospital would rear her until she was sixteen, during which time she would be sent to primary school and then to high school. Having finished her education she would be offered a position as a domestic worker at the hospital.

When the time eventually came for Olive to leave Cairns Base Hospital she found saying goodbye to Frances very difficult indeed. Though Olive never saw Frances again she got news, many years later, through a second cousin, that he had attended high school at the same time as her. As a result of her ill-treatment early in life, Frances developed a hunched back but finished her schooling and worked at the hospital as planned. She wasn't one of the stolen generation, instead she had become one of the saved generation.

Olive's entry into the nursing ranks had coincided with the Battle of Britain. Australian pilots flew alongside British and European airmen to protect England from the German invaders. Czechoslovakia, Poland, Norway, Sweden and France had fallen. Britain was fighting for survival. In Australia the Volunteer Defence Corps was formed and tens of thousands of men, many of them veterans of the First World War, joined up. They were engaged in coastal defence, observation units, anti-aircraft operations and the like, leaving younger men free to fight overseas. By the middle of 1941 Australian divisions were fighting in North Africa helping the Allies repel the German and Italian armies, stopping them from taking the Suez Canal. The famous battles at Tobruk and El Alamein, which lasted for months, stemmed the tide in a war that until then had been going the enemy's way.

Neither America nor Japan was yet involved. Japan, like Germany in 1939, had continually stated a desire for peace. Nevertheless, they had invaded China in 1937 and within a year controlled the majority of northeast China, building a most formidable navy as well as army. The Japanese, who were obsessed with expansion, were determined to take over the whole of China as well as other areas in Asia and the Pacific. The Americans had watched Japan's progress in the Far East with anxiety and saw fit to restore their most experienced senior officer, General Douglas MacArthur, who had retired in 1937, to the Philippines as chief of the Far East Command. As America monitored Japan's military build-up, the two countries continued to talk peace.

The American people were very much against any involvement in a global war as they had been in 1914, even though there was a general belief that the Japanese navy and army would prove inferior to their own if hostilities arose. When Japan moved into Indochina in 1939, America cut off supplies of iron, steel and oil. England and the Netherlands immediately followed suit. Japan had a big decision to make: to withdraw from Indochina and have their vital oil supplies resumed, at the same time watching America build up its military forces, or to make a most momentous move.

The Japanese military were already convinced that war was the only option if their expansionist plans were to come to fruition. The embargo on oil gave further strength to their argument. The installation of their war minister, General Hideki Tojo, as prime minister meant opinions of those opposing the war were cast aside. Clearly they were worried that America's ties to Britain made them likely allies as the war broadened across Europe into Russia and North Africa. They were of the belief that Japan could win a short war with America but not a long one. Having been at war with China for three years they were in fighting mode. America was not, but this would change. In a long campaign American forces would be built up while Japan's resources would slowly ebb. A decisive, initial advantage was essential to their plans of forcing America to negotiate peace while Japan held the trump cards. Peace with conditions that would give Japan enormous power in Asia and the Pacific.

Olive had been in training just over twelve months when the Japanese attacked Pearl Harbor. The savage, audacious attack on the American fleet at its major Pacific naval base took them completely by surprise. So duplicitous were the Japanese that their diplomats were involved in peace talks with Washington at the very moment that the attack took place. Commencing at eight o'clock on Sunday morning, 7 December 1941, Pearl Harbor, on the island of Oahu, just a few kilometres west of Hawaii's capital, Honolulu, was bombarded by wave after wave of Japanese bombers and fighter aircraft. More than 350 planes, launched from eight Japanese aircraft carriers, kept up a relentless three-hour attack.

The element of surprise and the intensity of the attacks gave the Americans literally no chance. Men aboard ship were so unprepared that several admitted later they thought the first warning siren sounded as an exercise drill. Sailors rushed on deck to see low-flying torpedo bombers zooming in on them. The first torpedo hit the battleship *Arizona* amidships. Within half an hour torpedoes had struck three other battleships, *West Virginia, California* and *Nevada*, leaving them twisted, blazing wrecks. A fourth, *Oklahoma*, capsized. The harbour was an inferno. A large portion of the Pacific fleet, though fortunately not the aircraft carriers, was in the harbour or in dry dock. Military airfields on neighbouring islands were attacked simultaneously. The incessant bombardment saw America lose five battleships, 188 planes and over 2400 men. There were almost 1200 other casualties and another sixteen ships damaged. Just 29 Japanese planes were shot down. This was a brutal, well-organised enemy. Next day America declared war on Japan. Japan declared war on America, Britain and the Netherlands.

The US fleet at Pearl Harbor had proved too tempting a target for Japan to ignore. To destroy it was the first step in asserting an initiative from which America might not recover. The great irony was that American intelligence agencies had already broken the Japanese naval code so they should never have been caught napping. Within five hours the Philippines' capital Manila was also under attack. Japanese intentions were quickly evident. They planned to capture key territories in Asia and the Pacific, so that when the war ended and the spoils were shared they would control the Far East and the South Pacific.

With the involvement of Japan, Australia's situation changed immediately. Facing a potential invader from the north was a very different proposition to having men fighting overseas. Even before the Pearl Harbor attack, a site at Garbutt, six kilometres west of Townsville Harbour on the northern highway and the railway line, was selected by US army engineers to become a major military air facility. Work got underway on three intersecting runways. Olive's birthplace was to play a vital role in America's war with Japan. She watched as Cairns and Townsville, the idyllic towns of her childhood, underwent changes that she could never have imagined:

Before Christmas the first large contingent of US troops arrived in Australia when a convoy of nine ships was diverted to Brisbane on the way to Manila. It was a taste of things to come. Rescue ships were already bringing hundreds of evacuees to Townsville from Rabaul in New Britain, the large island north of Port Moresby. In a three-week period no fewer than five merchant vessels arrived in Cairns carrying civilian refugees. A Dutch DC3 airliner landed in Cloncurry, from Java, with a full load of Dutch refugees who had narrowly escaped the Japanese. Light commercial aircraft carried evacuees from Wau, among them my grandfather Alfred, who was suffering from malaria.

Manila was now under desperate attack. The 200 000-strong Imperial Japanese Army, supported by its formidable navy, was determined to press home the advantage before American reinforcements could be mustered. In early January, less than a month after Pearl Harbor, General MacArthur's American forces were driven from Manila to the Bataan Peninsula and the island fortress of Corregidor, a few kilometres off the coast and 40 kilometres south of the capital. On Corregidor MacArthur's headquarters were set up in the 250-metre long Malinta tunnel. Above ground no fewer than 25 huge, 12-inch (300-millimetre) mortars and sea guns with a minimum range of fifteen kilometres kept up constant firing against the enemy. Every day the Japanese forces could be repelled meant reinforcements from America came closer.

On the peninsula new hospitals had to be set up immediately. Fifty nurses, including 25 Filipinas, were trucked to a fishing village at Limay Beach on the eastern side of the peninsula, overlooking Manila Bay. Fifty other US nurses went in boats to Corregidor. Eleven remained in the naval hospital and were forced to surrender to the Japanese a few days later. A single US army nurse, Second Lieutenant Floramund Fellmuth, on a makeshift hospital ship, arrived in Australia in early January.

At Limay Beach American nurses, soon to play an important role in Olive's life, set up the main hospital in a series of wooden barracks. After a very hectic month (during one 24-hour period 182 major operations were performed) the hospital was relocated to a more sheltered spot in the jungle. The new location was a former engineers' headquarters with running water. Converted dirt floor barracks and water buffalo stalls, set up for 500 patients, soon had over 1000 needing attention. The hospital was given the nickname 'Little Baguio' because it looked like the Philippines' beautiful summer capital Baguio. The injured lay on double- or triple-decked bamboo bunks, some with mosquito nets and burlap curtains to help cut down the billowing red dust clouds that prevailed during the dry winter season. The hospital's primary mission was to treat surgical cases.

A second hospital was set up several kilometres east. Bulldozers carved the hospital site out of the jungle from under bamboo and acacia trees. Triple-tiered bunks fanned along the hillside. Water buffalo, wild pigs, monkeys and snakes came and went from the wards as they wished. This general hospital received overflow and recuperating patients as well as new casualties and medically ill patients.

In their quarters, covered by canvas squares tied to trees, nurses set the legs of their metal beds in tins of water so that ants could not reach the mattresses. They bathed and washed their clothes in the stream that ran through the centre of the hospital. Constant hunger made their experience one unmatched by other wartime nurses. Everyone was hungry all the time. Retreating troops had left vital food stockpiles in Manila. Planners stored 180 days of supplies in the jungle, enough to last until relief came from the United States. But they had not allowed for 26 000 refugees. Rations were cut in mid January and twice more in the next few weeks. As supplies ran out people ate anything the jungle had to offer. Buffalo, pigs, monkeys, even pack mules and horses, in order to survive. Soldiers suffered from drop-foot, bleeding gums and ulcerated mouths caused by lack of vitamin C. Nurses, light-headed and weak from hunger, carried sandwiches in their pockets so that rats would not get them.

Undaunted they performed, without complaint, the endless tasks of battlefield nursing, administering morphine and soothing the fears of young men with combat wounds. Nurses, tired but displaying good humour, cleaned injuries with green soap, applied sulphanilamide powder and changed literally thousands of dressings. They washed bodies caked with dirt and sweating from tropical disease. At night they walked the wards carrying kerosene lamps with blue-painted glass, checking for the distinctive smell of gas gangrene. Japanese prisoners and civilians also profited from their care. Here was nursing at its most basic. The ability to improvise was of extreme importance. When Olive heard of their exploits, she was inspired.

Though the signs were very ominous with the fall of Manila, the desperate position on Bataan and the capture of Rabaul, there was confidence that the Japanese invasion could be halted at Singapore.

The island, roughly a kilometre off the tip of the Malayan Peninsula, inhabited mainly by Chinese, had been one of the British Empire's most famous outposts for well over 100 years. The city of Singapore was on the southeast end of the island. Because of its location in the narrow opening between the Indian Ocean and the South China Sea, it had become a great trading port. More important now was that it was one of Britain's most strategic military bases. The island was small but it had strong defensive forts and was heavily armed. Considered to be an impenetrable fortress, it now became a key Japanese objective.

The British had expected any attack on Singapore to come from the sea. Instead it came by air and on land. The Japanese army travelled down the Malay Peninsula on foot and by bicycle as Japanese bombers devastated the harbour. The army literally marched into Singapore. Retreating Allied troops had blown up sections of the Johore Causeway that linked the island with the mainland but the Japanese could not be repelled. They repaired the causeway. Heavy guns mounted for use against invaders from the ocean could not even be used. The battle was front page news in all Australian papers though reports on its progress varied. The people of North Queensland read the reports with as much hope as confidence. Surely the Japanese could not take Singapore?

On the very day that victory was claimed in Tokyo the BBC announced there had been a successful counterattack from the Allies and that Japanese reports of British surrender could not be substantiated. However the Japanese took control of the water supply and the 'impenetrable fortress' was lost in a few days of fighting. A force of approximately 30 000 had secured the surrender of five times that number. Japanese bombardment had largely spared business and residential areas so the city was intact for them. After the battle Australians witnessed the barbarity of the

Japanese for the first time. Chinese heads were cut from their bodies and mounted on stakes. The English were treated with cruelty and contempt. This barbarity was in direct contrast to the behaviour of the Japanese during World War I, when they were allies of the British. Their paranoia and hatred of British and Dutch colonisation of Asia had put compassion beyond reach.

The fall of Singapore in February 1942 was as big an embarrassment to the British as Pearl Harbor was to the Americans and came as an enormous shock to Australia. More than 150 000 British troops surrendered including 15 000 Australians. The most important military base in Malaya was in the hands of the enemy. Australia, with its thousands of kilometres of unprotected coastline and meagre military defence, was now an open target.

Just four days after the fall of Singapore Japanese aircraft bombed Darwin, the main port of northern Australia. The raid was led by the same architects of the Pearl Harbor attack and was carried out with the same precision. For the first time since British settlement the Australian mainland was under siege. Forty-six naval and commercial vessels were in the harbour as two separate raids involving 188 attack aircraft, launched from four large aircraft carriers in the Timor Sea, and 54 bombers from islands in the Pacific, began just before 10 am. The first wave of dive bombers, supported by Zero fighters, was concentrated on the city, its harbour and nearby aerodromes, including the RAAF base, and resulted in devastation and pandemonium.

The hills above Darwin Harbour contained many large oil reservoirs. Bombs burst oil supply pipes by the side of the wharves and blew apart an oil tanker. Oil blazed across the harbour, filling the sky with black smoke and making rescue missions extremely hazardous. The hospital ship *Manunda* was strafed repeatedly by machine-gun fire, then badly damaged when a bomb exploded below decks. Margaret de Mestre was the one nurse among twelve people killed aboard the *Manunda*. The American destroyer *Peary*, stopping briefly to refuel, was sunk with a loss of 91 American seamen. Eight vessels were lost and several others badly damaged. Most of the city's vital facilities were destroyed.

The second attack was concentrated on the RAAF base six kilometres from Darwin and involved the land-based bombers. In all, approximately 250 servicemen and civilians were known to be killed and a further 400 injured. Many more were never accounted for. Hundreds of panic-stricken people, fearing an invasion, were fleeing Darwin in cars, trucks, farm vehicles, on bicycles and on foot. Half the city's population was attempting evacuation. Morale was already low because of the fall of Singapore; there was a need to deny panic. Initially the real number of fatalities and casualties was not disclosed to the Australian public. In fact a figure of well under one-tenth of actual casualties was announced. Apart from the US sailors who died on the *Peary*, four Kittyhawk fighter pilots from the US Army Air Force 33 Squadron also lost their lives. They were the first of many US airmen who would perish in Australia's north during the coming months.

Despite the government's downplaying of the real damage in the Darwin bombing, shockwaves travelled throughout Australia. Barbed wire fences suddenly appeared on beaches and harbours from Cairns to Sydney. Submarine cables were laid across entrances to major harbours. Searchlights fanned the skies in major cities across the nation. Invasion seemed much more likely in the north but people were also moving away from coastal cities in the south. A partial blackout, or 'brownout', was implemented from Queensland's coast to 160 kilometres inland. This included the masking of vehicle headlights — a real danger in remote areas where animals often strayed onto the roads.

Meanwhile Townsville had been designated as the major American military and air force base in northern Queensland. Senior US officers arrived to plan the construction of new airfields and the enlargement of others. Construction had begun on a large project adjacent to Garbutt. Seventy of 115 buildings urgently needed to house operational air force staff were already underway. Water supply problems were solved by the construction of a reservoir on nearby Castle Hill. Army air headquarters were established in a large commercial building in Denham Street. The Bayview guesthouse on Stanton Hill was acquired to billet senior air force personnel and the Empire Hotel, South Townsville, recently renamed The Republican, housed more headquarters' staff. Evacuees continued to arrive by sea and air as a permanent camp was set up at the showgrounds for miscellaneous persons.

Improvements to the highway to Charters Towers, 135 kilometres west of Townsville, became a priority with convoys of troops travelling daily. Here two temporary airfields were established at the football grounds and one by the cemetery. Such was the urgency of the operation it took just seventeen days to build the new landing strips, hangars and associated buildings required for a major airfield. Hundreds of giant termite mounds were crushed and used as foundations for the runways. Bombers and heavy fighters took off as the tarmac was drying. Old goldmine shafts were used to store explosives, ammunition and fuel. Near the northern runway, which is still being used 60 years later, visitors may read a tribute to those involved during the war years: 'This plaque is dedicated to the 15000 members of the armed forces of the United States of America who served in the Charters Towers district during World War II.' Perhaps a second plaque should be dedicated to those who built it in the time it would now take to read the plans.

The bulk of airfield construction was carried out by black American units, the 91st and 96th engineers' regiments. It caused a great deal of controversy that these black servicemen were allowed into Australia, contrary to Australia's strict White Australia Policy. The fact is they did a magnificent job on airstrips and roads desperately needed to create the massive staging areas called for by US Command. Theirs were the 'non glamorous' units like construction and transport. Controlled by white commanders whom they generally resented, they were supposed to have no contact at all with civilians during their stay and were generally billeted well away from the townships. Their establishments were completely self-contained, even to having their own hospitals and morgues.

Townsville was being transformed into a garrison city. It would continue to grow. Only those involved at the top level realised by how much. The 30 000-strong population would soon escalate to well over 100 000, despite the fact that some 5000 civilians had left to travel south to avoid the impending invasion. The military would outnumber civilians by four to one. Before the arrival of American troops government authorities had encouraged civilians to evacuate. Now they encouraged them to return. However, the top military brass were happy with the evacuations. As homes became empty they were quickly filled with American servicemen.

In the cause of security, many troops, American and Australian, were sent to Townsville without knowing their destination. When they wrote home the censor did not allow them to disclose where they were. Blackouts were now a regular occurrence. Air-raid wardens patrolled the city on pushbikes ensuring people did not show even the smallest light during the blackouts. Curtains were drawn, windows blacked out and lined with masking tape to minimise damage from shattered glass in case of bombing. Candles became an essential household item. Lavatories were invariably outside the houses, but no lit torches were allowed on associated comfort trips. The obligatory search for red-back spiders began only after shutting the lavatory door. Car headlights were masked so as to throw minimum light; bicycle lamps were not lit at all.

On the Bataan Peninsula it was clear the gallant holding action could not last much longer. Second Lieutenant Ruth Straube wrote in her diary on 27–28 March: 'We're out of ink, we're out of flour. Last bread was baked yesterday, had to clear another section of jungle for more beds, bombings were very close, one whizzed right over our heads, we all fell to ground. What a mess, we still have anaesthetics thank God. We literally have nothing else left but hope and each other.'

Lack of quinine saw 500 hospitalised per day. This number soon grew to 1000. Almost everyone suffered from malaria or dysentery. Food was so scarce soldiers, still fighting long and exhausting hours, existed on 1000 calories per day, less than a third of that required to maintain energy and normal body weight. As more casualties arrived extra bunks were fashioned from bamboo. By 1 April, casualties were so prolific it was decided there was no sense keeping count. On 5 April, Easter Sunday, the main hospital came under attack. It was 10.30 am when the first wave of bombers struck. There was a cry, 'Plane overhead!' The first bombs exploded near the hospital entrance blowing up an ammunition truck. As nurses scrambled to help casualties a guard shouted, 'They're coming back. Nurses cut tractions!' The second wave of bombs hit the mess tent and doctors' and nurses' quarters. The third wave scored a direct hit on the wards. Iron beds and patients were blown into the trees. Bodies and bedding were strewn through the jungle. Dozens of men died.

On 8 April the chief nurses were told to evacuate their staff, the enemy was less than two kilometres away. Around twilight, nurses learned they had ten minutes to be ready to leave. As they evacuated to Corregidor, 20 minutes across the water, they had to leave behind 7000 patients in the two hospitals. It was absolutely heartbreaking for them to see their patients left without help. The following day Major Edward King Jnr, the Commander on Bataan, tried to surrender but Japan's General Homma would not meet him. King did not speak for General Wainwright and therefore could not surrender the entire Philippine garrison. Eventually a lesser officer, Colonel Nakayama, accepted surrender from King, who pleaded repeatedly for a guarantee that the prisoners would be treated under the conditions of the Geneva Convention. No such guarantee was ever given. The only response to King's repeated request was a curt assertion from Colonel Nakayama: 'The Imperial Japanese Army are not barbarians.' In many cases the exact opposite proved to be the case.

The nurses who remained in the Philippines were forced to join the infamous 'death march of Bataan', from the peninsula to Camp O'Donnell, 135 kilometres north, on which thousands of malaria-stricken and starving prisoners died. For the nurses to be made to march was strictly against the Geneva Convention as they were noncombatants. On the death march the weakest prisoners who fell behind were bayoneted, beheaded, shot or beaten and left to die. Distressed nurses saw the pyjama-clad bodies of patients, taken from their hospital, lying in ditches by the roadside.

Australia now faced the real possibility of attack by the Japanese army. In Darwin people had no doubt they would be invaded, and quickly. They streamed out of the city in their thousands, heading south to safety. Continued bombing raids further convinced them it was only a matter of time before ground fighting ensued. Australia's meagre defence of the north terrified them.

While thousands fled the north others remained. Olive's family stayed in Cairns, and her father worked on the wharves throughout the war. With slit trenches being dug in every backyard, William decided to go one better. At the back of the chook run stood a magnificent cascara tree, perhaps a hundred years old, with large black pods and beautiful buttercup yellow flowers hanging in profusion. Olive had climbed and played in the cascara since she was a little girl. On one occasion she sat in the tree and ate all the beans from a split pod, not knowing cascara was a strong purgative. She recalls her mother feeding her grated cheese, hard-boiled eggs and cornflour 'for about a week'.

Below the tree her father built a lined underground shelter. His mission completed, he waited to test its efficiency. Olive looked forward to the first use of his elaborate bunker. A week or so passed before the air-raid siren sounded. The family dashed to the shelter and clambered in. Pandemonium resulted. About 20 large cane toads had taken up residence as well as a Rhode Island rooster and a supporting cast of hens. All objected strongly to the invasion by the family and their untimely ejection. Sure enough, the air-raid warning proved to be a false alarm. When no bombs were dropped William decided that next time they would take the risk of staying in the house.

Olive now saw aliens being arrested, even those who had been born in Australia or had been naturalised. People in prominent official and commercial positions became victims of suspicion:

Some of the Italian canegrowers and market gardeners, though not all, were sent south to internment camps. In places like Ingham and Innisfail people of Italian descent outnumbered others by ten to one. Forty were arrested in Innisfail in one week. We never understood why some went and not others. The men were taken while wives and families stayed and worked the farms. Some of the local newspapers were pressing the government into making everyone speak English in public. The poor old Japanese laundryman who had been a friend for years was locked up behind the police station in a barbed wire enclosure. People came down and poked fun at him. He'd been doing their linen for years. I felt very sorry for him.

In Cairns Olive and her family heard Prime Minister John Curtin make a national radio broadcast in March 1942 which was also filmed and shown in picture theatres across the land:

> The full Cabinet today directed the War Cabinet to gazette the necessary regulations for the complete mobilisation, and the complete ordering, of all the resources, human and material, in this Commonwealth, for the defence of this Commonwealth. That means, clearly and specifically, that every human being in this country is now, whether he or she likes it, at the service of the government to work in the defence of Australia.

I was inspired by that speech. When I heard it I didn't see volunteering as an option — we weren't being asked, we were being told to work in the defence of Australia. I was only young but I didn't think of myself in that light. I was Australian and I was needed. And I admired John Curtin. The whole family loved him. He became a hero to us. All through that early part of the war he argued with Churchill to get our troops home to defend us.

Olive decided there and then that her missionary work would have to wait. She went next day to see her commander at the Voluntary Aid Detachment to tell her she wished to help with the war effort instead. Senior VADs were now being sent abroad to work in military hospitals as well as in Australia. They were accepted into the AAMWS: the Australian Army Medical Women's Service. This seemed the logical step for Olive. She had been a member of the VAD for over two years and of the Red Cross before that. Her commitment, along with her studies at the base hospital, entitled her to be ranked not far behind a fully qualified sister. Though not quite sixteen, she was accepted, with her mother's permission, on a probationary basis.

No sooner had she begun training than her commander told her, 'The Americans have just arrived and are looking for nurses with training in tropical medicine. Nurses from the south, even the experienced ones, generally have had no involvement with it. Olive, we'd love to keep you here, but my instructions are to advise you to get over to US headquarters and tell them what you've done. You might have trouble being so young but perhaps they'll be able to sort things out.'

This was something Olive had never contemplated. Still, it sounded exciting. The impetuosity of youth was stirred. After all, it was the same war and the Americans had come to save them. As far as the age problem was concerned she decided to use her sister Betty's birth date. Would she need to show a birth certificate? Probably not. Provided she had her parents' consent, that should be no trouble. Also, she was tall and certainly looked older than her fifteen and a half years. Why should they doubt her? They hadn't bothered to check teenagers who had put their ages up to go to the first war or this one. Never being one to baulk at a challenge, Olive needed no further prompting:

I got my papers together, went to the US headquarters building and showed them my nursing record. I made sure they saw my experience with tropical diseases. The recruitment officer said I could be transferred from the VAD there and then if that was what I wanted. I couldn't fill out the forms fast enough. I used Betty's date of birth instead of my own. She was born in January 1924 so, with the aid of one white lie, I was suddenly eighteen. I wasn't even sure it mattered. I swore the oath of allegiance to the United States, signed secrecy agreements and there I was, in the American army. It all took 20 minutes. I still needed one parent's consent so hurried home with the relevant form. I knew Mum wouldn't object to my being employed by the Americans as long as I was doing my bit.

The first order Olive received on joining up was to get her hair cut. This she did before going home to see her family. When her mother saw her without her long blonde plait she was so upset she burst into tears. 'Oh, Olive, you've had your beautiful hair cut off,' she wailed. 'Yes, Mum, and as soon as you've signed this form, I'll be in the American army!' came the reply. When Olive explained the situation Alda was not only agreeable she was proud of her daughter's decision.

Chapter Three

LIEUTENANT OLIVE

Olive was about to get a new boss. Japan's entry into the war presented Douglas MacArthur with the opportunity to become the most famous American general of the twentieth century. Perhaps he had already achieved that status. The son of a former US general, Arthur MacArthur, Douglas graduated brilliantly from New York's West Point Military Academy in 1903.

When the US entered the First World War in 1917, MacArthur was made a colonel. By war's end, in 1918, he was a brigadier general. His star continued to shine. By 1930, at the age of 50, MacArthur had achieved the rank of general — the US army's youngest chief of staff since General Ulysses Grant more than 70 years earlier. MacArthur had spent literally every day of his 61 years in the military. Among his many assignments were commands in

Japan, Mexico and America. His final two years were spent in the Philippines where he developed a great affinity with the people of the exotic island republic. In July 1941, just a few months before the attack on Pearl Harbor, MacArthur, retired for four years, had been returned to service in the Philippines. Immediately after Pearl Harbor MacArthur was made commander of the US armed forces in the Far East. Shortly before the fall of Bataan, he was ordered by US President Roosevelt to vacate the Philippines and head to Australia to take command of all Allied troops in the southwest Pacific. It would be MacArthur's task to stop the relentless Japanese surge through the Pacific region.

Douglas MacArthur's escape to Australia was extremely dangerous. On 11 March 1942, with his wife Jean, four-year-old son Arthur, the boy's Chinese nurse and an entourage of officers, he sailed in one of four PT boats from the small rocky island fortress of Corregidor through Japanese waters to a military airfield on the island of Mindanao. It was a hazardous escape across the open sea. Leaving at dusk, the 25-metre boats, laden with passengers and luggage, travelled at full speed on a journey that took almost two days. In Mindanao they were to rendezvous with three B17 Flying Fortress bombers assigned to their rescue. Only two of the three planes arrived and MacArthur was not happy with the condition of the aircraft, or with the capabilities of the crews. He demanded the best three B17s available with experienced, dependable crews. What's more, they were to be military planes; he did not wish to be rescued by the navy, with which he was already at loggerheads.

Three more Flying Fortresses were despatched, this time from Townsville, but again only two made it to Mindanao. The huge bombers were equipped for combat, not for transportation, so most of MacArthur's personal luggage had to be left behind. When they taxied to the runway on the dimly lit airfield they were loaded to the hilt. Severe turbulence along with the danger of flying over captured territories in the Celebes, Timor and part of New Guinea made the five-hour flight a nightmare. MacArthur hated flying. Even when they reached Darwin they found their destination under heavy bombardment and were diverted to Batchelor airfield about 70 kilometres to the south.

In the comparative safety of Batchelor, MacArthur sought respite for his wife and son. The previous few days had been a dreadful ordeal for the pair, particularly young Arthur. He requested they go by car to the nearest railway station from which they could travel to Adelaide. When advised this was at Alice Springs, 1600 kilometres away, less than a third of which could be travelled by train and the rest over unsealed roads, the party settled for two twin-engine DC3 aircraft, which took them to the Alice. After the cramped conditions of the B17s it was not only luxury, it was also safe. After a night's rest at Alice Springs where MacArthur is reported to have relaxed with a trip to the open-air cinema, he sent most of his staff ahead by plane and chartered a special train, consisting of three wooden carriages and a steam locomotive engine, to take the rest of the party to Adelaide. On the old narrow-gauge Ghan tracks they set off on another 1500-kilometre excursion, stopping occasionally in remote areas to refuel and fill up with water. Top speed was less than 40 kilometres per hour.

There were no passageways between carriages so the train stopped at meal times to allow the party to walk to the dining car. MacArthur was amazed at the vastness of the terrain. When they reached the small township of Terowie, 250 kilometres north of Adelaide, they had been on board for more than two days. Here the tracks changed to South Australia's wider gauge and a new train was on standby to take the party to Adelaide. An admiring crowd gave the general a warm reception with much cheering and cries of welcome. The local press took photos, which showed young Arthur, now fully recovered from his ordeal, dressed in military uniform.

MacArthur inspected a guard of honour and told the local press of his intention to lead his troops back to recapture the Philippines. It was in this small country town he first uttered his famous quote, 'I shall return,' one he would often repeat and one that would be remembered for decades after the war had ended. Though surprised that his arrival in the town caused so much excitement, he was clearly in his element as he spoke for the first time to the Australian people. MacArthur was a charismatic performer, dashing, outspoken and single-minded, but every inch a gentleman. The 61-year-old veteran soldier was an impressive figure in a very positive mood. As Australia was soon to realise, recapturing the Philippines was his obsession.

MacArthur had requested as little fuss as possible be made of his arrival in Adelaide. Naturally this was complied with though people rushed to get a glimpse of the famous general. After just a few hours he set off for Melbourne in two special compartments on the Melbourne Express. His family and entourage were tired but happy when the eventful journey, which had begun in Corregidor ten days earlier, was over at long last. Good fortune had been with them.

In Melbourne MacArthur was treated like a hero. Cheering crowds flocked to see his arrival. He appeared in public wearing his uniform with the familiar peaked officer's cap and rows of medals on his chest. Stepping from his black, English limousine he was an impressive figure, but behind the confident exterior was a worried man. He immediately saw the need for more troops and more planes. Many thousands of American GIs, so named because of the words 'General Issue' printed on their equipment, were already in Europe to oppose Hitler. In time there would be one and a half million of them. MacArthur knew he would have to battle to get anything like the sort of numbers he wanted in the Pacific. He knew too that he would get plenty of opposition from Winston Churchill, who was as obsessed about the defence of Europe as MacArthur was about the Pacific. What was not as well known was the resentment that would emerge from US navy commanders who believed they should be making the major decisions in the Pacific. Japan now controlled vital positions in Guam, Wake Island, the Gilbert and Solomon Islands as well as French Indochina, Burma, Thailand, Malaya, Singapore and the majority of New Guinea. Australian authorities had arranged MacArthur's headquarters in Melbourne but he soon had different ideas. A week before his arrival American bombers had flown their first mission out of Townsville to New Guinea.

In Cairns, Olive was temporarily assigned to the signal corps while plans were in place to set up a number of hospitals to accommodate the increasing US military personnel. Within ten days she was given the rank of lieutenant and flown by army transport plane to her home town of Townsville where the large US 12th Station Hospital was about to be established. Three other Queensland nurses, recruited along with Olive from the VAD because of similar training in tropical medicine, were afforded the same rank. This ensured that they were out of the reach of noncommissioned men and that the GIs would not dare to harass them. The nurses were discouraged, if not forbidden, from fraternising with soldiers of lower rank. 'To keep us out of harm's way,' Olive was told. Olive's salary was seven pounds a week. It was a fortune compared to what the Australian Army nurses were getting. And the advantages did not stop there:

The Americans wanted for nothing. My issue contained several uniforms, short-sleeved blouses and skirts for daytime use, and long sleeves and slacks for evening shifts to protect us from the mosquitos. We also had overalls for everyday working gear. We washed our own underwear but everything else was laundered for us. When I met some of the Australian nurses I soon realised how lucky I was even apart from the pay. I found out I could get anything I wanted from the store, which they called the PX. Talcum powder, lipstick, brassieres, stockings, you name it, we had it, so I was able to look after the Australian nurses I knew. Some of our VADs had come down from Cairns as I had and I saw them around the town and at social functions. I was the best customer our PX ever had. Prices were so cheap and there I was earning a comparative fortune. Later on, if the Australian nurses were short on medical supplies, I used to requisition them from our store and pass them on. We were fighting the same war so I couldn't see the difference. At one stage I met a group of Australian girls who were sterilising needles in a sardine tin. My lot weren't going to miss a couple of new, stainless steel American sterilisers, were they?

When General Wainwright was forced to surrender the Philippines there were still 50 American army nurses on Corregidor. MacArthur wanted desperately to have as many as possible evacuated to Australia. With tens of thousands of US troops about to be transported to Australia he would need as many experienced nurses as possible. In Bataan the Filipina nurses who worked side by side with the Americans had been wonderful. They knew the jungle and the tropical diseases and adjusted well to difficult conditions as most had been brought up on the land. This is why he sought out young women like Olive, who had similar local experiences in Queensland.

Of the 50 US nurses, 20 were captured and a plane carrying ten more crash-landed on Mindanao en route to Australia. They too were forced to surrender to the Japanese. However, 20 others managed to escape. Olive was delighted to learn that nine would be sent to US hospitals in Brisbane and the other eleven were to be assigned to the 12th Station Hospital in Townsville. They were superb, experienced nurses and would be a tremendous help to the relatively inexperienced young Australians. She was mildly amused when Colonel Chew, chief medical officer, warned her, 'Don't get involved in any hard drinking sessions with them. They're great nurses but tough cookies. They can drink most of our GIs under the table.'

When Olive arrived in Townsville, the sleepy town she once knew was already a bustling and very noisy garrison city:

Thousands of troops were already living in khaki tents all around the town. They were mainly American, but Australian servicemen and women were arriving too. The demand on local facilities was soon overloaded. Townsville had little sewerage, limited electricity and very few bitumen roads. Council and military units worked together around the clock to establish bigger and better facilities in these areas. We saw heavy machinery arriving by sea for use in roadworks and airport construction. Large galvanised iron buildings were springing up all over the place. They were the shape of tall water tanks, split down the middle and placed on the ground with the arc at the top. Anything up to 150 metres long and 30 metres wide, they were used as repair shops, hangars, equipment stores, vehicle depots and that sort of thing. We all called them 'igloos' because of their shape.

It was very difficult for people who had lived all their lives in a quiet town to adjust to the changes going on all around them. Civilian and military traffic vied for space. Planes taxied down streets already crowded with jeeps, buses, trucks, cars and cyclists. As petrol rationing hit, the locals took to cycling everywhere. Tyres were as hard to get as fuel and the army took priority in everything. With so many men having joined up there was a shortage of timber-cutters so even wood was rationed. 'Friendly' aliens were put to work chopping timber for private use and civilians would load up billycarts and prams from the depot to take wood home for cooking and heating.

The noise of machinery and aeroplanes never stopped. You just had to accept it or you'd have gone mad. It went on 24 hours a day. Damaged planes limped back from missions and crash-landed nearby. The Flying Fortresses suffered more casualties taking off and landing than during their bombing raids. Some of the pilots were very inexperienced and if a large bomber like the B17 or Marauder crashed on take-off the crew had no chance as the bombs exploded and incinerated the plane. When planes struck bad weather they would often return dangerously short of fuel. We'd be waiting at the hospital for the casualties. Over 500 US planes had reached Australia between December 1941 and March 1942. Now only a quarter of them were still in commission. It was a never-ending job to keep them in the air. Technical crews worked all day and night to fix them. As they were repaired they were rolled out of hangars to be tested and lined up for the next assignment. There were invariably long queues of various aircraft standing nose-to-tail at Garbutt or alongside other airstrips.

Searchlights were installed and lit up the sky to look for enemy planes. Barbed wire fences were built along the length of the Strand and Rowes Bay. Armed sentries stood guard on every corner. Large slit trenches were dug in schools and other public places as well as smaller ones in private backyards. Some people made quite elaborate shelters that kids used as cubbyhouses. Every time I looked at a trench I thought of that night in Dad's masterpiece in the chook run at Cairns.

Several anti-aircraft batteries were established, including some on Magnetic Island where naval and air force units were operating. In

Flinders Street, the middle of town, fifteen large concrete pillboxes were built underground to shelter troops and civilians who worked in the centre of town, in case of air raids. Air-raid drills were regularly carried out. Once the sirens sounded people would come from everywhere, scurrying below ground.

Military hospitals, both American and Australian, were set up in several locations. The 12th Station Hospital, which would be Olive's headquarters for the next two and a half years, was established in Chapman Street, Townsville. Residents were advised that theirs was the ideal location and the army needed it. Those who were worried about their safety and were able to stay with family or friends in the south were happy to leave. Not all felt this way but they had little choice. Within a week, after some tough government negotiation, they were gone, not to return until after the war.

Thirty residences were acquired in all, on either side of the street in what was called the Mysterton Estate. The homes were typical 'Queenslanders', high up on stilts to allow for airflow to negate the tropical heat. US navy construction workers, known as 'seabees', worked around the clock to link all the cottages by covered walkways so that the staff need not continually go up and down stairs when they went from one building to the next. When the complex was completed a nurse could walk around the entire hospital at the one level. Walls were knocked out as homes were converted into wards and auxiliary service buildings. On one side were the laundry, kitchen, pathology laboratory, X-ray theatre, mess hall, maintenance workshops and the like; on the other were the morgue and several wards, including casualty and surgical. The finest home in the street became the psychiatric ward, complete with barred windows. Engineers worked day and night to improve drainage, vitally important in an area where malaria was a constant threat, and to install sewerage, extra water and electricity supplies.

Olive arrived a week before the hospital was due to open and witnessed 12th Station Hospital units, including 250 beds, arriving by train from Brisbane. Some medical officers and hospital staff were already accommodated in local homes or the Botanic Gardens camp, but nurses were billeted in Armstrong Paddock, a flat, open area two blocks from the hospital. Initially living in tents, they were soon transferred to rough, hastily constructed wooden huts barely big enough for two. Armstrong Paddock was exactly that, an open paddock. Huge, perhaps three kilometres by two, dry, very dusty and completely devoid of trees. It was a real eye-opener, even for one as pragmatic as Olive:

The area was a tent city. I guess it must have held 4000 troops at any one time. Maybe more. The 135th Medical Regiment set up a convalescent hospital. Also at hand were portable field hospital units, ready for departure to whatever destination needed them. Troops and equipment came and went from Brisbane to New Guinea and the Pacific via Armstrong, including the 500-bed 33rd Surgical Regiment, which was headed for Guadalcanal in the Solomon Islands. Large huts were constructed to accommodate boardrooms, telephone operations, a post office, quartermaster's store, covered recreation areas, a dispensary and several mess halls.

We had separate communal bathing and ablution blocks for males and females. Privacy was at a minimum and modesty quickly went by the board. You soon got used to it — you had no choice. I adapted to this better than some. A body was a body as I saw it. In the hotter months the heat was extreme. We locals didn't care so much but some poor devils who'd come from cold climates really felt it dreadfully.

Duckworth Street, which ran the full length of the paddock on the far side to the hospital, was cleared and used as an auxiliary army runway for planes, including the giant B17 Flying Fortresses. They taxied at speed to and from repair hangars creating a cloud of red dust that remained a constant companion. The dust became red mud when the rains came. We wore wellington boots over our overalls right through the monsoon season. The mud was almost up to our knees. Sartorial elegance wasn't high on our priority list. Our dress uniforms were used only when we went out on special occasions.

I'll never forget my first meal at Armstrong Paddock. I walked into the mess tent, the only female present, a young one at that, and queued for my meal. I wore no insignia, just a pair of khaki overalls. The nurses from Bataan had not yet arrived. I moved from one soldier to the next [at the servery] and was given a standard meal for the tropics: cold, diced pork, cold baked beans, diced apple and celery. It didn't look very appetising, even for army food, but worse was to come. The next man plopped ice cream and peaches on top of the whole lot. It now looked positively revolting. This was no doubt considered an appropriate introduction for the 'new girl'. I asked him, 'What's this?'

'That's what you get ma'am', he said in a very thick American accent.

I expected some respect and saw no reason to compromise so I threw the lot in his face. I didn't miss him. I then returned my empty plate to the first man so that we could start the procedure again. We'd reached an understanding and I had no more trouble. In fact in busy times later on I often requested food to be brought to my quarters out of hours and the mess duty detail always obliged.

Despite the town's upheaval, locals were, in the main, thankful for the American presence in Townsville. Their confidence grew with every American arrival. Civilians had watched in awe when the

Liberty Ship *President Pollock* arrived at Townsville's No 5 berth and lowered amphibious ducks and jeeps over the side. The vehicles proceeded up Ross Creek and went ashore in an area adjacent to the Flying Squadron Sailing Club. Shipping arriving in the harbour increased weekly. The first of many vessels to land aircraft, *Tophee,* discharged twenty-two US P39 Aircobra fighters. The single-seater aircraft were towed through the city to Garbutt.

Yet this caused mild excitement compared to the arrival of twelve huge Boeing B17 Flying Fortresses. These were the largest and best-known aircraft of the war, over 30 metres long with a wingspan of 22 metres. The four-engine giants of the sky came to epitomise the American air force. With a range of more than 3000 kilometres, they were the first of many that would launch bombing raids from Townsville on New Guinea and beyond. Throughout the war the Boeing Corporation produced over 12 000 Flying Fortresses. Many were given names and insignia by their crews, which were painted on the side of the plane. High altitude bombing was relatively new and they had limited success in the Pacific. It was not until they were deployed over Germany that their true worth was realised. Nevertheless the sight of a ten-man aircrew, in leather flying jackets and helmets, manning the big bomber was inspiring. Soon after, 51 smaller Martin Marauder bombers arrived in Townsville Harbour by ship. The four Marauder squadrons were assigned to different airfields.

This explosion of military population and equipment was not just happening in places close to the coast. When the US 93rd Squadron arrived in the outback town of Cloncurry, almost 800 kilometres west of Townsville, all eight hotels were occupied by the Americans. The town's dance hall and shire hall were transformed into makeshift hospitals and the RSL hall became an operating theatre.

Work on vital installations continued around the clock. Within three months there would be seventeen military airfields within an hour's flying time of Townsville. Several were on the outskirts of the city. One of the major bases was established at Mareeba just west of Cairns. Here workmen had a complete airfield facility operable in seven days. From Mareeba three squadrons of Flying Fortresses flew their missions across the north of the continent to New Guinea or more distant Pacific islands. These intrepid airmen were awarded a host of group and individual citations but their casualties were heavy. The state school in Mareeba was assigned for conversion into a US army hospital.

In spite of her rank Olive wore a uniform with no insignia of any kind. Her peers and superior officers did likewise. It was a deliberate safeguard against Japanese sympathisers and fifth columnists. US authorities were very conscious of spies operating in Australia, particularly around cities where military personnel were abundant. US servicemen were constantly reminded of the danger of 'loose lips'. Throughout the city copies of this simple poster were prominently displayed:

HEREUNDER ARE SEVEN SECURITY COMMANDMENTS.

1. WHAT YOU DO NOT KNOW — YOU WILL NEVER TELL.

2. WHAT YOU DO NOT KNOW — WILL NEVER BE REPEATED.

3. WHAT IS NEVER REPEATED — WILL NEVER BE OVERHEARD.

4. WHAT IS NOT HEARD — WILL NEVER BE LEARNED BY THE JAP.

5. WHAT THE JAP DOES NOT KNOW — WILL ALWAYS COME AS
A SURPRISE.

6. WHEN THE JAP IS SURPRISED — HE IS MUCH EASIER TO DEFEAT.

7. WHEN THE JAP IS DEFEATED — YOU, YANK, CAN GO HOME.

SILENT SAM

When the 12th Station Hospital opened in late March 1942 it contained 480 beds and had the look of an exclusive private hospital complex with its tall, handsome weatherboard cottages and white picket fences. As the military echelon and politicians grappled with the massive problem of how best to defend the country, Olive and her fellow nurses went about their task of treating American troops:

On our first day the hospital had just four patients who were ill, not battle victims. The numbers grew quickly enough as patients were transferred from other hospitals and air traffic increased, but we had no idea just how hectic things would get when the ground fighting started in New Guinea a few months later. Initially work was very similar to that in a civilian hospital. The arrival of the 'Angels of Bataan' saw the hospital move into top gear. We worked four hours on and four hours off, or eight hours straight, depending on a roster that in busy times became more of a guide than a schedule. There were no unions and no overtime.

Morning shifts were busiest as men arrived from sick parades from various units. We served breakfast, replaced linen, changed dressings, cleaned wounds with antiseptic green soap and covered them with white sulphanilamide powder. The hospital always had an antiseptic smell about it. It soon became obvious we would have more malaria patients than any other. Malaria, dengue fever and dysentery were our most common concerns. Malaria and dengue fever patients arrived with exceedingly high temperatures, sweating profusely. We gave them quinine three times daily as well as paracetamol and helped keep them cool by swabbing them with cold water. Fortunately we had no scrub typhus patients, although rare cases had been reported.

We all worked shifts in the various wards so as to become as proficient as possible in all areas. Afternoon shifts were less hectic though never dull. We served lunch, accompanied doctors as they checked patients, administered medication and folded linen as it arrived from the laundry. Dinner was served at six o'clock — 1800 hours, as we called it — and patients were prepared for sleep. The night shifts were pretty quiet in the early stages. We cooled malaria patients down throughout the day and night by swabbing them with cold water and changed their linen as it became soaked with sweat. The women from Bataan were wonderful nurses and I learned everything I could from them.

As a nurse finished her duties she woke her replacement. We were encouraged to take a nap when we finished our shifts. This wasn't a problem on moderate nights but during hot nights and in the daytime it was very difficult. Nurses and officers had the luxury of mosquito nets, though others didn't. We were ordered to use them as a protection against infection. It was imperative we took every step to avoid malaria and dengue fever. If you were caught trying to sleep without them you were charged. In the months leading up to the wet season the humidity made sleeping very difficult and the mosquito nets made you feel half as sweaty again, so there was a temptation to sleep without them.

We had four medical officers, really good fellows, and all surgeons in private life. Colonel Chew, the commanding officer, was a handsome, very calm man in his forties, always in control and never flustered. Major Gray, his second in command, was another thorough gentleman, a few years older. Captain Connolly was a specialist on Fifth Avenue, which apparently was pretty swish and no doubt very well paid. Occasionally he would tell us he could have been back home making a fortune and getting famous, and I think he meant it. He was the only one with any pretensions to the upper class, but he was all right and also well liked. Lieutenant Fitzgerald, being the lesser ranked, seemed to get all the menial tasks like filling out reports, but handled it with good humour. All four worked really hard in very difficult conditions and they were nobody's fools. When the occasional malingerers came in disguising a hangover or a simple desire not to work with the flu or a migraine headache they got a very short shrift. We only saw them once.

I remember my first operation when a soldier had lost some fingers in an explosion. The doctors were still operating and the poor devil started slowly coming out of the anaesthetic. Doctor yelled to me, 'Hop up on his legs, hold him still,' so of course I did while they kept operating. We didn't have straps on the table so I had to sit tight while he started groaning and trying to roll around. Was it any wonder M*A*S*H was my favourite TV show years later?

As the weeks came and went Olive settled into the routine of military nursing. Each shift and each ward brought different problems. There were always malaria patients, some GIs coming in several times as the fever flared up again. Apart from aircrew casualties there were occasional motor accident victims, often the result of blackouts making driving more dangerous than normal. In outlying areas, drivers not used to country roads sometimes lost control after hitting kangaroos or cattle. Soldiers came down with other tropical ailments, dengue fever, dysentery and the inevitable venereal diseases.

Once the Americans realised the prevalence of malaria and dengue fever, both spread by mosquitos, they sent a large contingent of men out to spray the swamp areas outside the town. A few weeks before the hospital opened in Townsville there had been an outbreak of malaria in Cairns, where the 500 victims included 50 servicemen. Authorities were concerned the epidemic might have been caused by evacuees arriving from New Guinea. The spraying in Townsville proved quite effective. To avoid contracting malaria nurses took quinine tablets each morning. In time quinine was replaced by

Atabrin, a treatment that made the skin quite yellow. 'We looked like a bunch of hepatitis victims,' Olive recalls.

Unless working under extreme pressure, nurses had one or perhaps two days leave each week. This was their own time and so they were free to go to the pictures or dances but were not allowed to wear civilian clothes:

I enjoyed the nursing and relished the hard work but the one thing that got me down a bit after a while was wearing the same drab khaki colour day in, day out. Even on leave we were never allowed to wear civvies. The temptation to do so became greater as time wore on. Just to dress up and 'be a female' was sometimes considered to be worth the risk. I think we all did it now and again. Putting a frock on as well as some 'lippy' was very daring. We had plenty of uniforms and on hot muggy days might have a quick shower and change our clothes three times to keep fresh, but to wear something with a bit of colour in it was quite exciting. We all found it slightly depressing to continually be in the one colour and for us all to look absolutely the same. After a while it was lovely just to get into your pyjamas because they were not military issue so you could choose your own colour. Our undies and pyjamas were the only personal clothing allowed. We also weren't allowed to wear any make-up on duty but had to look as good as we could without.

In her free time Olive loved nothing more than to talk with the Angels of Bataan about their experiences in the Philippines. She got plenty of opportunities to do so in the first three months at the hospital. She tried to heed Colonel Chew's advice about not drinking with them, but it was a temptation:

'Angels' was the term given by their troops but they referred to themselves as the 'Battling Belles of Bataan'. I found that once the ladies had a few gins they unwound and were able to talk freely. I was inevitably inspired by their stories. They were genuine heroes. Ruth Straube let me read her diary, and I marvelled at the bravery of the nurses as Edith Shacklette and Juanita Redmond recounted those last days on the Bataan Peninsula. Edith still carried the American flag given her by the commanding officer, Colonel Duckworth, from the hospital in Bataan. He couldn't bear the thought of the Japanese getting hold of it. She recounted her distress when ordered to evacuate immediately: 'I only had time to take off my gown and gloves, leaving hundreds of men lined up under the trees waiting for surgery and I walked out on them — I'll never forget that — they were devastated.'

They were quite a few years older than me and were hard cases, having had years of nursing experience before the war. I got into the habit of sharing a glass or two with them until one night I overdid it and suffered so badly the next day I didn't touch gin again for about 20 years. Occasionally one of their group who had been sent to Brisbane would be transferred to Townsville for a while and her arrival would cause tremendous joy. Floramund Fellmuth, who was the first of the nurses to escape from Bataan, sailing on a makeshift hospital ship, the *Maktan*, had arrived in Brisbane via Townsville two months prior to her comrades. When she returned to Townsville for a short stint with us I could only marvel at the camaraderie that had been created by their hardships in the Philippines. I wasn't aware of it at the time but I suppose they had a big effect on how I approached life later on. On the one hand I became very practical but I also became much more compassionate than I had been in the VAD. I hit my crossroad in life much earlier than most. It made me very appreciative of what so many people had given for the freedom we took for granted.

The hospital was very well run and I found the orderlies and other staff were efficient, very polite and genuinely friendly. When they found out my birthday was on the fourth of July they threw a party for me. The Americans loved to celebrate their special days. Of course Christmas and New Year were important to us all but celebrating Independence Day and Thanksgiving were new to me.

Sometimes we'd have spirits, either Scotch or gin, to make a punch, but if we didn't, well, we had a couple of chemists who were experts with the pure alcohol that was regular hospital issue! They mixed a potent drop. And the food was excellent. Always good steak for the fourth of July and turkey for Thanksgiving. The poor old Australians had bully beef. My friends used to ask if I felt guilty about this. I could truthfully say no. I'd always been a good eater and even apart from special occasions the food was first class. If I was hungry on night shift the kitchen could always rustle up good food in a hurry. Salmon and tuna sandwiches with olives on the side of the plate were no problem at all. Guilty? No, not a bit.

Not all the important servicemen fired guns or flew planes. Apart from being armed the military had to be fed, shod and clothed. Though there was plenty of produce for normal times, Townsville's appetite was now astronomical. This caused the establishment of the Base 2, QM Chicken Farm in Coconut Grove, Oonoonba, on Townsville's southern outskirts. Its purpose was to produce poultry and eggs for the regional army hospitals. Output reached almost 37 000 eggs per week. There were none left over. The bakery in Townsville was already producing 5000 loaves per day.

The army also set up a shoe, textile and equipage repair shop. Before equipment became available elsewhere all shoes and boots were flown to Townsville for repair. Even when the American troops went to fight in New Guinea it was some months before repair shops were up and running. The Townsville Steam Laundry, in a very run-down condition, was acquired by the army and brought to maximum efficiency to service shipping and hospitals.

Its lucky owners got back a much-improved plant after the Americans moved on.

In spite of regular blackouts, Townsville hummed at night. Pictures were shown in clubs and cinemas, and dances were held at a variety of venues seven nights a week. Wet canteens (as bars were called) were crowded with off-duty servicemen and women. Many Australian servicewomen from the army, navy and air force were now billeted in and around the city. The free-spending Americans also attracted several hundred 'camp followers' who travelled to Townsville as they did to other busy cities just to share time with them.

Local women attended dances run by American and Australian servicemen at the Country Club, Sailing Club and Golf Club, as well as hotels and halls. In outer areas local girls were transported by truck to and from functions where couples jitterbugged to the latest swing tunes. Depending on the venue, music might be supplied by a sixteen-piece band or a piano accordion and fiddle player. Occasionally American entertainers came to town. Joe E. Brown, a very popular comedian, appeared in a concert in one of the large hangars at Garbutt. Later, in New Guinea and the Pacific islands, concerts for the troops regularly featured famous artists. The nightlife meant little to Olive and her fellow nurses:

We got plenty of invites to the dances but I generally didn't go. I was the youngest of us but still I was generally too tired. We were working four hours on and four off, and the schedule was very heavy. I did see Joe E. Brown in the hangar at Garbutt and took some photos of him on stage. Now and again I'd go to the pictures with one of the American boys but I was pretty ordinary company. I'd often be asleep before the opening titles were over. Naturally enough, women were fascinated by the Americans. They liked their accents, their uniforms were very smart and they were different. Even little things stood out with them. People couldn't get over how much ice cream they ate. Locals thought of ice cream as a kid's treat but they ate it at breakfast time. Even that made them interesting to some of the women. And they had money to spend.

Lots of serious romances occurred and some women went so far as to marry and go to America after the war. Mind you, the American authorities didn't encourage it. A soldier had to get permission from his senior officers and sometimes that meant going right to the top brass.

The experience of Arch Fraley, a member of a US photographic unit, is typical of those who found serious romance:

> We were part of a big convoy bound for the Philippines when we suddenly altered course and the rumour went around we were headed for Australia instead. None of us knew anything about the place, not even what language was spoken. We pulled into Brisbane and I called out to the first guy I saw, 'Do you speak English here?' His good-natured answer was, 'perhaps a bit better than you, mate!' That was early 1942.
>
> Our unit was transferred to Charters Towers and the colonel called me in, knowing I didn't drink, and told me to pick two sober mates to attend a function at the mayor's home. I enjoyed myself very much and a pretty girl called Lorraine caught my eye and we hit it off really well. I eventually married her in 1943 and we had a little boy a year later. When time came for our troops to move to New Guinea, my commanding officer said to me, 'I can't see any sense you going to New Guinea to get shot up, you've got a wife and a

young son. I'll give you a couple of extra stripes and a lot more money and put you in charge of the photo section at Garbutt.' I felt a bit guilty leaving my mates but I agreed and we came down to Townsville. After the war we lived in the States until 1950, but Lorraine was very homesick so I brought her back and we've been here ever since. The hospitality during the war was wonderful. When you suddenly put 90 000 American soldiers in a small country town it asks a lot of the local people, but I was always made extremely welcome and had no trouble at all.

Some, however, did manage to find trouble. In any garrison town, particularly during wartime, there would be disagreements, some of which could lead to violence very quickly. Harry Boyle, a corporal in Australia's Special Z Force Commandos, vividly remembers his arrival in Townsville:

We were on our way to camp at Oonoonba to do special training in the hills. We had technicians with us who taught us to set up loudspeakers and amplifiers that had a range of about 800 yards. On them we played a whole host of recordings of Japanese love songs, bayonet charges and calls to surrender. The idea was to keep the ruckus going all night so the Japs got no sleep and harass them into surrendering. Some of us thought it was a bit of a harebrained scheme but that was our lot at the time.

Our train was pushed into a siding as an American troop train was given right of way. This was the norm and it upset us straight away. The Americans made the mistake of giving us Aussies some stick as they passed. When the call came, 'Don't worry, guys, we'll look after your Aussie girls,' it was too much for one disgruntled digger who lobbed an anti-personnel grenade into the American train. The grenade, with bakelite casing, made more noise than it did damage, but caused quite a stir. We had a good idea who it was but we weren't going to give him up.

When we pulled into Townsville station all our weapons were confiscated and not returned until we reached our destination at Oonoonba. Townsville was a wild old town, as I recall it. When they eventually sent us to New Guinea, the Japs still had plenty of fight left in them and they just bombarded us every time we started broadcasting. When Lae fell there was a group looking for sound gear to run a big concert. We let them have ours, we were glad to get rid of it.

Olive's job meant she heard more than most about what was going on around the place:

There was a fair amount of animosity from time to time, as you'd expect. It was a very volatile mix. Alcohol and soldiers with access to guns waiting to go into battle. The Americans were paid so much better they could afford to go out all the time and lots of them spent their money on the local girls like there was no tomorrow. The Australians didn't have this luxury and they missed out on a lot of fun because of it. Australians weren't allowed into American wet canteens but Americans were allowed into the Australians'. Naturally that caused a lot of friction.

There was segregation and that caused trouble too. The Negro soldiers weren't allowed into the American canteens and there was resentment when Australians allowed them into places where they weren't tolerated back in the United States. Some of the locals tended to treat them much better than their own whites did, particularly those from America's southern states, even though the White Australia Policy was very strong at the time and the government didn't want the black soldiers here at all. The policy was brought in to quell the rush of Chinese during the gold rushes. Ironically, they were made to do a literacy test in the same way as the American Negroes were in states that wanted to keep them out of the US army. MacArthur supported the government's proposal that no more Negroes be brought to Australia than had arrived already and those in the Islands and New Guinea would not be allowed to take leave here. So they were here helping us defend the country and we were saying we didn't want them. Hitler wasn't the only one with ideas of white supremacy.

The brothels at the back of the Causeway Hotel did a roaring trade. Prostitutes came from Brisbane and interstate and the queues would often be 200 metres long during the day and at night. The women had to be licensed and checked regularly by doctors, otherwise they were called in by police and charged. The government was very wise in this way but plenty of disease was spread nevertheless. We could testify to that. This was the one place I saw Negroes and white servicemen stand in line together. Black and white military police patrolled in pairs. Very few locals ever went near the red light district but sometimes kids would make a few bob minding a place for the soldiers. On one occasion there was a large fire when someone put a match to the brothels. It was pretty common knowledge that it was an Australian soldier who was irate that the prices had gone up and the Americans could afford them but the Aussies couldn't.

We knew of brawls and shootings and quite a few deaths in different places. The most infamous confrontation was the 'Battle of Brisbane', when a simple argument between a GI and a military policeman escalated into a small war that went over two nights. Literally thousands of GIs, Australian troops, military police and civilians were involved. One died, several were wounded by gunfire and hundreds were injured. I believe no official report ever got back to the United States. Townsville didn't have anything of that magnitude but there was a riot in the camp just out of the town on the way to Giru. A whole crowd of Negro soldiers wanted to come into Townsville and were stopped by a roadblock. One thing led to another and several men died of gunshot wounds. We didn't see the bodies; they had their own morgue.

I was at a dance one night in the US Officers Club in Cairns, on leave from Mareeba where the Americans had set up the 11th Field Hospital, when a couple of Australian 9th Division boys who'd returned from the Middle East arrived uninvited. They were not allowed in the American wet canteens so were stopped by the doormen. Even though they would have known the rules they were fired up about being barred. One thing led to another and they went down to the post office and rang for reinforcements. The 9th Divvy boys were stationed in tents near Ellis Beach. Half an hour later a few truckloads of them arrived and tried to gatecrash the Officers Club.

A big brawl developed that spilled out into the street and across the road. Of course more joined in and it looked like a brawl you'd see in a cowboy film. We stayed put in the club and next thing American and Australian military police arrived. It was mayhem. There must have been 200 troops involved. Three Australians were shot but the whole thing was hushed up. The nurses at Cairns would have had a busy night and I was glad to get back to Mareeba.

Once we got a paratrooper who had been stabbed in the throat after a brawl at the Rising Sun Hotel in Townsville. We were able to save him and got his story of the incident. Some Negro drivers had pulled up outside the hotel and went in to order a meal. This fellow was among a small group of white paratroopers from one of the southern American states who objected to them being served. An argument developed and he and his mates followed the drivers out into the street where he was stabbed. The military police arrived and one of the drivers was shot dead. We didn't get the driver's body, it went to the morgue where the black transport division was camped, but the paratrooper was with us for quite a while. Again the incident was hushed up.

When we got casualties at the hospital we didn't discuss them outside. Most of these incidents were fairly isolated and generally didn't involve any civilians. The great majority of people got on very well with the Americans and adjusted well to the situation. The troops were very appreciative of kindness from local people, who usually went out of their way to be nice to them. There was a saying about the Americans: 'Overpaid, oversexed and over here.' Well, what does overpaid mean if you might get shot next week? Oversexed? They didn't give me any trouble. Over here? I was just glad they were. We were all glad. With most of our boys overseas, who else was going to defend us?

Another group who didn't mind them being 'over here' were the cab drivers. The Australian monetary system of pounds, shillings and pence was quite complicated for the new arrivals. They were issued with a booklet explaining the currency but it did not come easily to them. If the numbers one and nine appeared on the cab meter it was a fairly simple matter to convince a well-heeled and tipsy soldier that the fare was nineteen shillings when in fact it was one shilling and ninepence, less than a tenth of what was charged. When the fare really was nineteen shillings it often became £1 9s, or 29 shillings!

A surprising number of soldiers who had come from cold climates cracked mentally under the strain of the tropics. Isolation, homesickness, constant sweating under oppressive heat, sandflies and mosquitos proved too much for them. Locals were used to outsiders going 'troppo' even without the pressure of the war, but one incident was too much, even for Olive:

One night the police rang to say one of our staff, a night cook, had gone troppo and was walking down the main street cracking a whip. They picked him up and brought him back to the hospital. When he saw me he started yelling, 'Oh, I've been looking everywhere for you,' which was absurd because he didn't know me from a bar of soap. Anyway, he started to be very precise as to why he wanted me. Then they sedated him and took him away but I was very upset. In my young innocence no one had ever said things like that to me. I kept telling Colonel Chew I wanted him court-martialled. He stayed calm as usual and said, 'Now, Ollie, you can't have that, you know he's not in his right mind at the moment. Just calm down and we'll attend to everything.'

Well, I calmed down eventually, but three or four days later I was asked to escort a patient to another hospital. I was in the front passenger seat of the ambulance when an orderly opened the back to put the patient in and, lo and behold, it was the same fellow. He saw me and started in again with the same thing. Two orderlies had to sit on him throughout the trip but it didn't stop his yelling. We were about to pull into the other hospital when a bee flew in the driver's window, went straight past him and stung me on the hand. We arrived with this madman yelling from under two orderlies, and me complaining loudly about a badly swollen hand. I felt a bit troppo myself. He never came good and they eventually sent him back to the States as a 'section 8'. Not suitable for military duty. The tropics can do that to you.

It has often been said, with very good reason, that the first casualty of war is truth. Often, justifiably, it is hidden in the cause of security or sugar-coated in the cause of national morale. Olive had seen evidence of this with the censorship of reports on the bombing of Darwin. Just as often, truth is buried for indefinite periods to hide measures taken in wartime that would never be contemplated or tolerated in peacetime. Amid the continued bombing of Darwin and Broome in the north of Western Australia, intelligence and counter-intelligence agencies issued information, accurate and otherwise, depending on their reading of what advantage could be won or lost. It is not surprising that decades after the conflict ended and military secrets were revealed, historians, devoted to unravelling the mysteries of wars, still argued passionately on certain issues. They continue to do so today.

One very contentious issue was the infamous 'Brisbane Line'. Rumours were rife that in the event of any invasion, the top half of Australia would be left to the Japanese and the rest of the country would be defended from Brisbane southward. If the plan were true then civilians who had decided to remain in the north would be helpless in the face of the fury of the brutal Japanese army. Eventually this so-called 'Brisbane Line' was openly discussed in federal parliament and naturally caused a tremendous furore. The Labor Party, ruling from October 1941 with a minority government supported by two independents, made much play from it and the Opposition was routed in the election of 1943. It was claimed by Labor's opponents that paranoia played a major role in Labor's one-sided victory. Whether the plan was ever likely to be implemented is still debated to this day, but it was certainly discussed by the military well before it became a public issue.

The US hospital at Townsville, swarming with service personnel, was naturally a hotbed of information, accurate and otherwise. Nurses probably heard more rumours about military actions than any other group. They also became aware of the movement of

Allied troops as a result of the number of casualties arriving from certain areas as well as the loss of planes and ships as they treated patients airlifted from the Pacific. Olive, along with her fellow nurses, had signed security documents that forbade her from disclosing information gained in service for 30 — and in some cases 50 — years. Olive was not troubled by this. Cryptographers, who spent their entire war service encoding and decoding Allied and enemy information, signed documents forbidding them from disclosing information for as long as 75 years.

Olive kept a diary, though not filled with the personal experiences and feelings one might expect from a girl still in her mid-teens working in the traumatic, frantic and sometimes chaotic circumstances of a military hospital. She kept a record of the movements of American troops, planes and ships in and out of Townsville. For one so young, and working under extreme pressure, she was remarkably analytical. Her ability to sort fact from myth was already one of her strengths. Olive could certainly be described as mentally tough. She had very good reason to believe the 'Brisbane Line' was real, even if not called by that name:

We heard plenty of talk about them leaving North Queensland to the Japs. We believed it, why wouldn't we? No one used the term 'Brisbane Line' in those early days but we knew the score. Before the Americans arrived there was no one to defend us anyway but, even now, it was made very clear to us that if there was an invasion then we were in 'no-man's land'. The politicians down south always denied it but we had no doubt North Queensland would be sacrificed if the Japs landed. Everyone knew it. There were so few of us spread over the whole of the north that they couldn't have defended us anyway, even if we'd been their main concern, which of course we weren't. That's why people were pouring out of the north. It was a hard thing to swallow but we would have been left to our own devices. First they said there was no 'Brisbane Line', then later they said there was never going to be an invasion. I showed people Japanese invasion money after the war and they still said there was never any intention that they would land. Try telling that to people who were there at the time.

We nurses were made to take quinine tablets every day to fight against malaria. Anyone who forgot was due for a real dressing-down. Then we were shown tablets of a very different kind. Cyanide. Colonel Chew addressed us personally and told us cyanide tablets were kept aside for us and would be issued in the event of a Japanese invasion. The tablets were to be taken if capture was inevitable. We were told simply, 'Don't be captured. You will assuredly be raped, tortured for information and beheaded. You know what has happened overseas. It is not worth it for any female to be taken.' I can't recall anyone ever mentioning it afterwards. Maybe no one wanted to broach the subject. We all understood but I doubt I could have taken that tablet. I didn't actually discuss it with the other girls but I think most of them felt the same. We didn't really have fear. That was why we were doing what we were. It would have seemed a coward's way out, I guess. I was brought up as a Roman Catholic so suicide really wasn't an option no matter what the circumstances. And I was a fatalist. I believed God had set my path out for me. Colonel Chew spoke to us on other occasions later on, keeping us informed of progress being made in research against malaria and lecturing us once on the dangers of venereal disease, but it was this talk I remembered most.

Prime Minister Churchill and President Roosevelt had agreed that Britain should defend the Middle East and Indian Ocean while America assumed control of the Pacific, including Australia and New Zealand. Douglas MacArthur had been amazed on his arrival that Australia had so few troops and such a limited number of planes to defend it. A little over 30 000 fighting men and less than a hundred planes, including unarmed single-engine aircraft used as training craft for novice pilots, hardly seemed enough. He called for a massive increase in American troops and aircraft. He also told John Curtin that Australia should recall its soldiers from the Middle East to defend the country. Unless Australia could be defended he could never recapture the Philippines. Winston Churchill was adamant this was wrong. The Germans had to be defeated in Africa first. Not surprisingly, while the establishment argued on priorities, vast numbers of civilians were literally pouring out of the north, some to enlist in Brisbane, but most to escape the likelihood of capture.

At Ramsay Street, Garbutt, close to the new airfield, the Townsville Harbour Board constructed a large bunker. It was built like a fortress with enormously thick reinforced concrete foundations, walls and roof. Measuring 20 metres by 40, it was the nerve centre of US Army Air Force Pacific Zone. The downstairs operation room was below ground level and the building was further strengthened by a buttress-wall that was believed to be capable of withstanding any bomb blast.

The Japanese army had been ruthless in its march south. The speed with which they had conquered the Philippines, Java, Sumatra and Singapore had shocked the Allies. The next objectives were Port Moresby in New Guinea and Tulagi in the Solomon Islands. If these were won then Japan's complete dominance of the Pacific seemed inevitable. It intended to take Port Moresby and Tulagi by combined naval and land operations.

MacArthur was desperate to defend Port Moresby. If the Japanese took Moresby it would be the perfect staging area from which to attack Australia. Two great naval battles, fought in the

Pacific in May and June of 1942, were crucial to the defence of Australia and the result of the war. The first, the Battle of the Coral Sea, was remarkable in that, for the first time, a large naval battle was fought without a shot being fired from ship to ship. Planes launched from huge aircraft carriers, the length of three football fields and carrying crews of almost 3000 men, attacked enemy ships with bombs and torpedoes. Anti-aircraft guns blazed away from the decks of the carriers. Dogfights were waged above the ships as fighter planes defended their bombers. American B17s from Townsville and Charters Towers complemented aircraft from the American carriers *Lexington* and *Yorktown*. In these sorties casualties from the long-range bombing missions were negligible. They flew so high they were out of range of Japanese fighters but the height from which they dropped their bombs made strikes on moving targets almost impossible.

On 7 May 1942, Olive was summoned to the bunker at Garbutt. Every line on the two-man switchboard was flashing with news. It was obvious to Olive something very big was happening. Unbeknown to her the Battle of the Coral Sea was in full swing. The American destroyer *Sims* had just been sunk and the oiler *Neosho*, used to refill the fighting ships, was ablaze. Three Australian-based US Flying Fortresses had mistakenly bombed a group of their own ships. Fortunately their aim was poor.

The Coral Sea battle, which lasted five days, saw both sides suffer heavy losses. As well as the *Sims* and *Neosho*, America lost the great carrier *Lexington*. Its loss was a tremendous blow to US strength and morale. Damaged beyond help the *Lexington* was scuttled. Before her demise, 2735 seamen were rescued from the vessel and the bodies of 216 dead seamen, some from the carrier *Yorktown*, were placed on her. Then the shoes of the 2735 rescued men were placed on her decks in the positions they would take as the crew traditionally assembled on deck upon a return to port. A torpedo sent the blazing wreck to the bottom. One hundred and twenty-three survivors from the US oiler *Neosho* arrived at Townsville's 12th Station Hospital with many very badly burned. Nurses cared for them as best they could before sending them on to Brisbane by rail ambulance.

In the battle Japan lost a large carrier, *Shoho,* and another carrier, *Shokaku,* was severely damaged. The Japanese also lost no fewer than 144 planes. Both sides claimed victory but the most important thing was that the Japanese juggernaut had been stalled. The drive towards New Guinea's capital Port Moresby had been thwarted.

As the next major sea battle loomed Sydney Harbour suffered its one and only maritime attack. It was an invasion, small by any standards, but one that had an enormous impact on the city's psyche. Three midget submarines, 24 metres in length, launched from larger submarines a few kilometres off the Heads, made their way into the harbour. A torpedo, intended for the USS *Chicago,* sank the ferry *Kuttabul* which had been commandeered by the navy, killing 21 seamen. Suddenly the war was no longer in the remote north. Evacuation from Sydney was not as chaotic as it had been in Darwin but it was happening nevertheless as people headed inland and interstate. Had they known of the reconnaissance flight on the evening prior to the attack and the circumstances by which the pilot evaded defences, even more may have been inclined to leave.

Susumo Ito, a Japanese aviator, recalled his exploits some years after the war. The submarine carrying his small seaplane surfaced approximately 50 kilometres northeast of Sydney in the early hours of the cloudy morning. He was catapulted into the air and flew over Sydney's North Head at a height of about 500 metres, coming down to 200 metres over Garden Island, allowing his observer to sketch the position of the cruiser *Chicago*, which had been deployed in the Coral Sea battle, and four destroyers. Having avoided searchlights over the harbour, flying as low as 50 metres above the water while his observer did more hasty sketches, he then lost his bearings, left the harbour and attempted to find Mascot Airport. Suddenly the airport switched on its lights for him. As he recalls 'it was very helpful'. Ito flew back towards the harbour and out to sea, noting a hospital ship with many lights on as he headed towards North Head. Despite a rough landing and a hazardous swim back to the submarine, he and his observer survived and later flew more reconnaissance missions over Sydney, Brisbane, Auckland, Wellington and Noumea. He admits that without the obliging lights at Mascot, his war record may have been much less impressive.

The damage to Japan's two major carriers kept them out of the next big sea battle fought at Midway Islands. MacArthur told John Curtin that the Battle of Midway would be the most important battle of the war. He again told Curtin that Australia should insist that the 9th Division of Australian troops come home from the Middle East. Success at Midway could not be assured and a Japanese victory would mean that Australia was totally isolated. The Japanese fleet was much bigger than that of the United States and their sailors were more experienced. Again, planes from the Australian mainland supported those launched from carriers in the Pacific.

Against the odds the US navy, supported by ships from Australia and New Zealand, scored a dramatic victory at Midway. Though outnumbered, their tactics proved superior and their knowledge of the Japanese naval code invaluable. In another battle that featured plane versus ship, Japan suffered her first defeat. In three days of fighting the Japanese lost four aircraft carriers, *Agaki*, *Kaga*, *Soryu* and *Hiruya*, the heavy cruiser *Mikuma,* 320 planes and 3500 men. American losses were the carrier *Yorktown*, one destroyer, 150 planes and just over 300 men. Victory for the Allies was still a long way off but Japan's supremacy on the seas had been shattered. The immediate threat of invasion was averted. The decimation of the Japanese fleet meant they were now vulnerable, with bases scattered across the Pacific. However, the Japanese army was still a very potent force and they were committed to capturing Port Moresby. Morale at the hospital was given a tremendous lift by the victory at Midway:

We all knew how important that battle was. While reports in the press were always open to interpretation there was no doubting this was our first major success. You could feel it with the doctors, the staff, the inmates, everyone. MacArthur had made no secret that this was crunch time and his men had delivered. The Angels had an extra gin that night.

Soon after the Battle of Midway Olive was transferred to Mareeba, high up in the mountains west of Cairns, where the 11th Portable Field Hospital had been set up using classrooms and office buildings and tents in the state school. Here the temperature was vastly different to Townsville. During June and July, while Townsville experienced temperatures in the mid twenties, Mareeba's nights were so cold shallow puddles of water froze over. It was in Mareeba, alive with the sounds of Flying Fortress aircraft taking off and returning from bombing missions to New Guinea, that Olive had one of her few flirtations:

I formed a friendship with a nice young fellow, a dental nurse, and we saw a bit of each other while I was there. His name was William

Henry Conga and everybody called him Hank. He came from Indiana and his family had a lot of property. He was a bit keen on me and was a lovely boy. We went to a couple of dances and to the pictures. He was a Mormon, the first I'd ever met, who took his religion very seriously. He tried to explain it to me but as a simple country girl brought up in the Catholic faith I found it all a bit confusing. I certainly couldn't quite come to grips with the idea of polygamy. He was transferred back to the States, which was probably just as well. Apart from our differences I was too young and too busy to look for real romance.

When MacArthur had first arrived, Australia's military chiefs established his headquarters in Melbourne but he saw little point in being so far from the action up north. With North Queensland being the main staging area for American troops he relocated into the ten-storey AMP building in Brisbane. From here he was in the ideal spot to organise the defence of Australia and New Guinea and the subsequent counterattack to regain the Philippines. Brisbane's best hotel, Lennon's, became home for the general and his family. Though still 1350 kilometres south of Townsville, the move to Brisbane was appreciated by those people in Queensland's northern cities. MacArthur was now in control of the US air force as well as the army. The bunker at Garbutt would be his headquarters when in Townsville. It was here that Olive had her first meeting with her new boss:

I'd been nursing about four months when I was summoned to the bunker, along with other members of staff. I was interested if not excited about meeting him. He was simply the commanding officer and whatever he said would obviously be obeyed. Still, I got up near the front to get a good view of him. We'd heard rumours that he could be arrogant and rather aloof but I saw none of that. He was very polite and called the women ma'am or by our rank, in my case lieutenant, which of course he pronounced as 'lootenant'. He was a tall, very good-looking man who spoke slowly, carefully but firmly, and gave a general talk, a pep talk really, with a lot of importance on secrecy and just what a struggle lay ahead of us.

Talking without notes he told us there were 130 000 American troops on the high seas or already landed in Australia and that a big percentage of them would be staged in and around Townsville. We found that very comforting though he assured us they would take some looking after. He spoke with great affection of these young men who would protect Australia by repelling the Japanese, driving them out of New Guinea and recapturing the Philippines. He thanked us for our efforts so far, wished us luck and assured us that God was on our side. At the conclusion of his address he answered questions willingly, though few were asked. I think most were in awe of him. As I watched him I couldn't help thinking he must have so much on his mind, that his must be a very lonely job. Perhaps that was why he was seen as aloof.

So far Japanese bombing had been restricted to the northernmost cities of the Northern Territory and Western Australia. That was about to change. Olive was on duty at Townsville when, a few minutes before midnight on 25 July, headquarters received a yellow and then a red alert air-raid warning. The entire city was quickly blacked out as searchlights scanned the sky. Fifty minutes later the drone of aircraft was heard over Cleveland Bay and the searchlights picked up the silhouettes of three long-range, four-engine, amphibious Kawanisi bombers. Commonly known as Emilys, they had flown directly from Rabaul. No attempt was made to intercept them and locals watched as they dropped six bombs harmlessly into the ocean several hundred metres from the wharf area of

Townsville's outer harbour. It was the first time Townsville had been bombed but it caused no panic. In fact many people watched from vantage points rather than seeking shelter. It was an eerie sight to see the bombs explode in the moonlit sea, sending plumes of water skyward.

Further bombing missions occurred in the early hours of the morning on 28 and 29 July. Again some civilians ignored the warning, preferring to watch proceedings from Kissing Point, but the less foolhardy quickly took cover in air-raid shelters. People in the city hastened to the large pillboxes in Flinders Street where community singing was heard as the raids took place. Each time a lone Emily dropped its bombs without causing any damage. The first dropped eight bombs in the foothills of Townsville's Many Peaks Range and the second jettisoned six bombs into the sea by Ross River and a seventh which exploded in the vicinity of the Animal Health Station at Oonoonba, sheering the top off a large coconut palm and causing quite a commotion at the American chicken farm. The bombs dropped at the mouth of Ross River were known as daisy-cutters, containing metal scraps, blades and fragments. The topless palm trunk became a landmark.

On both occasions anti-aircraft guns blazed and four American Aircobra fighters, taking off from Garbutt, attempted to intercept the planes. They made six passes as tracer bullets lit up the sky. Though the second plane was hit several times it was able escape into the darkness with only minor damage and both invaders made it back to Rabaul. The American pilots, Captain John Mainwaring and Captain Bob Harringer, gave graphic accounts of the operation, both expressing disappointment they had not brought down the damaged bomber. The following day the *Townsville Bulletin* carried pictures of the topless palm as well as a bomb disposal squad digging in a crater by the racecourse and others looking for an unexploded bomb in shallow waters in Cleveland Bay. Olive took time to have a look at the damage:

I saw the blown-off palm which became the best-known tree in North Queensland. It was amusing to think that was all that had been damaged even though we knew how awful it could have been had the daisy-cutter fallen in the main part of town. They were a terrible weapon capable of inflicting horrific injuries. But the palm tree wasn't quite as amusing as the story that quickly did the rounds of the airman who responded to the alert, arriving minus his trousers. Whether he had come from the Causeway or more salubrious surroundings was not ascertained but his sense of duty was the subject of much mirth when reported in the press at a later date. We were never bombed again though the following night an Emily bomber returned, dropping eight bombs on Mossman, just north of Cairns, so again missing vital targets. There were to be no more raids on the Queensland's east coast. The purpose of such isolated bombing missions was hard to fathom. Still, it certainly caused plenty of anxiety and kept us on our toes. Perhaps this was its aim. It was a reminder, if anybody needed one, that the Japanese were not far away.

With damage restricted to the lone coconut palm, two large craters and some terrified chooks, many of whom apparently did not lay for some days, Japanese propaganda broadcast on 1 and 2 August made interesting listening: 'All-important military installations at Townsville were smashed in three raids by the Japanese naval air units. On July 25 oil tanks, shipping and supply dumps were raided. On July 28 airfields, oil tanks and supply dumps were attacked and on July 29 the remaining military installations were bombed. This attack on Townsville was one of the heaviest since the fall of Singapore.'

Radio Berlin went even further, broadcasting in Europe that the railway line to Brisbane had been rendered unusable, that Townsville was burning and that the particularly violent Japanese raids had prompted the Queensland government to completely evacuate the town!

With the setting up of the 150-bed 60th Station Hospital at Gordonvale, Olive's nursing duties now involved three separate locations. In the coastal township south of Cairns, two main street hotels, the Commercial and the Central, were acquired as hospital quarters. A large contingent of American paratroopers was camped in the nearby bush and most patients came from their ranks. Olive was billeted in a private home in Gordonvale and the Railway Hotel in Mareeba. Both places were far more luxurious than Armstrong Paddock, though much more isolated.

On one occasion, during a severe electrical storm, Olive was alone on duty in a ward at Gordonvale's Commercial Hotel. The phone rang and just as she connected the metal tip of the patch cord into the switchboard, lightning struck a telegraph pole four kilometres down the road. She was thrown backwards right across the room, momentarily stunned. When she came to she had no idea how long she'd been unconscious. A quick look at her watch assured her it had been only a short while but she was badly shaken for the rest of the shift.

Through her trips to Gordonvale Olive became good friends with a young Texan medical orderly who carried a saddle with him wherever he went. He had acquired the obvious nickname Tex, and Olive never heard him called anything else. She assumed he carried the saddle as a reminder of home or perhaps his favourite horse. He was an accomplished horseman and offered to take Olive riding. Tex was the first 'American cowboy' Olive had met. Though she had never been on a horse in her life it was typical of her that she did not tell him. She agreed to go and her air of confidence was such that Tex arranged her a mount with plenty of dash. When Olive tried to change course she could not control it and suddenly the fiery steed took off. Having no hope of reining it in, terrified, she held on and hoped for the best. She was very fortunate to suffer only minor cuts and bruises when the horse hit a tree and threw her quite heavily. That was her one and only horseriding experience. She lost track of Tex when he left, saddle in hand, for New Guinea some time later.

It was also at Gordonvale that Olive stood outside the Commercial Hotel while Douglas MacArthur and General Blamey, Australia's chief of staff, flanked by several high-ranking officers on a specially constructed platform, watched a display by a large contingent of the US paratroopers. It was the second time she had been in MacArthur's presence:

There must have been four or five hundred paratroopers from the camp just outside the town. We were quite excited by it. Planes came over us and dropped their parachutists into the open cane fields on the edge of town. The sky was full of them. Suddenly we saw one falling far too quickly. His chute didn't open and he fell to his death. One of the officers told MacArthur that news had come from the field that it was not a man who had fallen but a dummy that was deliberately used to keep the paratroopers aware of how accidents could happen. MacArthur was nobody's fool. I could see from his reaction that he was very upset. Not for any reason, I think, other than that the man had died.

The other officers made no sign that anything had gone amiss. I'm sure MacArthur loved his troops, every one of them. He was convinced they were the finest of men. I watched his face closely and it confirmed my belief that rather than being aloof he was a man made lonely by his position, knowing decisions he made would cost lives. We got that boy's body back at the morgue late that afternoon. He was buried in Gordonvale but later his body was exhumed and buried in the military cemetery in Townsville. Eventually he was laid to rest in the United States.

Chapter Four

VICTORY, FEVER AND CIVVY STREET

The whole balance and nature of the war was changed by America's naval victory at Midway. Stalled in their efforts to invade Port Moresby by sea, the Japanese were now determined to take the city from the other side of the country. This meant sending their army through the most rugged tropical jungle in New Guinea, across the Owen Stanley Range. Almost all of Moresby's 2000 inhabitants had been evacuated to Australia. Australian forces, bolstered by local militia, were in defence of the city. Only a handful of RAAF Kittyhawk fighter planes, inferior to Japanese Zeros, remained in service. Port Moresby, just 400 kilometres from the Australian mainland, was very vulnerable.

The long, tail-like peninsula which makes up the southeastern part of New Guinea is only 160 kilometres wide. On the far north coast, directly opposite Moresby, stood the Anglican mission at Gona and a government station at Buna, fifteen kilometres apart. Between them was the Sanandara rubber plantation. The Owen Stanley Range, which separates Gona from Moresby, boasted craggy mountain peaks as high as 2000 metres. There was a track across the mountains, barely a metre wide in many places, which the natives had used long before Europeans came, but no vehicle, or even a horse, could use it. The jungle growth was extremely thick and deep gorges and sheer cliffs made every step a dangerous one. Mosquitos carrying the malaria and dengue fever viruses bred in swamps and pools throughout the jungle. After a typical downpour mud became knee deep and the terrain was virtually impassable. The few white men who had walked the track could not believe an army would try it. Other than the natives, just a few plantation owners and missionaries remained on the far side of the range. At the foot of the mountains on the northern side was the village of Kokoda. It was here the legend of the Kokoda Track was to be born.

As Japan prepared for its New Guinea offensive, Olive spent a short time at MacArthur's headquarters in Brisbane being briefed, along with other hospital staff, on the action about to hot up in New Guinea. This is what the American ground forces had been training for. There was a most impressive array of officers at headquarters: ten generals, ten colonels, ten lieutenant colonels, nine majors, twelve captains, twelve first lieutenants and three second lieutenants. She was inclined to wonder who made the coffee! Olive returned to Townsville knowing full well things must get busier.

Olive had been in the service only a few months but had experienced a lot of pressure for one so young. She already realised it was important for nurses to relax when off duty. Sharing a gin with the Angels of Bataan was one way. She also found another, very different way, but one she enjoyed just as much. Water had always been a problem in the dry season, even before the influx of servicemen. Now the supply was continually strained. It had to be used frugally when washing or bathing. The luxury of lying in a tub had become a thing of the past, but the girls constantly yearned for a good long soak. Being a local, Olive knew the waterholes like the back of her hand. Moonlight skinny-dipping was one of the few luxuries left from her childhood:

I knew the creeks and waterfalls around Townsville and Cairns and soon got to know those at Mareeba and Gordonvale as well. After a long, hot day at the hospital there was nothing like having a naked dip in a stream and sitting under some cool cascading water. I took different girls depending on who was off duty, just a few of us each time. The Battling Belles were particularly appreciative. We stayed away from the estuaries where the crocs were, but I knew beautiful little waterfalls that ran through the wet season when the weather was at its stickiest. It was just beautiful to let that cascading water run over your body. Sometimes I'd lie in a pool of cool water looking at the moon, thinking how peaceful it was, then realising boys were being shot and maimed at that very moment. It all seemed like a dream. It was madness, really. We never did tell the men where we did our skinny-dipping. They would have spoiled it, I'm sure.

Though hospitalisation was always serious there were inevitable incidents that caused some mirth. The Bataan nurses could not believe the number of times GIs were admitted for treatment of rashes on their backsides caused by stinging nettles:

Soldiers would squat in the scrub not knowing just how painful a sting could be caused by simply brushing the nettle. When the nettles were in flower they were much more noxious and the pain could recur for twelve months whenever the area got wet. We painted embarrassed patients' bottoms with picric acid, which was bright yellow, on a regular basis. On one occasion a young soldier had been stung on the penis by several bees, and was swollen to many times his normal size. We worked quickly to remove the stings. Naturally he was in great pain so there were no smiles at the time but they did come later. Humour was our safety valve and in the next few months it was to get a real workout.

The initial stage of Japan's assault on Port Moresby began in mid July 1942. Transport ships carried the first landing party to the beautiful, remote, black-sand beach at Gona. Over the next two days 2000 engineers, infantrymen and anti-aircraft personnel disembarked on the coast. Their aim was to prepare a base at Sanandara and airfields at Buna. From here they would track over the Owen Stanley Range to Port Moresby. The surrender of the Americans in the Philippines meant Japan had enormous numbers of personnel available to them.

At Gona, Father James Benson and two missionary nurses, Sister Hayman and Sister Parkinson, had fled into the jungle on the arrival of the first landing party. They narrowly evaded capture for two weeks but eventually became separated. Betrayed by natives, the two sisters were captured by a Japanese patrol and bayoneted to death beside a shallow trench. Another party of eight from Sanandara — two priests, two sisters, a lay preacher, a local woman, a plantation worker and his six-year-old son — were also captured and beheaded on the beach by a Japanese officer. The six-year-old boy was last to die, having witnessed the others executed before him. All those assassinated were noncombatants. Colonel Chew's offer of cyanide tablets at the hospital back in Townsville had not been a melodramatic gesture. Father Benson eventually surrendered and, remarkably, was treated quite well, being sent back to a prison camp in Rabaul. A prisoner's fate depended entirely on the character of his captor.

Australian patrols engaged the Japanese within days of their landing, in a preview of what was to come. The Japanese, though no more familiar than the Australians with the rugged terrain, proved to be expert jungle fighters and greatly outnumbered them. Equipped with machetes and shovels as well as weapons, they were ready for the long haul. By mid August Japan had 12 000 men in and around Gona and Buna, and now controlled that area from the coast to the Owen Stanleys. More shiploads of troops arrived and pushed into the mountains. The bitter fighting that followed, in the morass of mud and slush under the canopy of the dense New Guinea jungle, was now absolutely vital to the defence of Moresby and therefore Australia.

MacArthur, controlling the action from Brisbane, sent the crack Australian 7th Division, just back from the Middle East, to defend Moresby and Milne Bay, a vital base near the southernmost tip of the peninsula. The 7th Division, bolstered by Australian troops already in New Guinea and a small number of American engineers, were ordered to hold the Owen Stanley Range and then to retake Buna. It was an awesome assignment.

Japan launched an all-out offensive on the Owen Stanley Range in late August. When they were thwarted by the Australians they launched a second attack at Milne Bay, on the far eastern tip of the peninsula, 370 kilometres from Port Moresby. After a fortnight of desperate, bloody warfare fought in mud, slush and torrential rain, Australian troops won the battle at Milne Bay. After several weeks of jungle warfare, aided by the local natives — the 'Fuzzy Wuzzy Angels', who acted as carriers of supplies, ammunition and wounded men — they also triumphed by regaining Kokoda. They won against enormous odds, then pushed the weary, starving, malaria-stricken Japanese back to Buna after prolonged jungle fighting in the most atrocious conditions. Port Moresby was safe for now, but while Buna belonged to the Japanese it remained vulnerable.

Meanwhile the bombing missions continued from Townsville, Charters Towers and Mareeba, now fully sealed with bitumen, an important factor with the monsoon season approaching. Further north more airfields were being constructed. Medium- and long-range bombers kept up constant attacks. Tropical storms made flying extremely hazardous but even in good weather take-offs and landings were often as perilous as enemy fire. Pilots were unfamiliar with their surroundings and many quite inexperienced. Crashes and crash-landings were a regular occurrence and a steady flow of air force casualties resulted. Most fliers were lost in mishaps involving the big Flying Fortresses, which carried crews of ten, but all planes were vulnerable. Some took off on bombing missions, lost radio contact and were never heard of again. The New Guinea jungle is still reluctantly giving up its victims 60 years later.

Many planes, short on fuel or disabled, effected emergency landings on the hard sandy beaches between Townsville and Cape York. Four Mile Beach at Port Douglas, now a popular tourist destination but in those days totally isolated, was typical of the stretches of hard sand ideal to land on. There were some miraculous escapes among the tragedies. A group of fifteen US Aircobras left Townsville and refuelled at Cairns on their way to relieve the Australian 24th Squadron in Port Moresby. Hugging the coastline they headed for their next refuelling stop at Horn Island but ran into severe tropical storms. No fewer than nine were forced to turn back and, low on fuel, ditched their planes on beaches. All pilots survived.

Amid a host of crashes, three terrible disasters occurred in the months of August and September, casting gloom over air force and army personnel. One of America's best-known airmen, Major Dean C. 'Pinky' Hoevet, commanding officer of the 30th Squadron of 19th Bomb Group of Mareeba, took his B17 Flying Fortress out to test a new flare-dropping mechanism. A flare exploded in the plane causing it to crash into the sea killing Major Hoevet and the entire crew. Pinky Hoevet was extremely popular with his men and from then on the airfield at Mareeba became known as Hoevet Airfield.

At Charters Towers a Douglas Boston bomber drifted offline on take-off and hit another plane which was being serviced beside the airstrip. Thirteen died in the worst accident at Charters Towers during the entire campaign. The very next day another B17 Flying Fortress of the 19th Bomb Group (named Hoobalibali, which in Hawaiian means 'kid 'em along') crashed on take-off at Hoevet Airfield, killing the captain and crew of twelve. A plaque exists at Mareeba Airport in memory of those who died. Olive was at Mareeba Hospital when the charred remains of the crew's bodies were brought from the airfield in buckets:

I'd been at Mareeba for several weeks and we'd had a couple of very bad crashes involving US planes and had to recover several charred bodies. This was the worst task of all. The smell of burning flesh is one of the most shocking odours and takes weeks to get out of your system. I felt almost at breaking point. I was due for two days leave so I decided to get out of the place and spend the time with my Aunt Ettie in Townsville. I got on a courier plane and was in Townsville in a little over an hour. Ettie and I sat around having cups of tea, talking about everything but the war, and I felt quite a bit better when I went down to MacArthur's bunker to organise a flight in the regular courier plane to take me back.

Unfortunately I couldn't get on. It was unusual but the flight was fully booked. My only alternative was to get the 'midnight rattler' to Cairns, a train that took anything from six to eight hours. It was crowded with troops and not comfortable enough to sleep in, so I was pretty tired when we got to Cairns next morning. Sometimes there would be a truck or ambulance at Cairns headed for Mareeba but this wasn't the case so I had to wait for a rail motor to go up through the rainforest at Kuranda. It was crowded as well. The trip was very slow, up steep inclines, through several tunnels on a narrow gauge. Even though it wasn't very far it took about two hours. There had been quite a few workers killed when the line was being built and it could still be very dangerous. Seven US servicemen had lost their lives some months earlier when the brakes failed and their carriage had hurtled back down the track.

I returned to camp almost 24 hours late, knowing I would be in serious trouble as the nurses had worked extra shifts to cover for me. I'd never been in trouble before so I was very nervous. My commanding officer, Colonel Chew, was in Mareeba at the time and gave me a real dressing-down, which was fair enough, and I was confined to barracks for a week. I hadn't intended to go AWOL but that's how it turned out and it was my responsibility to get back in time. The colonel understood, though, and could have been tougher on me. I think he might have been lenient because he knew how distraught I'd been after the crashes. We nurses were expected to perform but were treated very well in that way. The American officers were more empathetic than the British would have been, and probably the Australians as well.

The 4th Air Depot Group arrived in Townsville from Melbourne and chose Mount Louisa to install a large depot in which aircraft were to be assembled, overhauled, repaired and, where necessary, modified. Thirty-five large igloo type buildings fanned outwards towards the east, with an interconnecting road system and 102 residential buildings. Townsville was still growing. Hospitals remained busy.

On 28 September 1942 MacArthur sent in the first American combat troops to help regain Buna. These were the 32nd Division, the Red Arrows, national guardsmen mainly from Michigan and Wisconsin. Now Australian and American ground troops fought side by side for the first time. The battle conditions were as dreadful as on the Kokoda Track, the injuries as prolific as they were horrific. Casualties were immediately heavy. Constant torrential rain turned the battlefield into a quagmire. Tanks were bogged, men fought and died, by gunshot, shrapnel and bayonet wounds, in mud up to their knees or water up to their armpits. Thousands suffered from malaria, dysentery, dengue fever and scrub typhus. Only those involved could ever imagine the conditions. Maimed and injured men lay in the muddy foxholes waiting to be carried to field hospitals and transported to Port Moresby, and from there to Australia for treatment.

Casualties came to Townsville by sea and air. Two thousand six hundred Americans reached the 12th Station Hospital from Buna in November and a further 3200 in December. The less urgent cases were sent on to Brisbane by rail ambulance with nurses looking after them on the way. Some went south on the ambulance ship *Ormiston*, and the rest were treated in the now frantic and crowded hospital. Olive had been deployed at Mareeba for some weeks but when the casualties reached such large numbers she was sent back to Townsville to experience the most hectic period of her nursing life:

In a normal day, if there was such a thing, we worked four hours on and four hours off until 20 hours had elapsed, then had a spell for eight hours. When the emergencies came pouring in from New Guinea we just kept working until the job was done. It was chaotic, absolute pandemonium. We didn't have time to think. At one stage we worked 36 hours straight. Until we actually cleared the rush we had to try to keep going. You did this by drinking black coffee and putting your head under the tap when you thought you couldn't stay awake any longer. We were like zombies but they had to be sorted. The stretchers came one after the other. There were hundreds of men on stretchers groaning, covered in muddy, blood-soaked bandages. Sadly, some were beyond help.

We got them through the triage as fast as we could. The casualties were sorted into groups even before we actually got them into the hospital. They wore a tag, usually of cardboard, pinned to their uniforms by the medics in New Guinea, indicating their injuries or symptoms of illness and the treatment they'd been given at the field hospitals. They also wore dog tags so we knew who they were and from what unit. Nearly all of ours were from the 32nd Division, the Red Arrows.

Emergencies went straight to one of three operating theatres. Some had been shot, others hit with shrapnel or bayoneted and left to die. Once we'd got the rest into wards we redid the dressings of those with external wounds. They were washed with green soap and new dressings applied with sulphanilamide powder. We put powder on every wound. In the tropics wounds become infected very quickly. Some were in a very bad way. It was common to take a boy's boot off and find all the skin and a great lump of flesh would come away with it. They were covered in lice. This was a common problem in the mud from New Guinea. Lice and maggots in the wounds.

A boy who had no hope would have a red cross drawn on his forehead. You went to the next patient because at least he had a chance. The fact was that if you spent time trying to save someone with little chance of surviving, you were denying someone else with a better chance. You knew some wouldn't survive but it didn't make it any easier. That was the worst part of all, seeing a boy with that cross, knowing that back home he had a mother waiting for him.

Those who hadn't been wounded but had succumbed to tropical disease generally came by ship. There were hospital ships for this purpose but, when things got hectic, casualties were transported by any ship available in Port Moresby. We cleaned them up, bedded them down and gave them appropriate medication. You can imagine how pleased they were to be in a nice clean bed, surrounded by smiling, if exhausted, faces. We must have looked a mess, come to think of it. Once they were all bedded down we were able to go off duty hoping we got our full four hours sleep. We were so tired we had to be driven to Armstrong Paddock, a short walk away.

The nurses from Bataan were fantastic during this period. I don't know what we would have done without them. When blood supplies ran low we often gave blood ourselves. We thought nothing of it. It was hard to think that we were saving them so they could go back to the same conflict. A lovely boy would leave the hospital, thankful for what you'd done for him, and you would never know if he had lived or died. All you could do was say a prayer for him.

During my early training at Cairns Base Hospital a nun had told me that no one should die alone. It was advice I never forgot. Now, with casualties continuing to pour in and fatalities occurring around us, it was appropriate to heed that advice. I sat with dying American soldiers, many delirious, some still clear of mind but wounded beyond help, listening to their last words. I held their hands, pretending to be mother, sister, wife or girlfriend, whatever they wished. I just let them talk and tried to pretend I was the person they thought they were talking to. The other girls did the same. We would call them by name and we never took their dog tags off until after they died and were identified for burial.

The things they told me will go to the grave with me. Just boys they were, most of them, 18, 19, 20 years old, thrown into that terrible situation. They never wanted to talk about what they'd been through; they just wanted to relate to those closest to them back home. You knew then they were on their way out, in a world of their own. I can still see some of those faces, even now, 60 years later. They're always there in those cobwebs in the back of my mind. They just pop up out of nowhere every now and then.

When you walked up to the top of Castle Hill and looked across to the Belgian Gardens military cemetery, you saw where they were buried. The number of graves increased every day. Soon after the cemetery was officially opened boys who had been buried at Charters Towers and other places were reburied at the Belgian Gardens. After the war the bodies were exhumed and taken back to the States for their final resting place.

General MacArthur visited Townsville during this hectic period, speaking to key personnel at the bunker and inspecting units including the 12th Station Hospital. Accompanied by Colonel Chew he spoke with patients back from New Guinea. He was obviously very concerned about how things were going. No doubt he had reasons for coming other than seeing the troops, but I'm sure that was part of why he came. He had the ability to make people feel important, there was no doubt about that. He got his fair share of criticism but I'm sure some of it came because he was an American calling the shots in Australia. It was hardly a secret that Blamey resented him.

A small but significant number of patients at the hospital were suffering from what was commonly known as shell shock. Men brought back from the hell of battle lay in beds in the psychiatric ward, some crying, some shaking uncontrollably, others motionless, staring blankly, faces showing no emotion, unaware of things going on around them. Olive remembers one man continually tearing paper into strips and trying to set them alight and another who became very upset when she put some make-up on before leaving the ward to go off duty.

Shell shock had long been a sadly misunderstood condition. In the First World War men who had succumbed to mental breakdown were generally regarded as cowards or, at best, malingerers. Many were court-martialled, some poor devils shot as deserters, while others were forced to remain in the area under heaviest bombardment in the absurd belief that this would somehow bring them to their senses.

By the time of the Second World War much research had been done on post-traumatic stress disorder, as it was properly known. There was still much argument as to exactly what the condition was and how best to treat it. Why an apparently strong-willed man would suddenly break down, or how long the trauma was likely to last, was not really understood. The one thing agreed upon was that the condition was real and not an attempt to evade duty. Still, long periods of convalescence for traumatised men would not help the war effort. As soon as they were diagnosed by the MO as being unfit for service, they were shipped back to the United States for psychiatric treatment in veterans' hospitals. Some would recover, others would suffer for life.

What Olive did not learn until after the war was that thousands of such men were treated with massive injections of insulin, a substance that had been discovered and commercially produced in the early twenties specifically for the treatment of diabetes. This happened across the world. When injected into the bloodstream in large quantities it caused the body to suffer severe convulsions. Such convulsions were deliberately induced in mental patients in the 1930s in the same way they were by electric shock treatment a decade later. It became an accepted though controversial treatment for mental patients, particularly those suffering from schizophrenia and depression. It was being widely used in America, England and Australia on victims of shell shock.

Many never found out they had been subjected to the treatment. Others believed their condition was made much worse in the long term but were given no chance to complain. The army, in wartime at least, was a closed society. Once a man signed up he was the property of the force and accepted, without question, any instruction given by his superiors and any treatment ordered by military doctors. There was no avenue of redress even long after the war. Neither Olive nor her fellow nurses could do much but keep an eye on them and call medical orderlies if they needed constraint. They were all under strong medication so a nurse's main objective was to see that the patient did himself no harm. She found working in the psychiatric ward most depressing.

General MacArthur's orders to General Eichelberger, in command of the Buna campaign, were to capture Buna or not to come back. He meant it. Win the battle or die in the attempt. It was an extraordinary directive. Commanding officers were invariably evacuated if surrender became inevitable, Australia's Gordon Bennett from Singapore and MacArthur himself from Corregidor having been recent examples. MacArthur gave Eichelberger no such option.

Late in January 1943, four long months after the first American troops landed in New Guinea, the allied American and Australian army proclaimed a magnificent victory. The jungles of New Guinea, first at Kokoda and now at Buna, had provided the first defeat for the Japanese army, one that would soon be followed by another, at Guadalcanal in the Solomon Islands. The exhausted nurses at the 12th Station Hospital had no time to celebrate, casualties were still coming in their hundreds, but they knew that, for the first time, Japan was on the back foot. Australia's safety was again boosted as it had been by the naval victory at Midway. MacArthur's promise to rout the Japanese and retake the Philippines was looking decidedly more likely.

Neither MacArthur nor Australia's General Blamey had gone to New Guinea during the battles at Kokoda and Buna, preferring to run the campaigns from Australia. MacArthur made flying visits to Townsville. On one occasion Olive saw him walking around a compound munching on a head of lettuce talking to himself animatedly. He was obviously under pressure, not only from the enemy, but also from the US navy hierarchy and the US president. Both MacArthur and Blamey badly underestimated the atrocious conditions in New Guinea, a fact that made them both extremely unpopular with their troops during this period. The gallantry of troops in New Guinea and the magnitude of their triumphs were appreciated more after the war than during it. Strangely, the American people knew almost nothing of the battle at Buna but were fed abundant reports from Guadalcanal.

Despite the hostility of fighting in New Guinea and the Pacific islands, far more soldiers fell victim to tropical disease than to enemy fire. The debilitating effects had added enormously to the horror of war in the area. Military authorities realised that if they could significantly reduce these effects, particularly of malaria and dengue fever, then the army's efficiency would be increased accordingly. At one stage Olive was sent to Cairns to report on the results of research being done by a special malaria unit:

Going to Cairns gave me a chance to see my family, if only for a short time. Dad was busy on the wharves where work never stopped during the war. With so many young men joining up they were always short of labour. The malaria unit sent soldiers out, carrying pumps on their backs, spraying obvious breeding grounds while civilian and army entomologists and parasitologists worked to determine the carriers of the malaria and dengue fever viruses. It was a complicated study because there were something like 60 different species of mosquitos carrying several forms of the diseases. In the month after the spraying there was quite a drop in reported malaria cases but, ironically, a huge increase in dengue fever victims.

As far as the troops or nurses were concerned the two were on a par. The patients arrived at the hospital in a feverish condition, sweating profusely and shaking uncontrollably. We gave them two or three doses of quinine each day. Fortunately we had plenty, unlike the girls at Bataan and Corregidor. Later on we were able to give them Atabrin tablets, which were more effective for malaria and a lot easier to take. Quinine was dreadful-tasting stuff which repeated on you for hours. We nurses could vouch for that. We also gave them paracetamol to help reduce their temperature. Those with milder forms of the disease generally recovered in a fortnight or so and went back to the front line when they were strong enough. Some went a bit before we thought they were ready but it was wartime.

Scrub typhus was a different thing altogether. It was brought on by a small tick that latched on to the surface of the skin and was often fatal if it wasn't detected and removed quickly. About 200 deaths were reported from scrub typhus in the fighting at Buna. Again the victims developed a raging fever. We would have to check their bodies closely to find this little tick. It was much smaller than a dog or cattle tick, something like the size of a small plant seed, so it took some finding even though it was easy to extract. Once we'd removed it we wrapped the patient in sheets that were soaked in cold water to keep his temperature down. He could get up to 104° Fahrenheit (40° Celsius). We kept wetting the sheets as they dried. The typhus was so deadly, a lot of research went into developing a repellent for the tick. The boys called it Betty, and it was sprayed on uniforms and blankets.

We didn't get too many beriberi cases but we lost a few because of it. Mostly it affected the kids in New Guinea because of their poor diet, but now and then a soldier would come down with it. Their stomachs distended dreadfully, becoming as large as a pregnant woman's, and we often got them too late. There might only be two or three scrub typhus and beriberi cases but a whole ward full of malaria and dengue fever sufferers. If a man was wounded and also suffering from malaria, he would be in a dreadful state.

The end of hostilities in Buna signalled a return to normality at the hospitals in Townsville, both American and Australian. Malaria and dengue fever cases again dominated the wards. Accident victims, military training casualties and the inevitable venereal disease sufferers were sufficient in numbers to make shifts busy enough, but with the wild chaos now behind them, nurses again had a chance to relax:

It was lovely to finish a shift and be able to go to a movie or have a skinny-dip at night or a swim at the Strand in the afternoon and a rest under the banyan trees. Just to go back to your quarters and listen to the radio or the gramophone was a treat. We often went to the dance at the Aquatic Club even though we were very tired. It was almost part of your duty. Female company was very scarce and we were in high demand. The American band music was all the rage, Glenn Miller and Benny Goodman especially, but others like Artie Shaw and Harry James. My favourite was Woody Herman's 'Golden Wedding'. That was the music the American boys danced to. We all learned to jitterbug. Some of us were better than others but we all learned.

The radio was full of American singers, Bing Crosby, Kate Smith and the Andrews Sisters. They helped lift the boys' spirits because they were very homesick, but we liked them too. On a couple of occasions I was able to get away and visit my grandfather Alfred, whose health was getting worse. Living in the tropics all those years had brought him undone.

In wartime it was only to be expected that some patients would arrive at the hospital in unusual circumstances. Such was the case, late in 1943, with Staff Sergeant Grady Gaston, who owed his life to an Australian military unit known as the Nackeroos. This was the NAORU, Northern Australian Observation Reconnaissance Unit, formed to monitor the vast coastline from North Queensland across the Gulf country to Exmouth in Western Australia: thousands of kilometres of uninhabited and in some cases unmapped territory. Little was known of this commando unit, whose soldiers lived liked bushmen, isolated for months on end and aided by Aboriginal trackers from outback stations. Their purpose was to observe and report on any enemy activity on land or in the air. In the case of an invasion they were to remain behind enemy lines and feed information of the enemy's movements using morse code.

Sergeant Grady Gaston was a crewman on the US Liberator bomber 'Little Eva', which ran out of fuel during a severe storm while returning from a bombing mission and crash-landed in a remote area northwest of Burketown, near the Gulf of Carpentaria. Six parachuted to safety having arranged to meet at the crash site. Thirteen days later two survivors staggered out of the wilderness and were rescued at Escott Station. A group of Nackeroos, aided by Aboriginal trackers, retraced their steps and found the wrecked Liberator 60 kilometres away. Four members who had not bailed out had died in the crash. This left four, including Sergeant Gaston, unaccounted for. The rescue party found their tracks and followed them for 130 kilometres but eventually lost them. They assumed they had drowned crossing one of the many flooded streams or been eaten by crocodiles.

Gaston and three second lieutenants, Grimes, Spelts and Dyer, wrongly assumed they had crashed near Cairns, on the east coast, 700 kilometres away. They had no food and just two pistols, both of which were soon rendered useless by salt water. After three weeks they found an empty shack where Spelts, whose feet were in a shocking condition, was left behind while the others went on in the hope of finding a settlement.

Lieutenant Grimes drowned swimming a flooded creek three days later. Dyer and Gaston pushed on for another 40 kilometres before deciding to turn back. On their way back to the shack they found Grimes's body. Five weeks later Dyer died of malnutrition. The Nackeroos found Grimes's body and sent out a search party which passed within two kilometres of the shack where Spelts and Gaston were clinging to life. Spelts lasted another fortnight before dying of starvation. Gaston, now alone, set out in a last ditch effort to find help. When an Aboriginal stockman found the feeble, starving Gaston wandering deliriously on a beach at the Gulf, the airman was within days, perhaps hours, of death. He had survived by sucking moisture from plants and eating insects and rodents and an occasional fish.

The stockman was able to contact the Nackeroos, who took two and a half days to reach them in an old blitz wagon. They drove Gaston and the three bagged bodies of his crewmen 270 kilometres to the nearest airfield, from where he was flown to Townsville. When he arrived at the 12th Station Hospital he was still in a very bad way, being too weak to walk and unable to eat. He was suffering from malnutrition and exposure and weighed just 55 kilograms, 30 below his normal weight. It took some weeks for him to regain his health, after which he was repatriated back to America where he told his remarkable story.

The Nackeroos were also involved in a remarkable sequence of events that occurred along the western shores of Cape York Peninsula near Arakun. Panic and confusion was caused by their reported sightings of submarines and a Japanese landing party. An American infantry company, airlifted from Cairns by flying boat, carried out an extensive ten-day search to no avail. Nevertheless, rumours were rife, in Townsville and elsewhere, that 500 Japanese soldiers had been killed in the Northern Territory and buried on Rutland Station. This tale was later strengthened by Aboriginal elders who told younger tribesmen that they had seen a large number of dead foreign soldiers being buried by Australian troops. The story remains in Aboriginal folklore. Authorities always maintained the story was a myth but Olive was one of many who found the rumours of landings easy to believe:

There was no doubt the Japanese had gained a lot of knowledge of northern Australia before the war, proven by the fact that they had better maps than the Allies in many remote areas. There were lots of Japanese in the pearling and fishing industries, so you'd be a fool to believe there hadn't been spies planted among them. They'd had their eyes on Australia for a long time. Japanese submarines had been unofficially reported in Queensland waters well before the war. We had no reason to believe there hadn't been landings. How easy would it be for the Japanese to come ashore at any number of places along hundreds and hundreds of kilometres of unprotected coastline? If they had landed and been wiped out by the American or Australian infantry, there is no way that sort of information would have been released to the public. There was enough panic with the bombing of Darwin. We heard the rumours at the hospital. There was no way of knowing if they were true but plenty we heard had been spot on.

One 'rumour' that was not a myth was the exercise carried out on Australian and US ships in Townsville Harbour. This was a secret test run for a raid planned on Singapore Harbour. Z Special Unit men, on an old, former Japanese fishing vessel renamed the *Krait*, carried out the exercise which was called 'Operation Scorpion'. The Z Special Unit had been in training for nine months, working on an extremely dangerous plan to secretly infiltrate Singapore Harbour and blow up Japanese shipping. The fact that the old craft had been hidden away in the mangroves at Smith Creek in Cairns, a spot Olive knew well, was what she described as one of the town's worst-kept secrets. Nevertheless the *Krait* and her crew were to cause considerable embarrassment to US and Australian authorities. Using the same audacious methods they intended for Singapore, they were able, under cover of darkness, to infiltrate the defence and attach magnetic, dummy limpet mines to several Australian and American warships which were anchored deep in Townsville Harbour. The exercise went perfectly. The furore caused the next day by the discovery of the mines was amazing but little was said publicly for fear of jeopardising the proposed raid on Singapore.

Six weeks later, eleven commandos of the Z Special Unit and three British servicemen left Cairns on the *Krait* to begin the 3860-kilometre journey to Exmouth Gulf in Western Australia, the launching point for what was now called 'Operation Jaywick'. Hidden in the bottom of the *Krait* were three two-man rubber canoes. Avoiding Japanese patrols by pretending to be local fishermen they made their way to within 30 kilometres of Singapore. Here six commandos left the *Krait* by canoe, carrying magnetic limpet mines and rations. Avoiding all patrols, they made their way through Singapore Harbour where they attached mines to seven Japanese vessels. Having rowed to a safe distance they saw all seven ships explode into flames. Remarkably they were again able to row past now increased patrols, hide in the jungle and keep their rendezvous with the *Krait* a week later. During a remarkable 47-day adventure, 33 of which were spent in enemy waters, the frogmen blew up 37 000 tonnes of shipping and returned to Exmouth without losing a single man. Japanese security had been no better than that at Townsville.

After eighteen months at the hospital Olive believed she had seen most things: servicemen critically ill and dying from battle wounds, invalid soldiers badly affected by weeping tropical ulcers and infested with lice, men who had damaged or lost limbs or eyesight, victims of typhus, malaria, beriberi, dengue fever and the tragic, disoriented shell-shocked figures whose minds were temporarily or perhaps permanently destroyed. There were also those coyly attending the venereal disease clinic after frequenting one of the Townsville brothels or being stitched up after brawls with other service personnel. Nothing came as a surprise. Whatever needed to be done was done.

Then came an entirely new phenomenon. She found herself confronted with men who had obviously been burnt by chemicals. Chemical warfare was nothing new. Chlorine had been used during the early stages of the First World War and the most lethal of the chemicals, yperite or mustard gas, was used extensively by the German army in 1917. Horrendous stories came out of France where soldiers engaged in trench warfare had been overcome by the gas. Many who had inhaled it had died long cruel deaths, sometimes extending over weeks, as the gas caused severe internal bleeding and destroyed the bronchial and respiratory systems. Even in circumstances where gasmasks were available the odourless gas had often been inhaled before its presence was detected. Several hours passed before symptoms became evident. The gas also entered the body through the skin's pores causing huge weeping blisters and the victim's eyelids to stick together. Over several fronts during World War I, more than a million soldiers had been struck down by chemical weapons. More than 90 000 were believed to have died. Those lucky enough to recover all too often suffered from respiratory problems and serious skin disorders for the rest of their lives.

Gasmasks were at a premium in North Queensland. People had rushed to buy them as soon as war threatened. But these victims at the hospital were not coming from battle stations. How could this be? The answer was that these were guinea pigs, Australian and American troops used in experiments. Here again was a secret that could not be disclosed until decades after the war. It was one of the rare occasions Olive got to tend Australian soldiers in the hospital.

While the effects of mustard gas in European trench warfare had been well documented, the Allies wanted to check its effectiveness in hot, tropical, jungle-like conditions. The Japanese had used mustard gas against the Chinese prior to their involvement in the war. It was feared they might well use it again. Britain and Australia had signed international agreements banning the use of chemical warfare after the First World War but America had not. Now huge amounts of bulk chemicals were arriving in Australia from Britain and the US. Though Australia could not produce the gas, they had developed the facilities to fill empty bomb casings with it. This was not disclosed at the time but the vast deposits of chemicals found dumped all along the Queensland and New South Wales coasts after the war indicate the Allies were not just concerned with the likelihood of the Japanese using chemicals. They were equipping to reply, or in fact to initiate, ready to justify their use by saying that, though many would be killed, many more would be saved in the long term by shortening the war.

In the tropical heat and humidity of places like Innisfail, young volunteers were put through a series of strenuous exercises and running drills until they were sweating freely. They were then bombarded with mustard gas and later locked in a large metal chamber into which more gas was systematically introduced. Sadly for the volunteers, it proved infinitely more effective than in cooler climates.

In another experiment, volunteers were landed on Brooke Island, in the Barrier Reef, after it had been bombarded by US Liberator aircraft carrying hundreds of tonnes of mustard gas bombs. The purpose of the experiment was to discover just when it would be safe for ground troops to go in after the bombing. Some volunteers wore protective clothing but others did not. Though these experiments were carried out under controlled conditions the men had no real idea of what the effects would be. Many victims arrived at the hospital in a very distressed state as Olive vividly recalls:

These poor devils started coming in with their skin all blistered. We weren't told anything about their injuries or how they got them. We treated them for normal burns and tried to stop the irritation as we did with chicken pox. We used vinegar and calamine lotion on those who were very itchy. Many developed huge blisters on their arms but were even worse in their groin and under their armpits. Where they sweated, you see. We eventually realised what had happened and the MO confirmed it was mustard gas. I felt so sorry for them. You had to wonder why they volunteered but obviously they didn't know what they were letting themselves in for. They certainly didn't know how long it would affect them or they wouldn't have done it, I'm sure. We didn't even know that.

Why would servicemen enter into such dangerous experiments? A typical answer came from an Australian volunteer still suffering some 60 years later:

> We were young blokes, around 20 years old, desperate to get up to New Guinea to get into the action. We were all set to go and then things got put back. So we were bored out of our wits in the training camp, not getting the call. Then we were asked to take part in some experiments that they said could be important to the cause and we'd be paid an extra two bob a week. Two bob was two bob in those days. We'd also get out of camp, up to Innisfail, between Townsville and Cairns, and maybe see a few girls around Mission Beach, so we thought, why not?

Popular film and show business stars frequently flew in on military planes to entertain American GIs in the Pacific, sometimes stopping over in Queensland to perform there as well. Comedian Jack Benny and harmonica player Larry Adler performed in one of the large igloo hangars at Garbutt. Olive recalls their appearance caused great interest among the locals and Australian servicemen:

A lot of people got a kick out of them because they'd already seen them on the screen. Prior to the arrival of the GIs, they were the only Americans they'd ever seen. There was one very funny episode with the most popular comedian of them all, Bob Hope, who visited Townsville after performing in the islands. He was flying in a Catalina flying boat with another comedian, Jerry Collona, well-known singer

Frances Langford and dancer Patti Thomas. That was a typical entertainment troupe for the servicemen. Just the right combination to keep the boys' spirits up.

Their plane was headed for Sydney from Guam, in the Pacific, when the pilot struck trouble about 500 kilometres further up the New South Wales coast. Having jettisoned their luggage, which to Hope's dismay included three cases of Scotch whiskey, the pilot crash-landed in Camden Haven River and the plane came to rest on a sandbar near the little town of Laurieton. A local fisherman, Bunny Wallace, rescued the damp entourage and took them to the local post office where the post master thought it was a joke when Bob Hope introduced himself. They sent telegrams advising what had happened then went on to the local pub to stay the night.

The town only had about 600 residents but when the news spread they came from everywhere to say hello. An impromptu dance was arranged at the School of Arts and the Americans entertained until the early hours, with the locals taking delight in performing the 'hokey pokey'. Next morning the artistes were driven to Newcastle and then flew on to Sydney, leaving the crew to look after the plane. Fishermen dragged the estuary looking for the Scotch but found nothing. The Catalina was repaired a few days later and farewelled by the townspeople, who received cards from Bob Hope at the Laurieton Hotel each Christmas for years and years. By a strange coincidence I bought a house, exactly 20 years later, on the edge of the estuary where the plane had landed.

In March 1944 the inevitable happened: Townsville was hit by a cyclone, which caused considerable damage and was a frightening experience for those who had not been through one. The unpredictability of just where on the coast the cyclone would strike meant there was little warning to batten down. Winds of almost

100 kilometres per hour tore through the city as 12.5 inches (30 centimetres) of rain fell in 24 hours. Armstrong Paddock became a bog within the first couple of hours as tents were flattened and scattered by the fierce gusts. Aircraft were pushed into hangars and workshops and doors were locked shut. Men worked feverishly to tie down those that remained in the open in the last few minutes before the storm hit.

The cyclone destroyed four floating metal beacons that guided shipping past Magnetic Island, through Platypus Channel, into Townsville Harbour. Several smaller boats were thrown onto the shore. Wind completely devastated the 500-bed Australian 2/14th Hospital located in tents on the northern outskirts of the city. Over 200 patients, almost half of them casualties from the Gona and Buna campaigns in New Guinea, were relocated to other hospitals in Townsville and Charters Towers. A new experience for some, it was the fourth or perhaps fifth cyclone for Olive:

If you'd been through a few, as I had, then you knew the ropes. No one can move around in hundred kilometre winds so all you can do is batten down, sit tight and wait for it to blow itself out. We were quite safe in the hospital because the homes were built to resist them. Tents of course were completely useless so Armstrong Paddock was awash with them. The worst part was the flash floods and the cleaning up when it was all over. Streets became rivers in a matter of minutes. When it was over we answered the usual questions about why a person would live in the tropics, but we just laughed them off.

The war was now turning the way of the Allies. Allied troops were slowly assuming control of Japanese bases in the islands. While there was still fierce fighting and plenty of ensuing casualties, they were being treated out of Australia. As servicemen departed Australia and the influx of casualties dried up, the various US military hospitals around Townsville began to close down. The new US 44th Hospital 20 kilometres north of Townsville, at Black River, commenced functioning and gradually accommodated all patients from Townsville, Charters Towers, Aitkenvale, Woodstock and Gordonvale. Another new, prefabricated 750-bed US hospital was built at Cairns with almost 150 portable huts on concrete slabs complete with electricity, water and sewerage services.

The last 405 patients at the 12th Station Hospital in Townsville were transported, without mishap, to Black River using 16 ambulances and 25 buses. In just over two years the staff had treated more than 23 000 casualties of which 453 had died. Olive and the rest of the nurses were staged at Armstrong Paddock where they enjoyed a well-earned rest:

I had no misgivings about the hospital closing. I was glad it was all over and we had become superfluous. An important part of my youth had been sacrificed. I think the other Australian girls felt like me about that. We had played our part, and we needed to, but we really should have been going to university, planning our lives and having fun. Instead we were caught in circumstances where we had no say.

Defence had been turned into offence. Nowhere was this shown more graphically than when an armada was assembled in Townsville Harbour in readiness for MacArthur's drive into the Philippines. Olive climbed to the top of Kissing Point to witness the most exhilarating sight of the war:

It was a beautiful clear day and I stood on the point looking at Allied ships absolutely crammed into the harbour — all along the Strand, in Rowes Bay and further out still in Cleveland Bay. More than 260 of them, there were. Eighty thousand troops, the majority American and Australian, were being loaded at Townsville and transported to the Philippines. People crowded the Strand and lined the hill at Kissing Point. There was tremendous excitement. After all we'd all been through it was a very inspiring sight. On the way the convoy picked up ships and troops from Fiji, New Guinea, New Caledonia and the Solomon Islands. Two hundred and sixty vessels became 450. By the time he got to Leyte in the Philippines, there were over 900 ships in the convoy. It was MacArthur's crowning glory, his time of triumph and he orchestrated it accordingly. This was how he wanted to be remembered. We saw the photos after the war with him wading ashore, water up to his knees, with a group of officers wearing their peaked caps and dark glasses. He had returned like he said he would. Still, he must have had some doubts during the two preceding years and it wasn't till well after the war we found out just how hard he battled to stage his return just as he wanted it. He was ringmaster and this was his show.

In early October 1944, Olive boarded a Douglas DC3 bound for Port Moresby, along with several other nurses and hospital staff. There was no danger from the Japanese; the only risk was flying into bad weather. Two hospitals, one American and the other Australian, were still operating between Port Moresby and the main airfield. Most patients were malaria and dengue fever sufferers left behind after the rest of the troops had gone on to the Philippines or been evacuated to Australia. Combat casualties from the Philippines were now being flown directly to the United States.

At last Olive would get to New Guinea. But this once burning ambition, frustrated due to the war, no longer held any excitement. Her grandfather, suffering badly from malaria and tropical ulcers, had died in a nursing home in Charters Towers. Nothing of his fortune ever found its way to Olive's family. With the death of his wife Alfred had taken a mistress, a flamboyant woman who kept Great Danes as guard dogs. She was his sole beneficiary who, after the war, built the Lae Hotel and subsequently retired to Hawaii and lived on her fortune. His children did not receive a penny. More injustice, as Olive saw it.

Olive was now very ill. Fever that she had been fighting in Australia flared up in the sweltering, tropical conditions at Moresby. She was diagnosed with malaria, dengue fever and was also found to be anaemic. Her blood samples were so unusual she was asked to sign an agreement so that they could be sent to America for analysis. The American medical authorities were determined to find a cure for these diseases. After just a few weeks she was told she would have to come home. She was given an indefinite period of leave during which she would be expected to look after herself and get back to health, then she would be discharged from service.

Olive returned on the Blue Funnel liner *Charon*, sister ship to the ill-fated *Centaur*, sunk by a Japanese submarine off Brisbane with the loss of 268 lives, including eleven nurses. Because of the sinking of the *Centaur* all passengers did emergency drills twice a day and were not allowed to leave their cabins without wearing inflatable life vests known as Mae Wests. There were seven Australian nurses returning from Port Moresby, also suffering from malaria, who were looked after by a middle-aged Polish doctor who treated them like royalty. The nurses were given the exclusive use of a section of the forward deck on which they rested, soaking up the sun. They looked less than elegant in swimming costumes and life vests but they enjoyed a much needed rest. Olive was sunburned in the warm waters of southern Queensland and when the cold winds hit her face a day later she began to peel. She arrived 'looking a mess'. The *Charon* anchored at Watsons Bay in Sydney at 9 pm and next morning docked at Wharf 13 Pyrmont. Olive took a cab to Annandale in Sydney's inner west. She had arranged to stay a while with an aunt and then go on to Melbourne's cooler climate while waiting to be demobbed. Her first time in a big city came as an enormous disappointment to her:

I couldn't believe how dirty and unattractive Sydney was. I don't know what I expected but I was horrified. It was October 1944 so Australia had been at war for almost six years. Perhaps that's why it looked so rundown. There was garbage in the streets and everything needed cleaning and painting. When I saw kids playing on dusty, grimy asphalt footpaths I thought of how lucky I'd been growing up in Queensland with so much freedom and room for adventure. I found myself comparing the streams and gorges where we swam and the bushwalks of the rainforest with the back streets of the Rocks and Woolloomooloo. It was so disgusting I thought, I just can't stay here. If I'd been well, I'd have gone back home but I'd been instructed to make my way to Melbourne. The cooler climate would help me to recover faster. I decided Melbourne couldn't be any worse than Sydney and I'd been invited to stay in Williamstown with Aunt Harriet and Uncle Bob. I couldn't get out of Sydney fast enough. Next day I was on the train heading south.

Olive found Melbourne as depressing and rundown as Sydney, but she had no choice other than to stay. Williamstown was the end of the railway line and her aunt and uncle had lived there almost all their lives. Harriet and Bob made her very welcome. In her own words 'nothing much happened in Williamstown' so it was as good a place as any to recuperate. She had arrived shortly before the Melbourne Cup and Aunt Harriet convinced her that, as she might not get another chance to see the famous race, she should go. Neither Aunt Harriet nor Uncle Bob offered to accompany her so she went alone:

I was still a country bumpkin, really. I'd never even been to the races in the bush but I caught the train into Flemington with no idea about how to put a bet on. Having fought my way up to the stand through this huge crowd to get a view of the race, I then discovered I had to go back down again to put my money on, because all the bookmakers were down the bottom. By now the crowd was so thick I could hardly move. I think every soldier, sailor and airman on leave in Melbourne was there. Half the crowd was in uniform, as I was. I'd never seen so many people. By the time I had my bet and tried to get back upstairs the situation was impossible. I was clutching that illegible betting ticket and still struggling to get back upstairs when there was a huge roar. Obviously the race had started. I saw absolutely nothing and had no idea who had even won. I asked someone if my horse had won and they said no and then just laughed. Whenever anyone asked me, after that, if I'd ever been to the Cup, I used to toss up whether to just say yes and leave it at that or tell them the whole long story.

During my time in Melbourne Hank, my dental nurse friend, wrote to me from the States. He'd served in New Guinea, Guadalcanal and the Solomon Islands so he was one of the lucky ones. He was studying for a degree in dentistry back in Indiana. We exchanged three or four letters and in the last one he told me how beautiful it was to look out his window at the university and see the snow a foot deep on the sidewalk and feel the chill on his face. I recalled he suffered dreadfully in Queensland's heat. The thought of enjoying being cold was as foreign to me as the thought of a religion that accepted polygamy. We could never have been anything but good friends but I did enjoy hearing from him. It had been hard making any friendships, what with travelling between hospitals and knowing patients for such a short time, so I appreciated his writing to me.

I really felt a bit like an orphan once I came back from New Guinea. During my time nursing at the US hospital I'd lost close contact with the Australian girls even though I saw them occasionally when on leave. After all those dramatic times I had no friends to share those experiences with. This was the one disadvantage of having worked for the Americans. It was always one of my deepest regrets that even before the war ended they all left Australia with MacArthur and I lost track of them. Even though I was paid so well and had everything at my disposal, I've always envied the girls who made close friends and were able to keep them for years after the war. But for one chance meeting with one of the other Australian girls who worked with us, in Sydney some 20 years later, I had no contact with any of them. It was a very brief period in terms of actual time but people you had seen and worked alongside every day, you suddenly never saw again.

Olive spent the Christmas period recuperating, on full pay, with her aunt and uncle at Williamstown. Her fever disappeared completely but anaemia would haunt her forever. She was demobbed at Melbourne's Victoria Barracks early in 1945:

I was called in at 1100 hours one morning, signed a few papers, was thanked for my efforts and told I was once more a civilian. There was no parade, no saluting, no nothing. The whole exercise took about half an hour. I thought, Hell, I've got out as quickly as I got in back in 1942. I walked out of the barracks a free agent. All I had to show for my efforts were four standard Australian Service medals, an American uniform and a presidential citation that came in the form of a bar to be worn with the medals. Still, it was a damned good feeling. It was 1945, the war was coming to an end and I was still only eighteen years old.

Top: Two-and-a-half-year-old Olive with her mother, Alda, in Cairns, 1929.

Middle: Ten-year-old Olive in Cairns, 1936. The young tomboy took her share of bumps and bruises playing cricket with her cousins.

Left: Olive (*left*) with her family at a Railway Picnic at Fishery Falls in September 1936.

Above: Olive (*right*) with her sister, Betty, at the Cairns Show in the mid-1930s. Betty had been severely injured in a level-crossing accident, and Olive became her carer throughout their school years.

Left: Twelve-year-old Olive waiting for rain while on holiday near Bowen, 1938.

Top: Olive during Voluntary Aid Detachment (VAD) training just prior to enlistment.

Middle: Olive during her early training at Cairns Hospital with the orphan whom she named Frances and who called her Mummy.

Bottom: Part of the 12th Station Hospital, Townsville. Note the walkways between the buildings. COURTESY CHUCK HATHORN

Top: A group of Olive's VAD friends up to their ankles in mud during the monsoon season, 1941.

Middle: Japanese invasion money. Olive had no doubt an invasion was imminent.

Bottom: Olive's new boss, Douglas MacArthur, visits his Townsville headquarters, 1942. COURTESY ARCH FRALEY PHOTOGRAPHICS

Top: Olive (*third from left*) with the 'Angels of Bataan'.

Above: Olive in Sydney, circa 1950.

Left: Olive with 'Hank', on leave in Cairns, Easter Sunday, 1944.

Above: Frank aboard the *Mendi Palm.*

Right: Frank and Olive on their wedding day, 23 January 1953.

Above: Olive and Steven at Poole, England, 1955.

Left: Grandma Elsie with four-year-old Steven in Sydney.

Left: The ever-smiling Steven at five.

Below: Olive and Frank in Sydney in the late 1960s.

Top: Olive marching on Anzac Day in Adelaide, 1982. Lieutenant Dick Chugg is saluting.

Bottom: Olive with son Steven at a US Australian Association Coral Sea Dinner.

Above: Olive being congratulated on her OAM by South Australia's Governor, Sir Donald Dunstan, 1988.

Left: Olive at a dinner for the US Ambassador in Adelaide, 1988.

Top and bottom: Before and after: The Kapunda War Memorial as it was in 2000; and the magnificent War Memorial Gardens, September 2001.

Three remarkable women, representing three theatres of war, at the bust of the service nurse at Kapunda's War Memorial Gardens. Olive (*left*), the South Pacific; Vivienne Holmes (*centre*), Burma; and Nancy Wake (*foreground*), France.

Chapter Five

PEACE AND ROMANCE

Olive returned to Sydney to stay with her Aunt Mary in Annandale but found it very difficult to settle down. To resume any sort of stable life immediately after her extraordinary period in Townsville would obviously take time. Getting over the culture shock of the big grimy city was helped when she made some friends of similar age and discovered some of the beauty spots around the harbour. Still, overall she found it rather uninviting compared to the idyllic places of her childhood in Townsville and Cairns. Olive followed the fortunes of the war, which continued to turn the way of the Allies. The 32nd Division, the Red Arrows, having returned to Australia after Buna, campaigned again in New Guinea and then went on to the Philippines, accumulating 654 days of combat, the greatest number of any American division in the war. MacArthur continued to argue with Washington, his chiefs of staff and the navy.

In Townsville and Cairns, where her father was still working on the waterfront, operations continued to diminish as troops were sent north to the Philippines, Bougainville and to Europe. The giant B17 Flying Fortresses had much more success in bombing raids over Germany than they had in the Pacific. Nevertheless when Mareeba Airport was later returned to civilian use it was the propeller of a B17 that was placed by a plaque that reads: 'This aerodrome played a decisive part in keeping Australia free from invasion during the Second World War 1939–1945. Allied aircraft from the 19th and 43rd Bombardment groups of the USAAF and from the RAAF launched an air offensive against the Japanese in June/July 1942.'

Olive had been at her aunt's house for only a few months when Prime Minister John Curtin died of a heart attack, aged 60. The tall, bespectacled, inspiring orator had taken office six weeks before the attack on Pearl Harbor and had been a popular and courageous leader. His death occurred just six weeks before the war ended and his funeral was broadcast across Australia. Olive felt genuine sadness as she listened:

He was a wonderful man who worked so hard during the war it wore him out. He was very strong and always spoke up for the defence of Australia. Being a diehard socialist family we appreciated what he stood for but we also liked the way he stood up to Churchill and got the Australian boys back from Africa to Australia when Churchill wanted to send them on to Burma. We knew the score there. It was only that Curtin appealed to MacArthur and told Churchill where to go that got them back. Churchill was happy to let Australia fall and recapture it later, but Curtin would have none of it. It was quite a brave move on his behalf to turn so openly to America. Australia had always been so tied to England and the Commonwealth. MacArthur described him as a great statesman. It was a shame he didn't see the end of the war. He was a hero to us. I think almost everybody loved John Curtin for his fairness and courage, no matter what their politics were.

Even as the Germans capitulated in Europe, with the Italian people having overthrown the government and turned against them to support the Allies, the fanatical Japanese continued to defend their bases in the Pacific. On the volcanic island of Iwo Jima 20 000 Japanese, including 2000 suicide pilots, died along with 4000 American marines. Olive found it easy to picture American nurses working night and day as she and her colleagues had done in Townsville. It was not until the dropping of atom bombs on Hiroshima and Nagasaki that the Japanese were forced to surrender. The announcement of peace brought crowds of revellers into Sydney on trains, trams, ferries, buses, bicycles and on foot:

I'd been listening to the radio because we all knew something was about to happen. Once the announcement was made everybody came flocking into the city to celebrate. I came in by train with two girlfriends and we just couldn't get up the steps at Town Hall. People were jammed in like sardines in a tin, hugging and crying, singing and kissing. There were thousands of us trying to get up into George Street.

When we eventually forced our way up to street level, George Street was filled with confetti and strips of paper thrown out of office buildings. People were dancing on the roads, hugging and cheering, it was a once-in-a-lifetime thing. The pubs were jam-packed with drinkers and when they closed at six o'clock the publicans just couldn't get them out. Eventually they came pouring out onto the streets. The sly-grog shops must have done a roaring trade, men kept finding bottles of beer. We didn't drink at all, just danced and hugged people we'd never seen before. Especially if they were in uniform. People were going home in trams, singing at the tops of their voices.

Public transport stopped at midnight so when we decided it was time to go home we walked along the tram tracks to Lilyfield then up into Annandale. There was a huge crowd in Prince Alfred Park and we stopped for over an hour to join in community singing. We sang all the popular war songs: 'Coming in on a Wing and a Prayer', 'We'll Meet Again', 'The White Cliffs of Dover', 'The Last Time I Saw Paris'. As one song ended the strains of another would start in the crowd and we'd all join in. 'Three Cheers for the Red, White and Blue', 'Bless 'em All', 'Kiss Me Goodnight, Sergeant Major', we sang the lot. Large sections of the crowd linked arms and swayed as they sang. There were still hundreds of people around at four in the morning. People were sitting out on their verandahs chatting away. No one wanted the night to end. Even though we knew the war had been coming to a close, when it actually happened it was just so special, people went crazy. Some didn't go home at all. The party mood lasted for a week.

Victory marches occurred throughout the country. The troops came home in their thousands to be greeted by cheering crowds. Australia set about adjusting to peace as searchlights dimmed, barbed wire entanglements were removed from the beaches and rations were lifted. In Townsville, locals who had seen the town's population explode from 30 000 to a 120 000 in a few months watched the exodus of military personnel with the same fascination as they had watched their arrival. The noise and excitement of a garrison city filled with young American and Australian troops faded with the same speed at which it had grown. Suddenly it was all over. The old town would never be quite the same. An advertisement from the *Townsville Bulletin* told the story:

Buildings for removal, Department of Army, under instructions from Commonwealth Disposals Commission. Will sell by public auction all the buildings comprising the USA camp area known as Armstrong Paddock at Aitkenvale. Approximately 100 buildings comprising:

a) 8 mess halls with all fitments and appurtenances (various sizes from 53 x 20 to 184 x 40 feet) and including mess tables, shelving, counters, cool rooms, tanks, Sampson ranges, skillions etc.

b) Workshops 56 x 16, recreation building 56 x 16, office, QM store, canteen and storeroom buildings all 56 x 16 feet.

c) Telephone exchange 27 x 20, large headquarters, dispensary and post office buildings.

d) Another recreation hut 106 x 40 feet. These buildings contain counters, tables, map boards, wall desks, partitions, sinks and switchboards.

e) 26 shower and ablution buildings 30 x 9, 48 x 16, 51 x 15 and other sizes with all fitments.

f) 35 latrine buildings 10 x 7, 18 x 9, 24 x 8, brick incinerator, cinema box, boxing ring, complete stage and fittings.

In Sydney, Australian and US warships anchored in the harbour as thousands of servicemen enjoyed peacetime leave. Families, reunited with returned loved ones, flocked to picnic areas all over the city. Kids played backyard cricket with fathers and uncles they had not seen for years. The city sought relief in sport and recreation. Crowds lined the harbour foreshores to see the first Sydney to Hobart fleet sail out through the Heads. The American Davis Cup team arrived to regain the tennis trophy lost to Australia just days before the war had commenced in 1939 as England prepared to send her cricket and football teams to Australia. Sure enough, the Americans were interviewed eating ice cream at breakfast time. These were heady days.

Olive had been at a loose end. Now, well rested and needing to earn some money, she decided to take a job, though not as a nurse. Instead she applied for and attained a position as a receptionist at Sydney Hospital, Australia's oldest, in Macquarie Street. She found it strange that she earned more money with much less taxing hours by answering a phone than by nursing. She was no longer convinced that nursing would be her long-term vocation. At Sydney Hospital, Olive met Sister Nell Savage, the only survivor from twelve nurses on board the hospital ship *Centaur*, which had been torpedoed off Brisbane with a loss of 268 lives. The *Centaur* had been very clearly marked as a hospital ship and as such should have been immune from attack. Ironically, earlier in the war the *Centaur*'s crew had picked up 62 German survivors, including the captain and several officers, from the *Kormoran*, which had sunk off the West Australian coast after sinking the ill-fated HMAS *Sydney*.

Nell, who had won the George Cross for bravery on board the sinking *Centaur*, was asked to address the nursing staff about her wartime service. Later Olive took her around to the various wards to meet the sisters. She was very impressed with Nell and they spoke at length about each other's nursing experiences. The deliberate and deplorable action of the Japanese submarine commander in sinking a hospital ship helped reinforce Olive's deep abhorrence of injustice. Still unsettled, she found herself continually thinking of certain aspects of the war:

I was deeply troubled that certain people could determine that other people were expendable. The idea that Churchill could decide that my family and friends along with all those hard-working people in the north could be left to their own devices infuriated me. The people in the big cities in the south were to have a chance but we weren't. It still infuriates me 60 years later. I guess I had the socialist ideas of my father instilled in me. The mustard gas victims were exploited because of their naivety. They had no idea how much they would suffer or for how long. They couldn't even talk about it for 30 years. Then we learned about the massacres of the missionaries in Gona and the Australian nurses who were marched into the sea and machine-gunned to death in Malaya. If that marvellous woman Vivian Bullwinkel hadn't survived, we would never have known about it. How many atrocities did we *not* know about? The stories of extreme cruelty and murder that came out of the prison camps were devastating. I found it impossible to understand that sort of brutality being carried out, often on defenceless noncombatants. It was more than I could ever comprehend.

Despite her feelings about such appalling aspects of the war Olive joined the Australian American Ex-Services Association and regularly attended the dawn service on Anzac Day, after which she marched with the American ex-servicemen and women. Between 80 and 90 in number, they were always placed at the end of the long procession. She wore her uniform proudly, looking every inch American but feeling very much Australian.

After just five months at Sydney Hospital she decided to take a post at Royal Prince Alfred (RPA), again as a receptionist. Her reference from Sydney Hospital, signed by J. Stevenson, staff supervisor, on 19 July 1946, described her as 'conscientious and courteous and having carried out her duties with credit'. Olive began work at RPA just ten days after leaving Sydney Hospital and stayed with them for just over two years. She refers to these two and a half years as her 'lost period':

I was really trying to work out what to do with my life. Pay for nurses was appalling and conditions not much better. At RPA nurses were billeted in Nissan huts in nearby Alfred Park. There was no checking up on them, they came and went as they wished, but still they were living in huts being taken for granted as they always had been and still are today. There is great satisfaction in helping others and this sense of duty is what kept young women in the profession. I found I could sit on my tail answering the phone for twice the money the nurses were earning and not have shiftwork interfere with my social life either. So I was in a quandary as to what I should do. I had plenty of images in my mind from the war that I wished I could forget and working at the hospital obviously kept those images fresh. I was still trying to adjust. It was difficult to knock back the easy money on the switchboard to go back to the wards and the trauma.

Still, Olive did just that. Despite her enormous practical experience, jammed into two hectic years, she was not yet fully qualified, having missed out on obstetrics because of her hasty decision to join the army. She quit her receptionist job in order to complete a nine-month course across the way at the new King George V Hospital. Again her reference, this time from the medical superintendent, was excellent. She tucked it away with the other. A small pub across the road became a meeting place for off-duty nurses and helped in making this period more enjoyable. Soon after, her family sold their home in Cairns and moved to Sydney. She went to live with them in Broadway, a fifteen-minute walk from the hospital complexes.

She finished her obstetrics course without difficulty but was still finding it hard to settle down. Now a fully qualified nursing sister, Olive had short stints at the Padua Private Hospital and the Alma Mater in Randwick. At the Alma Mater she had an experience that did not actually change her life there and then, but had a profound influence on her. She met Freddy:

Freddy was 22 years old and had been at the hospital longer than anyone could remember. He was looked after through some sort of fund that had apparently been set up for him, but he never ever had a visitor. He had the body of a nine-month-old baby and still wore napkins, but his head had grown to normal size. What his real name was no one knew; he was just Freddy. I'd been taught, when training, that it was necessary for a nurse to have an 'invisible barrier' so that she would not become involved with any patient. 'Do not become emotionally involved,' the nuns warned us. If you did then your work would suffer. I'd been able to retain this barrier, even when the GIs were dying in Townsville and the little black girl Frances took a shine to me in Cairns, but somehow, for some reason, Freddy broke that barrier.

I used to take him out in his cot into the garden and he would pant like a little dog. He couldn't talk and this was his only way of showing pleasure. I fed him and sang to him and I know he appreciated it. He died while I was there. I don't know why but Freddy was the one who somehow got through to me. I'd always had a feeling for the underdog from the time I used to bring little orphaned animals home when I was a kid. Mum let me keep them all except the baby crocodile and I was very upset at having to take him back. Now I knew I had a responsibility to look after those who weren't able to look after themselves. That was simply how it was. God had put me here to care for the underdog.

The chance meeting reinforced a belief that she had long held. She had a special purpose in life. But still she was unsettled, leaving the Alma Mater to take a temporary job as a receptionist, this time with the Australian Broadcasting Commission. Her salary was much better than that of a nurse and she remained for four and a half months. In 1948 a polio epidemic broke out in Brisbane as it had done when Olive was at St Joseph's School in Cairns. A special unit was set up in the Royal Brisbane Hospital and volunteer nurses were sought. Olive decided to heed the call. Her reference from the ABC simply noted that she was moving interstate:

I read about the epidemic and knew how traumatic it had been when I was in Cairns as a kid. It was a terrible viral disease, mainly affecting children, whose muscles became paralysed and wasted away. There was no cure for it and no way of preventing it. Epidemics occurred every now and then but could never be predicted. No one could be sure why it had broken out in Brisbane, though there was speculation that birds had carried the virus. Anyway it was a genuine epidemic so I replied and was accepted immediately. Polio was regarded as highly contagious and people had a real paranoia about catching it. For some reason I never had that fear. I had been immunised as a child when that little boy died but whether that was an effective protection against the disease I didn't really know.

I got there to find we had 60 patients in one ward. There were kids from a few months old to men of 60. And then on top of that there was an outbreak of chicken pox. Some of the younger ones were in casts and corset type things and they itched so much with the chicken pox it was terrible for them. The poor little beggars suffered dreadfully. We swabbed them with vinegar and gallons of calamine lotion and at the same time they were very ill with the polio. I worked there for two years and it was tough going for the patients and the nursing staff but we never lost a patient. When they eventually brought out the Salk vaccine, a few years later, the disease was beaten.

Towards the end of my two years at Brisbane Hospital I became aware that nurses were wanted by the occupational forces in Japan. Authorities were looking for nurses, particularly those with military service and those with experience in midwifery, to look after the spouses and families of British and American servicemen, under the command of Douglas MacArthur. I went out to the Brisbane army barracks and was advised I could sign up. I told my mother, who was visiting me at the time, and she rang my father in Sydney. Well, he hit the roof. He flew up immediately and positively forbade me to go. He said, 'You've done enough, Olive, you've got to start looking after yourself for a change.' I'd never seen him so agitated. I know they had both suffered seeing so little of me during the war, so perhaps that was also part of his frustration. I wasn't totally convinced I wanted to go, so, while I was used to making my own decisions, this time I took his advice and dropped the idea.

I was then offered a position with a wholesale supply company, Surgical Supplies, where I dealt directly with hospitals and doctors. I took the job and found I liked it mainly because it was a bit different. I'd just had enough of nursing. They put me through a crash course to prepare me for the job and I spent some time with the Berlei Company, who made special garments for people with ruptures. I did a quick course on prosthetics that I found very interesting. I recall a lovely nun coming in one day suffering from curvature of the spine.

She was well into her forties and very modest of course, no one was ever allowed to see their bodies. She had another nun with her and she had to strip down to be measured and fitted for a spinal brace. I explained everything to her and made her as comfortable as possible with what had to be done. I kept a sheet over her as much as I could and she thanked me at the finish. She was very sweet and I respected her situation.

I stayed with the company for a bit over a year before deciding I needed a complete change in my life, so in 1951 I decided I might go overseas. While I was thinking about travel Douglas MacArthur had finished his duties in Japan and was commanding the United Nations forces in the war in Korea. He must have been 70 years old. I wondered if anything would ever stop him.

Olive came back to Sydney where her Mum and Dad were still living and brought some furniture down for them. She returned to Sydney on the Orient liner RMS *Ormonde*, which was sailing on to England via the Suez Canal. Hers was only a short leg of the long trip, one she almost missed, and one that would change her life. She was running late and when she arrived at the wharf the gangplank had just been pulled up. As she hurried down towards the ship it was lowered again. This was a most unusual occurrence and one that did not go unnoticed by the ship's radio operator and the chief engineer, who witnessed her arrival from the deck. With infinite masculine wisdom the pair decided the attractive young lady now boarding the liner must be very important indeed, perhaps the governor's daughter or someone of that stature. A wager was made as to who could be first to meet her.

After dinner on that warm, balmy evening Olive was relaxing on the deck of the 15 000-ton luxury liner when one of the pair appeared, resplendent in his well-pressed, all-white tropical uniform. He strode confidently around the deck, had a look over the side and appraised those passengers relaxing in the deckchairs. A few metres away sat an attractive young lady who seemed, to Olive, to be the focus of his attention. Olive waited for him to make a move toward her, so she was totally surprised when he walked over and sat beside Olive instead. Then, very courteously, he introduced himself as 'Frank Wilson-Weston, radio operator, RMS *Ormonde*.' His manner was very charming and she found herself smiling politely. As they sat chatting, Captain Blake appeared and enquired as to whether Olive and Frank intended going to the dance that evening. It was traditional to have a dance on the first night out of port. Her first inclination was to say no as she was rather tired and had been looking forward to bed. She had often been told to be wary of sailors but here was the most perfectly spoken and delightful man inviting her. Acting on a whim, and pleased with the company of Frank and the ship's captain, she agreed.

This was Olive's first night at sea and the setting for the dance was entirely new and exciting to her. Quite a difference, she thought, to the air force hangars at Garbutt. As a 'country kid' from Townsville she was quite adept at the standard old-time favourites like the 'Pride of Erin' and the barn dance, and she had done pretty well learning to jive with the young American GIs. Now, as Frank guided her effortlessly across the deck to the jazz waltz, she realised she had not met anyone of Frank's charm. Their eyes met several times as they danced to 'Some Enchanted Evening' from the musical *South Pacific*.

In the two days it took the *Ormonde* to travel from Brisbane to Sydney, Olive became well acquainted with the thorough English gentleman. She was somewhat amused to learn that his full name was Frank Charles Ulrich Gladwin Wilson-Weston. His father and grandfather before him had lived all their lives with the British aristocracy in India where Frank was brought up. In this environment, manners and protocol were extremely important. After serving in the RAF he had joined the merchant navy and was on his third successive journey to Australia.

When the *Ormonde* berthed in Sydney he was there to help her with her luggage, to meet her parents and to ask her to accompany him, that night, to Sammy Lee's Chequers' nightclub, a place Olive had never even heard of. She agreed to go. Though certainly not swept off her feet, she could not help but enjoy his charm and gentlemanly hospitality. Next evening they went to the cinema and then to dinner, where Frank admitted his wager with the chief engineer, a fact that they laughed heartily about. When Frank left on the following day to continue his voyage to England, Olive farewelled him at the wharf. As she boarded the bus he put his arm around her and kissed her goodbye. It was the first time their lips had met. That evening she reflected on the last four days, the likes of which she had not experienced before.

Within a week of Frank's departure Olive received a parcel that had been posted in Melbourne, the *Ormonde*'s first port of call after Sydney. It contained Olive's white gloves, which she had inadvertently left in the pocket of his tuxedo at Chequers' nightclub. Each of the ten fingers was stuffed with a piece of paper on which was written a romantic message. Also in the parcel was a long and beautifully written letter that, to her great surprise, concluded with a proposal of marriage. Olive decided the man was not only a romantic, but perhaps somewhat mad as well. She had heard of shipboard romances but this was going too far. After all, there had been no real romance.

Happily she wrote a letter of reply, ignoring any mention of the proposal, and posted it to Fremantle where she knew mail would be delivered to the ship. Frank's next letter, eight pages in length, which he posted at the next port, Ceylon, was even more romantic than the first, and again he proposed. She read this letter several times, savouring every word of the small, neat, backward-sloping handwriting. Again she replied, this time suggesting he was rushing things just a little, but she made it clear she appreciated his feelings for her. Encouraged, he wrote again from London with a third proposal. She now realised he really meant it. He was in love with her. Olive was not as besotted as Frank but she found him attractive and liked him very much for his charm, his manners and his company. After much thought she wrote back saying that, though she had not been contemplating marriage, she agreed they could be considered engaged.

Thrilled with Olive's reply, Frank requested work on a ship headed back to Australia but instead was posted, again on the *Ormonde*, carrying troops to Korea. He wrote to her several times during the three-month trip.

Hello my dearest adorable darling Olive.

I am sitting in the wireless room. It's almost 11 o'clock and I am listening to Radio Luxembourg. Plenty of dance music, but at the moment Perry Como singing 'I Will Love You Forever,' voicing my thoughts of course Darling. Each minute I'm away from you seems like an eternity. This feeling is something I have never experienced before. It's wonderful. The very thought of you makes me tingle and my heart is thumping thunderously Darling. You make me feel so alive even the crew notice it and kid me about it.

Meanwhile Olive's family went to live in the sunny seaside suburb of Manly. She took a job as a bookkeeper at the Manly Pacific Hotel overlooking North Steyne on the Pacific Ocean, enjoying the work and the surrounds where a long row of Norfolk Island pine trees separated the beach from the hotel. The Manly Pacific was a family owned hotel that attracted holiday-makers from all over the country. One frequent visitor from South Australia was the young scientist Marcus Oliphant, who had worked on the development of the atomic bomb and much later became Sir Mark, Governor of South Australia.

Back in London Frank, again, requested a Pacific cruise. Once more he was denied, this time sailing on the 4000-ton oil tanker *British Commodore* to the Persian Gulf. His letters continued to flow. Sometimes Olive would get three delivered on the one day. There was always news of his voyage but his thoughts continually went back to romance.

Hello Olive, Sweet Darling Olive.

Thank you for my letter. I look forward to all of your letters my dearest one. Each one is a treasure, all of its own. God bless your sweet self. Darling I too am impatient to take you in my arms again. I say this as if this has been so many times before — when really, lovely lass, that's not true. Let me see we had one dance that night on the ship (first time in my arms) and that night when I hurriedly kissed you as you got on the bus (second time when I had one arm around you and had to force myself to hold the other arm rigid by my side when I was just longing to enfold you in my heart which you had just stolen). As the time draws closer when we shall be Mr and Mrs, Olive Darling, that one kiss returns to me so vividly and I die to repeat it, but this time knowing that you love me. I shall be satisfied with just one arm around you and Darling to you who are so virginal and sweet, not having known me for long before

we parted, I'll understand completely if you feel a bit reticent
when we meet again at home.

Try as he did, Frank was unable to get out to see his future bride.
After voyages that took him on the *Amersham Hill*, carrying wheat
to Canada, and the *Biographer*, cruising the Caribbean, the
frustrated couple agreed that unless Frank's next venture was
'Down Under' she would sail to England to marry him. Olive
resigned from her position at the Manly Pacific when it was
purchased by nightclub owner Sammy Lee, reasoning the
bookkeeping job could well become stressful under entrepreneurial
management. The clientele certainly changed rapidly.

When Frank was posted on the *Mendi Palm* to the Belgian
Congo in West Africa, the pair decided they had waited long
enough. By the time *Mendi Palm* returned to London over eighteen
months would have elapsed since his first letter, written from the
Ormonde in Melbourne, so Olive agreed to set sail for England.
Overjoyed, Frank made arrangements for her to be looked after in
case he was away when she arrived. Before she left she received a
telegram, sent to her care of the Manly post office, from Takoradi
on the West African Gold Coast: 'No letter Takoradi. Cheer up
Olive darling. Bon voyage 11th. Dying to see you. In my thoughts
and loving you truly always. Frank'.

Olive's parents and sister Betty saw her off to England on a perfect
spring day in October 1952. By coincidence she was again booked on
the 15000-ton luxury Orient passenger liner *Ormonde*. It was the
ship's last ocean voyage. The *Ormonde* had a wonderful record,
having done around-the-world trips for many years before the war.
When hostilities commenced she was used as a decoy ship, sailing at
the head of naval convoys inviting submarines to attack her. She was
said to be a blessed ship. Despite several repaint jobs a crucifix always

reappeared on the interior of her bow. As it was her final voyage before being broken up at English wrecking yards, she proudly flew a large pennant from her funnel when departing each port, and three blasts from other vessels farewelled her as she sailed across the globe. For Olive this added greatly to an already exciting voyage.

Olive shared a cabin with Beverley Borger, a young woman of similar age who was also travelling to England to marry. Her fiancé was the heir to the Bachelor canned foods fortune. They had much in common and hit it off immediately. Before the *Ormonde* departed Sydney, Captain Blake asked Olive if she would look after a seventeen-year-old orphaned English lass who had come to Australia to live in the Barnardo's Homes but who had got into bad company and subsequently prostitution, and was being deported. She was also asked to take care of a sixteen-year-old youth, Michael Haig, returning from boarding school in Perth to his parents in Cairo. Olive agreed to both requests.

The liner struck very bad weather on the way to Melbourne. The huge storm and mountainous waves smashed the porthole of Olive's cabin and water poured in, flooding the compartment. Olive and Beverley were forced to change cabins, taking what was still dry with them. Olive was one of only five passengers — from a total of 150 — who turned up for breakfast the following morning.

During a three-day stay in Melbourne Olive picked up her wedding cake, which Aunt Harriet had made. Olive was pleased to see her again, still grateful for her kindness when she was recuperating from malaria. The cake contained a full bottle of rum. By the time portions of the cake returned to Australia after the wedding, twelve months would have elapsed.

The *Ormonde* sailed for Adelaide, again to the farewell blasts of liners, ferries and tugs. The Great Australian Bight brought even rougher weather and Olive gave seasick tablets to passengers who had not yet found their sea legs. One man who had been suffering since the ship left Sydney had determined to abandon his trip in Fremantle but the tablets did the trick and he went on to London.

Among the passengers joining the ship in Fremantle was an Englishwoman who had come out from the cool English climate to Marble Bar, where temperatures topped 104° Fahrenheit (40° Celsius) week after week. She had suffered a mental breakdown and was returning to England. Again it was Olive who was asked to keep an eye on her. She now had three people under her care:

I didn't mind. It was obvious my nursing background prompted the authorities to ask me to look after them. It was not uncommon when young or infirm people were travelling alone to have some kind of chaperone from among the other passengers. The boy was very polite and well mannered. His father was the chief engineer at Marconi Radio in Cairo. It was Marconi, Frank's employer, which supplied ships' radio officers all around the world. The girl was a little older and she became quite close to me as the trip wore on. She was a nice kid and behaved herself very well. The woman slowly improved as we went. She kept very much to herself. I felt extremely sorry for her. I could imagine a gentlewoman coming from an English climate to Marble Bar. It would have been torture for the poor thing.

Captain Blake and his first officer were aware of Olive's and Beverley's situations and took good care of them. When the ship's fancy-dress ball was staged, Olive found just the costume to keep shipboard Romeos at bay:

I went as Tondalayo, a dark, native lass from *White Cargo*, a famous Hollywood film of the forties played by Hedy Lamar. Two gay cabin stewards helped me dress in a sarong and shells with dark brown greasepaint and oil all over me. Certainly no one with a white uniform would come anywhere near me, let alone ask for a dance. Nor would anyone else in good clothes. I thought it was rather clever to get a costume that looked seductive but kept the wolves at bay at the same time. The idea worked perfectly.

The first port of call after Australia was Colombo, capital of Ceylon, where mail awaited her. Having read a sixteen-page letter from Frank, Olive went to the Mount Lavinia Hotel and had a succulent Indian curry. At the next stop in Aden, Olive saw beggars for the first time. She found it was quite a distressing sight, even after her wartime experiences, with limbless children begging for alms and bodies lying inertly in the gutters as goats wandered among them.

Aboard ship the wedding cake was fermenting beautifully and in the heat of the Red Sea the already strong rum odour increased significantly. Each time one of the girls opened the cabin door they were greeted by the sweet smell of rum. When the *Ormonde* crossed the Red Sea and came to the Suez Canal, the Suez crisis was making headlines across the globe. Two British warships, one ahead and one behind, escorted the liner through the canal to Port Said:

From Port Said, escorted by two of the ship's officers, I had to take this young fellow to his parents' place in Cairo because they couldn't get out of the city to come and pick him up. Soldiers confiscated our passports as we left the ship to ensure that we returned. So there we were in Egypt, without passports, and soldiers carrying machine-guns on every corner. We took a taxi to Cairo where his parents were very relieved to see their boy was safe and sound. They wanted me to stay and have lunch and a drink but I was very dubious about Egyptian food and water so I just had a Coca Cola.

When we got back to the ship the soldiers were there to check our passports. They were a lecherous bunch too, making comments on how pretty I looked in my photo. I hid my utter disdain for them as best I could so as not to upset them. We were all glad to be away from Suez, going next to Algiers. Here I had a desire to visit the kasbah, although I knew women were forbidden entry. Having convinced a couple of the ship's officers to escort me I thought I might get in but was barred at the entrance. I was an Infidel.

Throughout her voyage Olive received several telegrams and radio messages as well as letters. Frank's ship the *Mendi Palm* was in the Belgian Congo as Olive passed through the Suez Canal. She had told him of her appearance at the ship's ball and his following letter began 'My darling Tondalayo'. It was apparent he would arrive home some months after Olive so he made arrangements for her to be looked after by family until he arrived. She still found it hard to believe that she had only ever spent a few days with him. Sailing into Gibraltar through wildly protesting local fishermen, upset that the liner had come so close to their nets, the *Ormonde*'s passengers enjoyed a brief stay before setting sail for Tilbury in England. Here November snow fell so heavily passengers were not allowed on deck as the ship berthed. Olive's new young orphan friend clung to her tightly, pleading not to be given up to the authorities, but Olive had no alternative than to say goodbye to her. She never saw her again.

Olive took the train from Tilbury to London. Frank had arranged for his cousin Peggy to meet her at Victoria Station. With most of her luggage stowed in the ship's hold, consigned to go directly to her temporary abode at Peggy's flat in Holland Park, a porter stacked her remaining luggage on a trolley as a public address announcement summonsed her to the stationmaster's office. Peggy had rung to say she was held up in traffic so would be half an hour late and suggested Olive have a cup of tea at the station while she waited. This she did, while the ever-patient porter waited in the extreme cold to dispose of her luggage. When Peggy arrived the porter placed all her luggage in the cab and Olive tipped him ten shillings. Peggy was aghast.

'My goodness, how much did you give that man?' she asked.

'Ten shillings,' Olive replied.

'That's a ridiculous amount, he would have been happy with sixpence and that is exactly what you should have given him,' said Peggy.

'Well, I wouldn't have been happy standing in the freezing cold for half an hour for sixpence, and I doubt you would either,' said Olive earnestly. She wondered if Peggy's attitude towards the porter was typical of the English attitude towards the working class. In this case it was. Peggy had also been brought up in India, the daughter of the minister for excise, an eminent man who had been awarded the MBE. Olive was moving into the 'upper class'. Not that it would make the slightest difference to her.

When Olive and Peggy got home to Holland Park they found that a friend had come down from Scotland to stay with Peggy, so Olive was obliged to spend a couple of nights on Peggy's lounge-room floor, rolled up in a carpet and blanket in front of the fire. Peggy was apologetic but Olive assured her she did not mind as long as Peggy did not expect a ten shilling tip! She was not all that impressed to have travelled halfway across the world to get wrapped up in a carpet and sleep on the floor. The thought of her own bed held a certain appeal. Not surprisingly she decided to head, posthaste, for Frank's Welsh hunting lodge, Athol Brae, to meet her future mother-in-law, Elsie Wilson-Weston. When she told Peggy she would be moving to the lodge Peggy said, 'Oh my goodness, you can't go up there to live with Aunt Elsie without

Frank. She's really eccentric, quite strange. Been on her own too long. You won't like it, you won't stay. You won't even understand what the locals are talking about. The place is really eerie and you'll be very lonely.'

Olive knew a lot about Frank's parents and their life in India from those first conversations on the *Ormonde* and his wonderfully descriptive letters. His great-great-grandfather had gone to India with a prominent British merchant company in the eighteenth century and the Weston family had continued on, always marrying among the British, until India's independence was granted in 1948, at which time they came back to England. Four generations of the family had lived with the British and Indian upper class in very opulent circumstances with a large number of servants. In stark contrast to Olive, Frank attended boarding school in Lucknow, travelled in a private carriage and ate his mangoes in the bathtub. Frank's father, Thomas Gladwin, held a very senior government position, that of special manager of court of wards. This meant he was responsible for looking after the business affairs of a maharajah who had died before his son, the prince, was old enough to assume office.

Thomas died prematurely from pneumonia while recovering from a serious car accident in 1932, leaving Elsie to look after four children. June, the eldest, was fifteen, George fourteen, Frank thirteen and younger sister May was nine. Elsie went back to work for a short period, nursing in Bombay, until she married her second husband, Guy Athol Wilson-Weston. Sadly, Guy died only five years later and Elsie was badly affected by his death. She had his body incarcerated in a lead-lined coffin which she refused to bury for six months. It was not until June came to see her that she was convinced to bury him.

Frank was nineteen when he joined the British air force in India and was posted to Burma. When the Japanese invaded he walked out of Burma in a party of 132 with nothing but the clothes he had on, intending to walk into India over the old Burma Road. Unfortunately the party became disorientated, took a wrong turn and ended up in China. They were missing for nine months and were looked after by the Chinese army, who fed and clothed them. Frank, always keen on electronics, built a radio and after much difficulty was able to contact India. Following several long and exhaustive sessions on the makeshift radio they convinced the Indian authorities of their identity and were rescued by plane. Frank served with the RAF until the war ended and then gained employment as a ship's radio officer.

When Elsie returned to England her family was well spread out. Younger daughter May was working for a goldmining company in British Guyana. Olive had corresponded with her during the two years she had waited to marry Frank. May was to marry an engineer from the mine just a month before Olive's wedding. June, married to the manager of a large jute mill, was living on the east coast of India while brother George was living in England with his wife Maureen and four children. Just what possessed Elsie to buy a hunting lodge in the far west of Wales, and to live alone at the lodge, was something none of her children understood. Her relatives seldom visited because the place was so isolated. Olive, not knowing a soul in Wales, approached the lodge with some trepidation:

I had to wonder just what a woman who had lived in the company of maharajahs would make of an unsophisticated Queensland country girl. Frank had assured me I would get on 'famously' with her but Peggy had warned me that she was eccentric. I arrived to find the hunting lodge — in Clynderwen, South Wales — beautiful, as Frank had promised, but the weather so cold I thought I might actually freeze. On my first morning at the lodge I was woken by Elsie knocking on my door, yelling, 'Get up, Olive, get up and look at the snow, it's beautiful.' It could have been the King of England knocking, there was no way I was getting out of bed. I recalled the American GIs in Townsville asking how we lived through the heat and humidity of the wet season. I already felt the same way about the cold. Nevertheless I rose not too much later and saw the beautiful sight of magnificent, large oak trees, which covered the property, their branches heavily laden with snow.

Soon enough I was sitting in the dining room having a cup of tea with Elsie, in front of a large open fire. I guessed her age to be about 60. She was very petite, spoke very quietly and politely with a clipped English accent, and was as ladylike as one would expect from a woman who had lived most of her life among the aristocracy in India. Despite her mild eccentricity, Frank was right, she was charming and we hit it off straight away. Then the postman came by with a letter from Frank. Elsie went out to greet him and I heard him say in a thick Welsh accent, 'Oh, so she's here then, she's here, is she?' Elsie invited him in to meet me and this little chap came in so well rugged up against the cold all I could see of him were his eyes and nose. We each said good morning and had a brief chat. As he was leaving I heard him say to Elsie, 'She's white then!' I couldn't help laughing. He had obviously expected to see a native girl. Tondalayo, perhaps?

Athol Brae was a three-bedroom wooden cottage set well back off the road on a property of about two and a half acres. The roads leading to it were signposted in Welsh and the neighbouring farmers always spoke in their native tongue. Water was hand-pumped into a bucket from a well 50 metres from the house. There was no electricity. Oil lamps provided light and a large fire, burning wood and coal throughout the day, supplied heat. The lodge was heavily wooded with dozens of squirrels living in the huge oaks and rabbits and pheasants the most prolific of game. Towards the back of the property a river meandered through the woods carrying an abundance of salmon. In winter the icy, gale-force winds coming off the Atlantic Ocean caused the oaks to sway violently and creak loudly as they rubbed against each other. Branches grated against the roof of the cottage. Peggy was right: at such times it was an eerie place and one that had changed little over several generations. In the spring and summer months it was stunningly beautiful. The village shops, a little over a kilometre away, numbered about six and supplied essential foodstuffs such as bread, vegetables and the like. The shopkeepers spoke English to Olive with a very pronounced accent but Welsh among themselves.

Since her return from India Elsie had lived at the lodge alone when Frank was at sea, except for the company of a cat called Myfanwy and a good-natured Irish sheepdog with the wonderful name of John Jeeves. Though Elsie seemed happy in the solitude of Athol Brae, she attempted few menial tasks other than the necessary drawing of water from the well. Her cooking skills were very limited as she had been waited upon by servants for most of her life in India. She was delighted to find Olive extremely efficient in this area and happily conceded the task to her. Try as she did, Olive found it impossible to understand why Elsie had chosen to live alone in such primitive conditions.

Elsie was also surprised and delighted to find that Olive undertook as a matter of routine so many duties normally regarded as men's work. Coal was expensive and Olive had always been taught to live frugally. Rather than use the coal by the hearth she dragged dead logs from the woods not far from the house, took an axe from the toolshed and set about cutting suitable lengths for the open fire, which burned all day. If there were no logs available she cut down a tree, chopping a horizontal V in the trunk as she had seen her father do since she was a child. She couldn't bear to see coal being used when fuel was available at no cost a short walk away.

One day Myfanwy brought a fieldmouse home and was playing with it by the front steps. The poor mouse was all but dead and when Elsie saw it she was aghast. 'Oh, Ollie, do something for the poor thing,' she cried. Olive simply picked up the mouse by the tail, dashed its head once against a tree and gave it back, lifeless, to the cat. Elsie was shocked at Olive's composure under pressure.

Olive knew of John Jeeves from Frank's letters and came to treat him as though he was her own. Elsie had brought the lovely old dog back from India. He was such a special part of the family she had paid £60 to have him travel on the same boat, then had to wait six months while he was in quarantine before he could be taken to the lodge. John Jeeves took a shine to Olive and Olive to him:

He was a lovely old dog, slowly losing his sight but his other senses were very sharp. I had an old green nylon wet-weather coat that hung behind the door and he got to recognise the sound of that coat. As soon as I took it off the hook he realised I was going out and he'd be ready to go too. John Jeeves became my constant companion. We wandered all around the lodge and down to the village together to go shopping. When the occasional car approached I'd call him off the road and he would stand beside me, his body against my legs, till the vehicle passed. I was his eyes and he was my protector.

Immediately on her arrival, Frank cabled Olive to tell her to have the wedding banns read so that they could marry as soon as he got home. They were duly announced in the village parish and the wedding was set for Saturday, 22 January 1953. The banns were current for three months, after which they would need to be posted again. As Frank's ship was not due back in London from the West Coast of Africa until late that week, it was obviously going to be touch and go. If Frank's boat were to be delayed then the banns would lapse.

It was fortunate that Olive and Elsie got on so well. It would have been a long, slow three months if they had not appreciated each other's company. When Elsie planned a trip to Cardiff to see Aunt Beattie and Uncle Cliff, she expressed disappointment that they could not take her a table bird from the lodge.

'Why can't we?' asked Olive.

'Well, there are no men here to either kill a fowl or prepare it,' she replied.

'But we've got an axe,' said Olive.

'Of course we have,' said Elsie.

'Then let's get on with it,' said Olive.

'Surely you're not serious,' said Elsie. 'You're not going to kill a hen?'

'Just watch me. Point out the one you'll miss least,' said Olive.

All the hens and the large rooster had pet names. Matty, the oldest hen in the yard, was the designated offering to be taken to Aunt Beattie. Elsie watched in awe as Olive took the axe from the shed, honed the blade on the grindstone wheel and put it by the woodheap. She then let herself into the chook run and began stalking Matty. This manoeuvre proved to be of considerable concern to Charlie, the rooster. As Olive stalked Matty, the big rooster chased her, rising up on his feet, wings outstretched, crowing loudly. Elsie suggested more than once to forget the idea but Olive was determined. She caught the hen despite Charlie's endeavours to stop her. When the hen's long neck eventually rested on the block it took just one swift arc of the axe to bring success. Olive held the headless chook at arm's length, letting its blood drip down as it gave its last few twitches, and the job was done:

I thought Elsie might pass out but she rallied. That chook must have been ten years old. I pumped some water from the well which I boiled in a big pot and that old bird certainly took some plucking. We took it down to Cardiff and Aunt Beattie had to boil it for such a long time to make it edible. Anyway, we'd got the job done. I thought, fancy asking a country girl if she could knock the head off a chook!

There were diversions during Olive's stay. Not all of her days were spent at the lodge. She was interested in history and historical places so found a lot to enjoy. While waiting for Frank to return, and later when Frank was at sea, she took herself off to famous places. Travelling alone never worried her so she got the train to Newcastle upon Tyne, on the Scottish border, and went looking for Hadrian's Wall. She didn't find it but finished up lost 'in the middle of nowhere with a lot of funny looking sheep with black faces'. She stayed a week in a B & B in Yorkshire to look at the places of interest, like the cave of the notorious old witch Mother Shipton, and walked on the famous step at Durham Cathedral where Bishop Bede had stood in the eighth century.

Olive accepted an invitation to attend Beverley Borger's marriage in Worthing, just out of Brighton. As one would expect of a wedding of the heir to a large fortune, it was a very glitzy affair:

I'd met a young chap on the ship whose parents had a unit in the city, at Grosvenor Place, right near Buckingham Palace, and I was able to stay with them. I went to afternoon tea at the Charing Cross Hotel where the groom's aunt had a whole floor of the hotel as her suite.

There were butlers and chauffeurs everywhere, not exactly what I was used to, but I was thrilled to be able to attend. I hadn't even met Beverley before the boat trip but was picked up in a chauffeur-driven Rolls Royce and taken to the ceremony in Worthing. The butler opened the door of the Rolls and there were several maids in attendance. It was a fairyland, really, and her fiancé Bob Bachelor seemed very nice. I felt very happy for her.

Olive stayed at the Bachelors' apartment in Knightsbridge when she came down to shop for her wedding outfit. She selected her ring at Ciros, one of London's very best jewellers, leaving it for Frank to pick up on his arrival in London, and she also did some shopping for Elsie. Then she set about choosing her bridal dress. She had no set idea about what to buy; she simply wanted something 'special':

I came across a beautiful, eggshell blue, Chinese silk brocade with a gold pattern running through the material. As soon as I saw it I thought, That's it. It wasn't a wedding frock but it was so unusual I knew it was right for me. Being a colonial in London, and having done my shopping, I took the chance to see Buckingham Palace and was wandering up the middle of the mall towards the palace when suddenly I heard the clip-clop of hoof beats behind me. I turned around to see the household cavalry in full ceremonial gear bearing down on me. I was so embarrassed I quickly shot off the road and onto the footpath.

After I was married and Frank was at sea again I came back to see Elizabeth's coronation. All Australian visitors to England had been invited to see the coronation of Queen Elizabeth. Beverley and I had received our invitations soon after we arrived. There were platforms all along the mall, one of which was for us Australians, so we had a clear view of the royal coach on its way to Westminster Abbey. This was a big thrill. Later on we went to the garden party at the palace to see

Queen Elizabeth and Prince Philip. We were excited about this too but it was a waste of time really. We just got the briefest glimpse of the royal couple because there were thousands there. Still, it gave me a close-up look at how wrapped up in royalty the British were, and also how important it was for some of them to be seen in the right places.

Frank's letters remained as prolific and passionate as their wedding drew closer, so Olive got to know the postman quite well. She received no fewer than five letters between 6 December and 17 January, each posted from different ports as the *Mendi Palm* approached London. Frank took every opportunity to contact her. An ocean-poste message arrived via telegraph from another vessel, the SS *La Quinta*, travelling to England ahead of the *Mendi Palm*: 'Hope it was a merry Xmas Olive honey and may the New Year be the first of many happy ones for you so help me. No word since the 8th, maybe adrift. Arrive Newcastle about the 13th. Yearning to be with you my darling. Love to you and Ma — Frank'. His final letter was from Newcastle:

9 pm. Hello 'Angel Face'. I expect this time next week we'll be a brand new 'husband and wife'. Gosh, I cannot, even now, realise that soon I shall be your husband Darling and that you'll be all mine. I seem to be sitting on a cloud all day despite the cold up here. I think, by your letters, you're a wee bit scared and nervous. I won't eat you, just caress your sweet soft loveliness with my lips dearest Darling. Glad to hear that you've been confirmed my Darling. God bless you and look after you always Sweet Olive. I have been 'confirmed' often you know. Once it was said I was a confirmed bachelor (Ma said that) and at others a confirmed drunkard etc. but now I'm a confirmed devotee of the 'darling of darling girls'. Olive by

name but a rose by any other. She is sweet and full of honey, a little bit of which I hope to force from her soft lips soon.

How is Ma, my love to her. Thank you Darling for doing that shopping for her. Remind me to take you through the woods Darling. Yes they're beautiful in the summer. We used to go swimming in the river where it bends below the woods. I'm sure you'd like that wouldn't you darling. You're a great one for the water, especially cold water if I remember rightly. Well Olive darling it's time for me to roll into my bunk and keep my nightly date with you. Do you know I've been waiting for you for two years. Now that I am on the same soil every minute seems an eternity.

Olive was well aware the circumstances were somewhat unusual. There had been no passionate affair; in fact there had been no time for such. Nothing had been further from her mind than marriage when she met Frank. As she was still in her mid twenties she had never had fears of being a spinster. Yet she went ahead, proceeding with complete confidence that she was doing the right thing:

Frank arrived on the Saturday we were due to be married. I guess some brides might have been worried about that but there was nothing either of us could do to expedite matters. I met him at the railway station and we decided to go straight to the minister's home and ask could we be married on the following day. It was most unusual to have a Sunday wedding so the minister rang the bishop and obtained special permission. As it was to be a very small wedding, with just a handful of relatives and close friends, we weren't concerned about putting it back a day.

I stayed the night before the wedding at the home of Mrs Williams, a good friend of the family, so that Frank could stay with his mother, and dressed for the wedding on Sunday morning. It was a lovely little stone church, hundreds of years old, and as it was to be a small ceremony the setting was perfect. I went down to the church in a taxi with Aunt Beattie's daughter Ann, who was my lady-in-waiting. The driver insisted on taking us all around the village, in and out of laneways, because it was important that I should be late. It was snowing and the place did look beautiful with the branches of the trees laden with snow. I was keen to get there as soon as I could because as usual I was freezing. Meanwhile Frank, dressed in his officer's uniform, and Uncle Cliff, his best man, waited in the comfort of the church.

When the driver decided that we were late enough he drove me to the door of the church and I walked into the portal. When I saw the place was absolutely packed I damn near walked out again. The whole village had turned up to see who was so important they had to be married on a Sunday. It was the first wedding in the church for a year. Anyway, there I was, a girl from Townsville, marrying a pukka Pom in a tiny Welsh village.

Having bowed to the traditional Welsh custom of running through a rope made of men's handkerchiefs tied together, and throwing loose change to the crowd, we drove back to the lodge for a reception which included some typical Welsh singing in front of the open fire. Intentions were that Frank and I would stay at the lodge while Elsie went to stay with Aunt Beattie in Cardiff. By evening's end Elsie had decided she would prefer to stay at the lodge also. This arrangement lasted just three days before Frank suggested we should stay with Aunt Beattie and Elsie should remain at the lodge. On Wednesday we boarded the train for Cardiff to continue our honeymoon. I was 26 and Frank was 33.

Chapter Six

STEVEN

Olive and Frank enjoyed their honeymoon in Cardiff, a city he knew very well, spending most of their evenings going to the cinema and to dinner. The weather was brisk by day and very cold by night. They took daytrips to the nearby fertile valleys that were stunningly beautiful. The Wye Valley, through which the Wye River meandered sluggishly, was full of historical interest. Each bend in the stream seemed to reveal a new secret with ruins of ancient Roman encampments, castles and abbeys that were many centuries old. They visited the most famous of all the abbeys, at Tintern, built in the thirteenth century, which remained, despite its missing roof, a classic example of grand, ornate architecture. This they followed with sandwiches, at the teahouse nearby. It was almost compulsory for holiday-makers and honeymooners.

Olive was somewhat bemused when special trains brought thousands of spectators into Cardiff from the Ronda and Cynnon Valleys as well as from England to witness a first division soccer match at Ninian Park. She was amazed to see visitors walking up the middle of the main roads, showing no regard for motor vehicles, and into the many pubs adjacent to the football ground. The street was a sea of blue scarves as more than 32 000 came to watch the Cardiff 'Bluebirds' do battle with the strong English club Preston North End. Unlike Cliff and Frank, who were fanatics, Olive had no interest whatever in football so was happy to let them go off to the game, during which they stood, chanting and singing continuously, and from which they returned home late, well lubricated and in good humour despite Cardiff's one–nil defeat. Cliff assured her things could have been worse — had Cardiff won they might not have got home until next morning. In any event they drank Scotch till the early hours while they replayed the game and several of the songs. Olive retired to bed some time before Frank, though not before he had reminded her several times that she had married a man who was a personal friend of Stanley Matthews, England's most famous player.

Just seventeen days into their honeymoon Frank received a cable from Marconi Radio telling him to report immediately to London as they wanted to send him to Singapore for two years. He was absolutely furious. After pleading unsuccessfully for most of the previous two years for a trip to the southern hemisphere, he was now expected to pack up and leave his new bride in England. He refused the request, telling his employer he was interested only in trips closer to Britain. Unless Marconi could oblige he would be forced to seek alternative employment. This time his pleas were heard and he was subsequently posted on the SS *Uskmouth* travelling from Newport to Italy and North Africa.

When Frank went back to sea Olive became bored with doing nothing at the lodge so she took a job as a bookkeeper at a victual company which supplied food and drink to the many large vessels that docked in Cardiff Harbour. She went to stay with Aunt Beattie and Uncle Cliff. At her office in the docks she employed a young secretary from Cardiff's Tiger Bay, an attractive, dark-skinned teenager with a lovely personality and energy to burn. Olive took a liking to the girl, whose brother was a promising young boxer. After a short while the youngster left to take a job at the theatre box office. She had her heart set on a musical career. The show business world obviously suited her. In time she became Wales' most famous popular female singer. Her name was Shirley Bassey. Olive resigned from the victual company after six months when a bout of German measles laid her low.

After a few months at sea Frank now found long periods away from Olive too much to take. She sometimes travelled to meet him when he returned to port but he was increasingly frustrated with his work. He resigned from the Marconi Company late in 1953 to take a job with the ministry of civil aviation and was posted to Hurn Airport, near the seaside city of Bournemouth, 150 kilometres southwest of London. Bournemouth was a popular year-round holiday resort, made most attractive by a beach and two piers. Olive was assured its milder climate would be a welcome change from the extremes of Cardiff. Olive and Frank rented a place in a lovely spot called Ferndown. For the first time in his life Frank worked regular hours. They were both extremely happy to be able to spend so much time together. Olive invited Elsie down to stay.

From the time Olive had arrived in England she had been keen to meet up with her maternal great-grandmother whom she knew would be well over 100 years old. The old lady lived in Paignton, part of the popular seaside district of Torquay in Devon, a further 100 kilometres down the coast. Olive had her address so when a neighbour offered to take her for a drive to Torquay she readily accepted and invited Elsie along. She was excited at the thought of meeting her grandfather Alfred's mother:

We hopped in the neighbour's car and headed south through some really lovely country and found the address I had for her. As I approached the house the postman was at the gateway and I asked him if this was her place.

'Oh yes,' he said, 'this is where she lived but sadly the poor darling's been dead for a couple of years. But her daughter lives just around the corner, let me show you her place.'

So I went around to the house with Elsie in tow and knocked on the door. In due course a lady appeared and I said, 'You don't know me, I'm a total stranger to you, but I'm your brother's youngest grand-daughter.' She looked at me a bit uncertainly and I said, 'Your brother Alfred.'

Well, she let out a yell and threw her arms around me and hugged me tightly. She just couldn't get over it. The last time she had seen him was when he ran away from England as a sixteen-year-old. 'Come on in, come on in,' she kept repeating.

So Elsie and I had afternoon tea with her and a very long chat. I told her how I'd planned to work in New Guinea and how much Alfred had meant to me as a child. Then she rang her sister Alda in Nottingham, saying, 'You'll never know who I've got here. It's Alfred's grand-daughter from Australia! I'll put her on so you can say hello.' No sooner had I finished talking to Alda than she rang her other sister Ettie. I then realised Grandfather had named two of his daughters in Australia after his sisters in the old Dart. She repeated the news just as excitedly for a second time and I had a long chat to Ettie as well.

She was a lovely woman and I was so glad I'd come to visit, even though it was a shame I couldn't have arrived before Great Grandma had passed away.

Though Elsie had seemed quite happy to be living in the solitude of Athol Brae she now decided she had no desire to return. Olive understood completely. A 60-year-old woman living alone in bitterly cold temperatures, with no electricity and braving the weather to pump water by hand from the well, made no sense to her. Olive and Frank offered her the chance to live with them and she jumped at it, selling the lodge and returning to Bournemouth. Except for her dislike of the cold weather, Olive had not been happier since her carefree tomboy days in Cairns. But snowy conditions took their toll. She suffered terribly from chilblains that affected her fingers, toes and ears and was forever applying nicotine cream to treat the blisters and frozen tissue below the skin. In the warmer months she loved Bournemouth but the English winter was too much for a girl from the tropics:

I was really disappointed that Britain was so cold and that it affected me so much. Bournemouth was not far from Robin Hood's Sherwood Forest and the New Forest was a beautiful place. In spring, when the rhododendrons were out, it was magnificent. There were lots of lovely ponies at New Forest and we went there often. One year the winter was so severe several had frozen to death. We also went to Poole, another lovely place on the coast, where they made the famous Poole Pottery. There were castles down the south just as there were in Wales. It's funny but I found I got depressed and homesick when the autumn came because nearly all the leaves died and all the deciduous trees made things too bleak for me. It was all too grey. I missed the Australian greenery almost as much as the sun.

You really had to experience an English winter to know how bleak and cold it was. Frank rode a bicycle, with a two-stroke engine attached, to and from Hurn Airport. When he returned in the evening his hands were frozen stiff from the handlebars even though he wore two sets of gloves. I used to help him off the bike, his body was so stiff, and walk him inside where I had a raging fire ready for him, burning pine cones I'd collected from a large tree which grew at the back of the house. I just couldn't believe I was living in one of England's milder climates. I did my best not to complain but no one in the whole of Britain looked forward to summer more than I did.

Olive corresponded regularly with Frank's younger sister, May, now living in West Africa. When May announced she was pregnant there was great excitement. Just four months later, in the spring of 1954, Olive also fell pregnant. The mothers-to-be compared notes and found, to each other's surprise, the two favoured girls' names were Susan and Stephanie. When May had a baby girl she opted for Susan so Olive resolved to call her child Stephanie if she had a girl.

Frank could only be described as being beside himself about Olive's pregnancy. He fussed over her to the point where she had to explain she was not an invalid. As the birth came closer he was so nervous she found it hard not to laugh at him. Olive was booked into a private maternity hospital at Barton-on-Sea, 25 kilometres away, and the ambulance driver who was to take her to the hospital lived four doors down the road. Each day he came to see how she was progressing. In her eighth month she went into labour and was rushed off to hospital. It was snowing heavily and the ambulance drove as quickly as possible with chains on the wheels. Frank was so nervous he was ill in the back of the ambulance.

When Olive arrived at Barton-on-Sea doctors were reluctant to take the baby, feeling it was too small. She did not give birth and returned home after two days. When labour came again a month later the whole snow-covered course had to be negotiated once more. Olive gave birth, without complications, to a boy weighing three kilograms. Stephanie became Steven. When Frank saw his son for the first time he wanted to see Olive immediately but was told she was resting. Unable to contain himself he threw pebbles at the window of Olive's room on the second floor, calling out, 'I've seen him, I've seen him! He's beautiful.'

He was a bundle of joy. Frank was a bit put out now and again because Steven took up so much of my time. Sometimes Frank worked shiftwork and the 2 am feeds were a bit inconvenient but for first-time parents we did very well. Like all in our situation, we got a thrill out of the first smile and couldn't wait for him to say his first word. He was very strong in the neck and sat in the crook of my arm really well. He had a good set of lungs and had no trouble letting me know when he was hungry. Because he'd been born with two bottom teeth I found breastfeeding too painful so put him on the bottle within ten days.

Olive now took a very practical view of religion. She was Catholic and Frank was Anglican and they had resolved, before marriage, never to argue about their differences. Although Olive's upbringing had been very strict, her ideas had been changed by the war. She saw great hypocrisy in people who espoused the virtue of their faith systematically killing others. Many were of the very same faith as their victims. Her belief in God was not threatened but her belief in mankind and religion had been. She no longer went to mass but resolved, very simply, to live her life by the Ten Commandments, knowing that by so doing she could never cause harm to anybody. She also remembered John Wesley's poem, taught to her when she was eight years old. When it came time to baptise Steven she happily went along to the nearest place of worship, which was a congregational church in Ferndown.

The Wilson-Westons were very keen on names. Charles had been a family name for generations and Gladwin traced back to the Norman invasion. And so the little fellow's full name became Steven Michael Charles Gladwin Wilson-Weston. Steven (spelt the way of the Normans) was almost twelve months old as winter approached. Frank decided it was too much to expect Olive to put up with another three months of suffering. He was happy to leave his job and take her back to Australia where he would seek work. Olive was ecstatic at the thought. But what of Elsie? Would she like to join them? Yes she would.

Frank booked passage for three adults and their thirteen-month-old son on the liner *Mooltan*, which belonged to the Aberdeen Shipping Company. The trip back to Australia, in contrast to the wonderful voyage on the *Ormonde*, which had brought Olive to England, was a nightmare:

We paid a small fortune to return. Steven was charged a quarter fare even though I'd brought all his food and he slept in our cabin. All the shipping line had to do was supply a cot. The boat was full of 'ten pound immigrants' coming to live in Australia and they were treated as cheaply as possible. Despite having paid our full fare we had to put up with the same. The ship was originally scheduled to leave from Southampton but then we got a late message saying its departure point had been transferred to London. We travelled by train through the snow to London, to find our luggage, which had been stored in a holding bay, had been misplaced.

We got into our cabin to find they'd forgotten to arrange a cot for Steven. The company couldn't find our luggage so Frank told them that if it wasn't there by the time we left they would have to pay for it to be sent to Australia. Obviously he knew, after all these years with shipping companies, about their responsibilities to their passengers. At the very last minute they found the luggage in a warehouse and as we were going through the locks out of King George Docks in London, they lowered it off a sling onto the ship, as we were actually moving. The crew then had to store it in a bar at the stern of the vessel. There were 29 trunks and cases.

Having paid about 260 pounds sterling for the three of us we thought things might pick up a bit, especially after the luggage fiasco, but we were treated no better as the cruise went on. It was shocking. The food was terrible, with one meal of rissoles actually containing maggots. Two months of torture, we called it. Travelling with a young baby would have been difficult at the best of times. As we were leaving Ceylon for Fremantle, Steven developed a carbuncle on his forehead and the ship's doctor placed him on sedation. One evening he failed to show up to treat Steven, who was screaming with pain. All the mothers were concerned for him. I took off to look for the doctor and found him at eight-thirty at a party. I gave him the 'rounds of the kitchen' and he was most apologetic that he'd forgotten but it didn't help Steven.

At Fremantle I took Steven to hospital where they lanced the carbuncle and when we got back to the ship there were police everywhere. The master-at-arms was a pig of a man and apparently some of the passengers decided they'd had enough so took to him and gave him quite a beating. There was blood all over the lounge. One of the shipping line managers arrived to take over his job before we sailed to Melbourne. The next thing the press turned up, not because of the fight but because a passenger had contacted them about the maggots which had been found in the rissoles. The ship's owners were trying desperately to keep the publicity down. Even when we got to Melbourne we were caught up in a strike at the dockyards so we were ten days waiting to sail for Sydney — not that we blamed the ship's management for that, but it just added to the 'trip from hell'.

Greatly relieved that the voyage was over, the family stayed with Olive's parents in Dulwich Hill, in Sydney's inner west, while Frank looked for work. The three-bedroom cottage was rather crowded but their financial situation was such that there was little choice, at least in the immediate future. Steven was approaching that time when he should have started to say a few easy words. Despite encouragement from Olive and Elsie, who was naturally keen to hear him say 'Nanna', he showed no signs of doing so. The best he could manage were some guttural grunts. Though Olive was aware children varied greatly in the time it took to begin talking, a mother's intuition told her something might be wrong:

I suspected his hearing might have been poor so I took him to the Commonwealth Acoustics Laboratory where it was found there was a most unusual impediment in his hearing, varying with frequencies. He could hear some frequencies quite well at a normal level but not others. In fact if I lowered my voice he could understand me better. We were advised to take him to a Macquarie Street specialist. The specialist examined him and recommended further tests by a neurologist. We waited for results of encephalograms, hoping for the best, but, to our dismay, they showed that he was slightly brain-damaged. They could give no answer as to how the brain damage had occurred and told us it was so slight it was barely detectable on the encephalogram. Perhaps it was the result of my false alarm at eight months, but no one could tell. I always suspected this to be the case and believed if I had borne him then he might have been all right. The most likely scenario was that he lacked oxygen at birth but there was no definitive answer. I'd had German measles, which can be associated with birth defects, but that was in Cardiff, many months before my pregnancy. Frank and I were shattered, but at least Steven was only slightly handicapped and was strong physically. There was a definite tendency at the time to put handicapped offspring in a home and forget them. We were having none of that.

Then I underwent tests as well and was told I would be unable to have more children. The specialist told us if we wanted more kids we would have to adopt them and we were both keen on the idea. In those days adoptions could be arranged through the lawyers of both parties so we were thrilled to bits when the specialist told us of twins who were available. There was a boy and a girl who had been born to unmarried university students. After several weeks of negotiations everything looked set, when the parents' lawyer asked us if we owned our own home. We had to say no, as we'd only just come back from Europe, but were saving to buy one. We were told that wasn't good enough and so the adoption fell through. This was the first time such a stipulation had been mentioned so we believed we had been cheated somewhere along the line. After all, I was a qualified nurse and had experience at bookkeeping and Frank was an expert in his electronics field. Financially we would have had no problems. We had already been planning the twins' schooling and talking about them going to university. It was so absolutely heartbreaking, we never got around to seriously considering adoption again.

Disappointment with the failed adoption attempt was offset to some degree by news of employment for Frank. He obtained a position with the commonwealth government, working for the Ionospheric Prediction Service, a division of the post master general's department, which dealt with transmission of high frequency radio communications through the ionosphere to distant planes and overseas bases. Olive was never exactly sure what the service achieved, other than that it suited Frank's knowledge of electronics, but his employment was suddenly to produce a wonderful surprise. Out of the blue they were posted to Townsville.

Frank purchased a light green, second-hand Morris Oxford sedan and the foursome drove slowly up the coast, staying overnight at caravan parks, stopping for lunchtime snacks at seaside towns along the way. Olive sat in the front passenger seat with Elsie alongside Steven in the back. The long but very pleasant trip of almost 2500 kilometres took a week, with all expenses met by the government. On the way, Olive considered the fact that, of the three adults, only Frank could drive. In an emergency she would be of no help. Since her early teens she had always shown the ability to deal with a crisis. Now that the family had a car she felt a responsibility to be able to drive it. She would discuss this with Frank later on.

It was well over a decade since Olive had seen her birthplace and the centres that had shaped her life during the war. She immediately went exploring. The homes in Chapman Street, where the 12th Station Hospital had been established, were much as they had been before the American troops had arrived. Armstrong Paddock was no longer a dustbowl. A school and housing estate made the place unrecognisable from the khaki tent city of the early and mid forties. MacArthur's bunker now housed commercial interests though the underground section was closed off as it filled with water in the wet season. Only the Strand seemed unchanged, being devoid of its barbed wire entanglements and not yet asphalted or guttered. Many families had come back after the war and the population had continued to increase slowly. To Olive, it would always be home.

While Frank sent signals into the ionosphere Olive set about ensuring that Steven would achieve whatever his mental capacity would allow. She began the onerous task of teaching him everything she could, encouraging him, hour after hour, to put words together. Her patience was endless. She found the only thing to which Steven reacted was repetition:

It was very wearing but Elsie and I would tell him things literally hundreds of times before he understood. Constant repetition was the only way. When it came to encouraging him to speak, I bribed him with a bag of jellybeans. I'd put him in his cot at night, take a jellybean from the jar and say 'ta', over and over again. He'd hold his little hand out for the lolly but I refused to give it to him until I heard that word. I felt terrible when I'd put the jellybean back in the jar. On the night he eventually said it I offered him every jellybean in the jar. He was smiling and I was crying. That was our first breakthrough.

Try as he did Frank was unable to get along with his boss. He knew Olive loved the township and had many friends there but, reluctantly, after six months he resigned. His regional director summoned him to the office. Knowing Frank was a most efficient worker, and not wanting to lose him, the director plied him with questions: 'You are the fifth person who has come up to Townsville and resigned. Please tell me the reason. You are obviously well suited to the job. Why are you going? Is it the place, the heat, the staff? What is it?' Frank refused to tell. He was English, trained in the air force, and not inclined to complain about his superior officer.

The family returned to Sydney and the family home at the top of Seaview Street, Dulwich Hill, from where there was an impressive view of Botany Bay. Occasionally one of two large sailing ships, still plying their trade between England and Australia, would appear in the bay and Steven would be held up to the window to see it. Olive's father was now a union representative on the Sydney waterfront. Frank felt a mixture of disappointment and anger at how the job in Townsville had turned out. Three months later he was having a beer in the Marrickville Hotel when, to his chagrin, he met his protagonist from Townsville. 'What are you doing here?' Frank asked.

'I've quit,' he said. 'They were going to transfer me to Antarctica!' Obviously the director had found the problem. How Frank wished they had planned to send him a bit earlier.

Soon after Frank found radio communications work with the Water Board, a job that took him to country locations as well as the city. This position sufficed for a few months until he applied and got a position as a senior radio technician with the department of civil aviation, designing, installing and maintaining navigational aid equipment for Mascot's Kingsford Smith Airport. It was a job that suited him perfectly, working initially at a large workshop located in a former Catholic school on the flight path at Mascot and later in a workshop in Marrickville. He was destined to remain with the department for the duration of his working life.

Having been in Australia for three years by this time, 1959, Elsie decided she would return to England to live her remaining years. She booked on the *Himalaya* and the foursome drove to the terminal in the Morris Oxford just as they had done all the way to Townsville and back. Steven walked around the deck, hand in hand with Elsie. It was an emotional farewell as Olive and Frank fully realised they would probably not see her again. When Olive put Steven on her knee in the front seat for the trip home, he looked into the back of the car, realised that his grandmother was gone, and cried uncontrollably.

With Alda and Betty still on hand to help look after Steven, Olive now decided she too should look for a job. She answered an advertisement in the local paper for a company secretary and bookkeeper with a motor vehicle repair firm called Lustreglo. It was the day after her 33rd birthday. Joe Palisi, co-owner of the firm, vividly remembers the circumstances of her attaining the job:

I had a small panel beating shop in Marrickville that was growing quite fast and my partner and I decided we needed a secretary. There would not have been too many women employed in the panel beating business then, even in the office, so we were keen to get a mature woman who could fit in with an all-male staff, not some young thing the boys would be too interested in. It was raining very heavily and Olive arrived for her interview dressed in bright red plastic rain gear from head to toe. Hat, coat and boots. I thought she looked like a pixie. Anyway, she made quite a dramatic entry for a smash repair place.

When she spoke she had a very distinguished accent and my first thought was she might be a bit highbrow for the job. We had plenty of rough looking blokes there but she had a look around and said she'd like to try it. She hadn't had a lot of secretarial experience and she started to tell us some of the things she had done. I found it hard to believe anyone her age could have had so many different experiences. Working for General MacArthur, being a lieutenant with the Yanks, the hunting lodge in Wales, going to the coronation, meeting all those famous people, going to society weddings, it all seemed a bit much. I have to admit I was a bit sceptical. Anyway, we agreed to put her on, not realising how influential she would become.

As it turned out, everything she said had been true. We had a tiny little office and she made it clear she wanted to be 'one of the boys'. She didn't mind sharing the one toilet with them, which was just as well because we only had one. We soon realised we'd made a good investment; nothing was too hard or too outlandish for Olive. She was very efficient and she fitted in well. She got on very well with our clients and the bank manager, which didn't do us any harm either. I thought he might have been a bit keen on her. He often had a drink with us. We were just around the corner from the hotel and on Friday afternoon we'd pack up and start carrying the schooners back for a drink. It turned out she really liked that part of the work too. She might have been the best drinker of the lot of us. In time she brought Frank down to the Friday night drinks and he fitted in very well with the boys too, even though he didn't drink as well as Olive. We were impressed that he was a very clever man, a wizard with electronics, but a bit of a giggler with a really funny sense of humour. No matter what you said or did he'd find something to laugh about, especially after a few beers.

I recall Olive had been working with us for some time and she handled everything well but one day she burst into tears and I asked her what the matter was. As it happened I'd put a young bloke on who was a bit backward. Everyone in the shop had a nickname so the boys christened him 'Nailhead'. They were having a go at him, not maliciously, just in a way that they did among themselves, but Olive flooded with tears. Then she said to me, 'I've got a son like him.' I could have fallen through the floor. She'd never mentioned him, we hadn't seen him and so we had no idea. It certainly pulled me up with a jolt. I felt really lousy that I'd let my staff sling off at a handicapped young fellow. We had a talk to the boys and things eased down a lot and we all made sure he got a fair go.

Later on we met Steven. I had to admire Olive, she just lived to make sure her boy got a chance and to make certain that one day he would be able to look after himself. The effort and love she put into Steven was really inspirational. What she achieved with him was amazing. She kept all the accounts so well we never had to worry about the money. She was as honest as the day was long; the money was spot on to the penny. And all the time she was one of the boys. She could knock those beers back, and the Scotch as well.

Olive loved being back in the workforce. Running the office was very satisfying, her concerns quite different to those that had occupied her mind at home. Joe found that once Olive said she would do something, then she did it. Her determination bordered on stubbornness. Over several years at the office her smoking increased to 60 cigarettes a day until one morning she arrived and told him she had decided to quit. He didn't see how she could do it. Frank drove her down to a doctor in Enmore who used hypnotherapy to cure the habit. He had a good reputation and was supposed to have cured other doctors. She went to him just once and that was it. She never touched another cigarette:

It was the best fifteen dollars I'd ever spent. Though I never mastered the drawback and half the cigarettes I lit burnt away on the ashtray as I answered the phone or did the books, I was buying three packets a day and sitting there in a smoke-filled office.

Joe had also shown some desire to quit but when Olive wanted to take him to the doctor he was not committed enough and refused. She did, however, talk him into doing a speed-reading course. The office received a lot of correspondence so it seemed like a good idea. It was supposed to enable them to read ten times faster but it did not have the desired effect. This was a rare failure for Olive.

STEVEN

One of the clients bet her she couldn't drink a bottle of Scotch at a New Year's Eve party but she did it, and walked out of there as steadily as you like. Despite her experiences she had not changed that much from the tomboy who took the dare to run up the sleeping crocodile's back in Cardwell all those years ago.

The only real difference Olive ever had with Joe was over politics, a fact he still remembers well:

> She was a dyed-in-the-wool socialist and I was from the opposite side of the fence. My father had come out from Italy in 1924 and had influenced me just like her father had influenced her. Olive believed in the worker looking after the worker. Dad believed that if the government managed things well, the worker was looked after anyway. We had many a schooner arguing that. I thought I might have turned her around once when we both disagreed strongly with Gough Whitlam's decision to grant so much money to the arts and to buy the painting *Blue Poles*. I asked her how that was going to help the poor. My joy was short-lived, however, as Olive explained that a girl whose father and grandfather were life members of the Labor Party could hardly give up on her leader because of one mistake. She voted for him again. I think she thought his first name was God, not Gough. Still, she was as loyal to the firm as she was to her political beliefs.

When Steven was five Olive attempted to enrol him in the Dulwich Hill Infants School in Seaview Street. After a short while she was told there was no point bringing him back as he could not comprehend what was going on and would hold the class back. From an educational point of view he was officially categorised as 'sub-normal' and therefore not accepted in mainstream schools.

173

There were other children in this same situation so Olive met with their parents and decided they should do something about it. Though sympathetic to the teachers' problems they saw a need to provide some avenue of education for their children. Olive and her fellow parents knew the kids had certain learning ability, albeit less than children with no handicaps, so they were not content to see the youngsters simply hidden away from public view. Parents in a similar position were contacted by word of mouth and a committee formed to act on their behalf:

We began by approaching the education department for some sort of assistance. They simply humoured us. They 'understood' our problems but could not help. We tried them several times but to no avail. Their apathy often riled me so I got uptight a few times and let them have it but it was a waste of time. It was too hard for them. We approached politicians at local, state and federal level but drew a series of blanks. Even Fred Daley, our wonderful federal member at Dulwich Hill for so many years, couldn't help us. My father knew Fred well and we used to work for him during election campaigns, so we figured if Fred couldn't help no one could. If the education department wouldn't give us a school we'd have to start our own. It was up to us. Once we'd made our decision it was 'all systems go!' Though we got no help, at least we got no interference. I think no one wanted to cross us.

We rented a large house at Campsie and found volunteer lay teachers who taught the children in what we believe was the only such school in Sydney at that time. We didn't make a fuss about it and there were only a handful of kids to start with, but word soon spread and more parents sought permission to enrol their kids. Once things settled down our committee decided to buy a bus so that the children could be taken to and from school together. Proceeds to buy the bus would come from fetes and raffles. The major fundraiser was a number of chocolate wheels run by the fathers in various shopping centres around the area on Saturday mornings. Shopkeepers willingly donated prizes: a chicken from the delicatessen, beer glasses from the gift shop, a meat tray from the butcher, and those sorts of things. Cooperation from the stores never ceased. We worked like navvies but it was very rewarding.

It was a very special day when, many months later, the goal was reached and a brand new, twelve-seater minibus proudly carried the school's insignia, Sydenham Bankstown School for Subnormal Children. A professional driver, whose wages were paid through further fundraising, was assisted by 'bus mothers', rostered to look after their valuable passengers:

From just three or four kids when we started the numbers grew to about 40, in three or four years. The school was not just a blessing for the children but also for mothers who had so much more time to spend on things other parents took for granted. There was a wonderful feeling of camaraderie among us and the relatives and friends who helped. We had set the benchmark, I suppose. Others would no doubt follow.

Our school at Campsie was essentially for young children so when Steven was eight, or maybe nine, Frank and I started to look around to see if he could continue his schooling elsewhere. We were very fortunate to get a chance to book him into the only private boarding school for disabled boys in New South Wales. We drove up to Kendal Grange, on Lake Macquarie, two hours north of Sydney, to check it out. The school seemed perfect. It was run by a Catholic order called the St John of God Brothers. All the pupils were mildly handicapped and the teachers were experts in their field. We booked him in,

THE HEROIC LIFE OF A WWII NURSE

naturally having some misgivings about leaving him because he'd never been away from us, but knowing he would learn to become independent and that we would be able to see him quite frequently.

It was a unique school, with very large grounds set in a beautiful location with its own poultry farm, piggery, cattle, sheep and goats. The youngsters were taught to look after the animals and to grow crops to feed them. They also learned the use of tools. Suddenly there was a purpose in their lives. They all had jobs to do, which gave them a sense of responsibility. At the same time they were learning about life. They weren't just being cared for; for the very first time they were doing the caring. The boys were never happier than when they were busy. As far as class work was concerned, they were taught the basic skills of reading and writing. This was natural for others but, for handicapped kids like Steven, it was very difficult, particularly writing. But he did well with his reading. We drove up each weekend and he came home for school holidays. We never came to regret, even for a moment, having sent him there.

No sooner had he been enrolled than I was asked to organise a parents and citizens' association which I did, with myself voted in as president. The Brothers wanted to build sporting fields that were to be rather expensive, so we needed a plan to raise money quickly. Having had enough of chocolate wheels, which were good fun but slow and very labour intensive, I convinced the committee we should take a risk and raffle two new cars. We were able to get them at cost from a sympathetic motor dealer and permission to raffle them without any trouble. The raffles were very successful and a lot of money was raised. With parents assisting paid professionals, the fields were completed in next to no time. I sensed I had a position on the P & C for as long as I wanted. We went up to see Steven play on the new field but he was totally disinterested in sport and stood in the middle letting people run around him or, in some cases, over him.

Olive believed it was important for Frank to get a complete break from his workplace so each year the family spent three weeks holidaying out of Sydney. They discovered the quiet coastal town of Laurieton, 25 kilometres south of Port Macquarie on the New South Wales north coast and a half-day's drive from Sydney. Laurieton, on the Camden Haven River, was the scene of Bob Hope's emergency landing during the war. Here they met up with Bunny Wallace, still the town's best-known personality by virtue of his rescue.

Bunny had a purebred, jet-black schipperke or Belgian barge hound which he called Skipper. Originally bred as a watchdog and hunter of vermin, the nuggety little fellow stood slightly below knee height, with strong sloping shoulders and a quizzical fox-like face. There were very few in Australia and Bunny had acquired him from a breeder in Cowra. The dog had a lovely temperament and Olive took a shine to him so bought a pup from the same breeder and called him Bosun. Frank became very attached to Bosun, who accompanied them on fishing and shopping trips as well as walks along the beach and river banks. Later on they won first prize with Bosun at Sydney's Royal Easter Show, a feat made somewhat simpler than normal by the fact that he was the only entrant in his class. The family liked Laurieton so much they made it their regular holiday spot.

In 1964 Olive and Frank left her parents' home in Dulwich Hill and rented a flat in Marrickville. Olive had now been working at Joe Palisi's smash repair company for five years. Joe was a rare boss for that time. His willingness to share profits with his staff of fifteen created a most harmonious working environment. He paid above award wages to his panel beaters and spray painters as well as those in the office. Within a few months of moving into their new flat Frank and Olive learned of a deceased estate, a two-bedroom bungalow, also in Marrickville, which they wanted to buy. The cost of the house was £6000 and they were £500 short of the deposit. When Olive mentioned it to Joe Palisi he immediately offered to lend them the money, which they were to pay back, free of interest, by very reasonable weekly instalments.

Delighted with events, Olive decided that now was the time she should get a driver's licence but Frank was very much against the idea. 'More to do with my independence than my safety,' she said. Frank's objections counted for nothing in this case as Joe paid for the three lessons needed for Olive to become a licensed driver. The licence was soon complemented by a sturdy 1947 Vauxhall Velox. Olive was not just licensed, she now had transport. She also had a job for life, with a man whose generosity had allowed her to own her own home. Joe Palisi never had cause to regret the confidence he showed in his company secretary.

Olive's father, William, in good health, stopped work at the waterfront in the late 1960s to enjoy retirement with Alda, his wife of 45 years. The house they had rented in Dulwich Hill for the past twelve years came up for sale for $8000 (decimal currency had arrived in 1966). Olive convinced him to spend his retirement package to buy it. With some financial assistance from Olive he did as she suggested. The house was purchased in Olive's name and she agreed to pay off the mortgage. It gave her great satisfaction to see her parents looked after. They were not rich by any means, but having struggled through the Depression and the war years with a disabled child, Betty, they deserved the security they now had.

Not long after the purchase of the Dulwich Hill house, a wonderful opportunity arose for Olive to buy a property containing two adjacent cottages across the river from Laurieton township, their favourite holiday spot. The cottages at Laurieton, or more precisely Dunbogan, were in a superb position with a vehicular ferry linking residents to the main township. It was a stunningly beautiful location on the edge of the peninsula with Pacific Ocean frontage. Behind the property was the expanse of water where Bob Hope's entertainment crew had crash-landed. Some of the locals still referred to it as Lake Hope and the Laurieton pub still had newspaper reports from the incident adorning its walls. The family had holidayed in the larger of the two houses during Steven's time at Kendal Grange. They needed some repairs but, at $16 000, it was a chance too good to miss. Olive now sold the Dulwich Hill house and bought the two cottages. It was a perfect retirement property. Alda and William and Betty adjourned to the smaller house immediately while the other was rented. Frank, Olive and Steven would join her parents when they determined the time was right.

Olive was now in her forties, Frank approaching 50 and Steven twelve. Steven attended school at Kendal Grange until he was sixteen. He enjoyed the environment as well as the discipline and made steady progress. By the time he left he was ready to do set, menial tasks under controlled conditions. Though he would never read the newspapers he could understand documents like a work roster, bus timetable or television program, so had done well. There were very limited opportunities for handicapped people but the Brothers had already booked him into a sheltered workshop in Marrickville where he began work dismantling old telephones and recovering parts for the post master general's department, with which the workshop had been granted a large contract. Steven was a British subject so Olive had him naturalised. She realised his full name was far too complicated for him so decided, with typical practicality, to make things easier. Steven Michael Charles Gladwin Wilson-Weston became, officially, just plain Steven Weston.

Olive had worked on the parents and citizens committee for the duration of Steven's schooling at Kendal Grange, at the same time maintaining her involvement in the school at Campsie, which continued to flourish. As youngsters left, fresh parents arrived with new enthusiasm. Her Vauxhall gave way to a Simca, then a Fiat and in turn a Datsun 120Y. Good advice on second-hand cars came easily at her place of work. Frank slowly overcame his aversion to Olive's driving and was content, on rare occasions, to be her passenger.

She now became involved with the people running the sheltered workshop in Marrickville. Among other duties she arranged holidays and excursions for the workers. Everyone contributed a certain amount from their wages each week into a holiday fund. The first Christmas holiday saw 30 excited people travel to Adelaide by coach. Accommodation was organised for them at the Wesley College by Frank's sister June, who had migrated to Adelaide with her husband Bill and sixteen-year-old twin boys, Eric and Bill junior. Here they stayed in students' quarters vacated for the holiday period. June, who had been a Queen Alexandra nurse in India, was deputy matron at Adelaide's North Eastern Community Hospital. She delighted in telling Olive that one of her nurses had worked in an Australian army hospital in Townsville during the war and distinctly remembered Olive giving her three brand new sterilisers from the US PX store. On a second trip to Adelaide they travelled by train to Melbourne and then did the rest of the trip by coach. Another highlight, much shorter in length but equally enjoyable, was a trip to a cattle station in the Upper Hunter Valley of New South Wales, again travelling by coach. Olive always accompanied them:

I thought it was important to have them do things they would not normally do and to see things they probably might not see again. They just loved the trips; they were so excited and were very proud of the fact that they had paid for their own holiday by working and putting their money away. It riled me so much that people didn't understand that they could appreciate what the rest of us did. In many cases they were even more appreciative than people who were better off and who tended to take things for granted.

It also riled me that youngsters with only minor disabilities were put in mental institutions, like Callan Park and Gladesville, with others who were insane and, in some cases, criminally insane. I believe a lot of blame here lay with the medical profession. They encouraged parents to put disabled children in an institution and forget them. They were told to start a new family, hoping that the next child would be all right. When I did my obstetrics at King George I saw doctors put deformed newborn babies out in a cot and we were not allowed to even give them a drink of water. They just had to die. People don't believe that now, but it's true. This attitude of ignoring the disabled ran throughout society. You didn't see any ramps or toilets for the disabled in those days. 'Keep them out of sight' was the principle.

The apathy towards even marginally handicapped people and the disregard shown them was terrible. I began helping the St John of God social workers identify and foster out poor unfortunates who were locked up simply because they had Down's syndrome, or similar minor disabilities like Steven. We had one big old home at Lewisham, with a housemother and a housefather, where they were looked after, fed and kept clean. They were able to come and work at the sheltered workshop at Marrickville. We couldn't help everybody but we helped a lot.

Frank, now in a very senior position at the DCA Marrickville workshop, was busy on a major project, the design and installation of a new, complex air-traffic control system for Mascot Airport, scheduled for completion some five years down the track. Steven was completely settled in his job at the sheltered workshop in Marrickville and keen to discuss the importance of his work with those willing to listen. Olive continued to help with the workshop and the placement of handicapped people in foster homes with the St John of God social workers she'd met through Kendal Grange. Life at the new home at Marrickville, though governed to some extent by Steven's disabilities, was, at the same time, enriched by the love and dedication afforded him.

Chapter Seven

ALONE AGAIN

The years from 1968 until 1973 had been happy and productive. Olive was very satisfied with Steven's location at the sheltered workshop and her own involvement with it. Her own work environment could not have been more rewarding. William, Alda and Betty had settled in well at Dunbogan and Olive flew up to Port Macquarie every few weeks, hiring a car at Port Macquarie to visit them and ensure they lacked nothing. William spent many pleasant hours fishing the river and the family became regulars at the Laurieton RSL Club, which was just a two dollar cab fare across a new bridge that had replaced the old vehicular ferry. Sadly, things were about to change.

Frank had been working under a lot of stress as the airport project approached its deadline. The announcement that the

Queen would officially open the new complex on her Australian tour added considerably to the pressure. There could be no extension of time. Weighed down with responsibilities and working long hours, he had developed high blood pressure. Always a poor sleeper he now became an insomniac, his mind constantly full of work-related issues. Workmates became accustomed to him starting the day with a headache powder taken without water. Olive was worried enough to go down to the Marrickville workshop and express her concerns to his boss. His hypertension increased. Eventually blood vessels burst behind his nose and the bleeding was so profuse he was rushed to Marrickville Hospital. Olive knew his problems were serious:

It was no ordinary nosebleed. He lost so much blood doctors monitored the bleeding and pinned his nose back in an effort to stop the flow. He was given blood transfusions and kept in intensive care. When he eventually improved enough to have visitors several technicians came to see him from the workshop. All Frank wanted to do was talk to them about how progress was going. He had a photographic memory, once he had seen and analysed something he never forgot it. The result was that people asked him things all the time. If they wanted an answer they invariably went to him. He didn't have the ability to leave his work at the office and was very worried about the schedule. He went back to work in time but his blood pressure never improved. I was terribly concerned that the problems would only get worse.

Sadly my concerns were well founded. When the Queen was opening the new complex that Frank had worked so hard on, he was in intensive care having suffered a heart attack. Fortunately he'd had the attack at home so I was able to get him to the hospital in very quick time. The Queen was back in England by the time he had recovered and gone back to work. He was still very British and was dreadfully disappointed he didn't meet or even see the Queen at the opening.

That same year, 1973, Olive lost her mother Alda, who died aged 69 and was buried in Laurieton cemetery. Her death, just two weeks before her fiftieth wedding anniversary, so upset William he had no desire to stay on so Olive organised his enrolment in a nursing home back in Sydney. He was 72. Betty, now approaching 50, refused to leave. Though intellectually impaired since the bus crash in her childhood, she was physically strong and capable of looking after herself at home so Olive agreed to let her stay. Betty enjoyed the eternal happiness of intellectually handicapped people who knew no worries and to whom each day was a new adventure. In this respect she was very similar to Steven. Olive flew up regularly to see her and make sure she was all right.

Olive was now more concerned with Frank's wellbeing than she was with Steven's. His nemesis was stress, most of which was caused by the pressure of his work. She ensured he ate sensibly and did her best to keep him free from worry. In spite of her best efforts Frank had a second heart attack eighteen months after Alda's death, one that was more severe than the first. Again he was rushed to intensive care at Marrickville Hospital. He was a difficult patient so every day for a week Olive went to the hospital after work and stayed the night in his private ward. She was his personal nurse. While Frank was in hospital Bosun, to whom Frank had become very attached, was stolen from the backyard. Olive kept the news from him, fearing it might have caused another attack. When he came home he opened the front door and immediately called the dog's name. Olive had no alternative but to inform him of their loss. His disappointment was obvious.

Frank's convalescence and recovery took much longer this time. When the immediate danger had passed he was examined by the commonwealth medical officer who found him too ill to continue work and discharged him from the DCA. Olive decided it was time for the family to join Betty in Dunbogan. It was a logical move given Frank's delicate physical condition. His doctors assured them that complete rest in a situation totally devoid of stress was the only medicine they could prescribe. Olive knew that Steven loved Dunbogan from his school days so had no regrets about taking him away from the sheltered workshop. Her only misgiving was leaving the employment of Joe Palisi:

No one could ever imagine a better boss than Joe. He was a friend and adviser to all his staff. He paid us well and showed everyone great respect. It paid off for him because we were very loyal. We loved coming to work. It was a place where everyone pitched in to help. I was bookkeeper, company secretary, odd job girl, nurse, whatever was needed at the time. After I got my licence I'd pick up cars to be repaired or drive across town to pick up spare parts. Lustreglo did very well. We got the contract to spray paint the hull of *Dame Patti*, Frank Packer's second America's Cup boat, in 1962. We were very proud of that. Lustreglo also painted the inside of the new airport tunnel.

I have some great memories of the fifteen years I'd worked there, even though not everything went according to plan. I remember when Joe went out to Cronulla for a demonstration in one of those new, high-powered jet boats. The boat hit a wave and Joe fell and broke a leg. When he got back to shore he rang his wife and told her he'd sprained his ankle. I was practically family by this time and when his wife Rosaline found out the truth she was so distraught she couldn't even ring Marina, his mother, to tell her the bad news. Nonna, they called her, she was the matriarch and a real sweetheart. It was left to me to phone her. She was so emotional it took me several minutes to settle her down. Joe was in plaster for months. I ran the place for six weeks while Joe was in St George Hospital and looked after Rosaline's and Marina's banking as well. They were a lovely family.

I always told Joe I didn't think I could ever give up work completely because I'd been so active all my life and we had such a close-knit group. But suddenly it seemed the natural thing to do. With Frank retiring it was time to put down my tools as well. I'd been working since I was fifteen and I figured I'd probably earned a rest so we sold up and headed north. Frank and I shared the driving. Of course Betty was delighted when we got there. I felt a bit like a mother hen with three lame ducklings, but I absolutely loved Dunbogan and Laurieton.

The weather was certainly milder than in North Queensland but still very warm in summer. The sandflies worried Frank, as did the humidity, though Olive did not notice either. Steven greeted each new day with a smile and a question, 'What'll we do today then?' The answer was generally what they had done yesterday, which suited him just fine. Frank wasn't any great shakes as a fisherman but he soon found it a pleasant way to spend the time, especially in a place as peaceful as Dunbogan. When the fish were biting it was generally Olive who had the most success and Steven would help Frank light the barbecue with much excitement. There were few sweeter tastes than fresh, barbecued bream or flathead. Apart from the estuary, where fishing trips were always made interesting by the number of times Steven got his line in a mess and the corresponding time Olive spent unravelling it, the Laurieton RSL became a favourite haunt as it had been with Olive's parents. She was delighted when Joe Palisi was able to come up for a holiday with his wife Rosaline and their five children.

187

Olive was pleased that Steven showed no signs of missing his workmates in Sydney. He busied himself cutting the lawn and the neighbour's as well. Occasionally, Olive and Frank took Steven to the cinema in Laurieton when a film was shown that suited him. Once a month they drove to Port Macquarie to stock up on groceries. Steven was particularly excited when they made a special trip to see a seven-metre crocodile known as 'Big Momma' that had been bred in Townsville and sold to a local crocodile farm. Olive played some golf at Port Macquarie. Though never becoming a fanatic, in time she reduced her handicap to the low twenties and never forgot her first birdie. A morning on the golf course was most relaxing. She would never complain about her burden, but always felt she was 'on call' when with Steven and Frank.

Despite much enjoyment attained from fishing, Frank's main interest was still electronics. He set up his own ham radio station with a call sign VK2 APW. Olive found this rather amusing. From the time she was quite young she had often heard her father refer to a person regarded as having no substance as being 'like the barber's cat — all piss and wind.' It was a common expression, particularly among working class people and she told Frank his call sign APW reminded her of it. After more than 20 years of marriage her irreverence no longer worried him. Frank's vast knowledge allowed him to communicate successfully with ham operators across the world, often with spectacular results. A distress signal picked up from a vessel near the Philippines led to a rescue attempt involving another radio operator in Tasmania and the US Coastguard. Though unable to ascertain if the crew was rescued he was able to help save a family of four when the father fell from the mast of his yacht and was badly injured near Palmyra Island, south of Hawaii. Frank was able to direct a naval warship to the scene. He spent countless hours, day after day, at his hobby. Olive was well pleased to see him so busy with a pursuit that involved no physical duress. Her only disappointment was that Steven could not understand enough to share his father's interest. Try as he did Frank was never quite able to accept Steven's disability as well as Olive did.

To Olive's great surprise Betty had found romance:

She came to me with a lovely old gentleman named Bill. He was a veteran of the first war, in his mid eighties, and the pair sat holding hands like a couple of teenagers while Betty explained how much in love they were and asked for my permission to marry. She was 54. I couldn't help but smile at the improbability of the whole thing as they spoke, always calling each other darling, but he was a real gentleman and as they sat there admiring each other I thought, What the heck. If it gives her a few years of happiness, why should I stop her? So I agreed. A few days later I went over to see her and she opened the door wearing a wedding ring. They had gone off to Taree during the week and tied the knot. I couldn't help but laugh. After giving my blessing I wasn't even invited to the wedding. Bill lived for three more years and Betty was very happy. When he died she was able to go into an RSL retirement village with a war widow's pension.

In 1979 Olive attended a special ceremony to mourn the death of one of Britain's most celebrated servicemen, Lord Louis Mountbatten, who was blown up by the IRA in Ireland at the age of 79. Mountbatten had directed the liberation of Burma and Singapore at the war's end. During the ceremony she met Nancy Wake, the 'White Mouse', whose exploits with the French underground had made her the most famous Resistance fighter during the Second World War. Nancy was living in Port Macquarie. They became acquaintances, if not close friends, who met again on Anzac Day and shared stories of wartime experiences.

About eighteen months after they had settled in Dunbogan Frank had a third heart attack. Olive drove him to the doctor at Laurieton and from there they went by ambulance to Port Macquarie Hospital where he stayed for two weeks. Upon his discharge from care, one of Frank's doctors, a former Adelaide man, advised Olive he would be better off in a less humid climate and suggested Adelaide would be ideal. There is little doubt Olive would have lived out her remaining years at Dunbogan but for Frank's illness. She had owned the property for almost ten years and, deep down, was quite devastated at the idea of leaving:

I loved the place. No one could ever imagine a better spot to retire. Steven loved it too but Frank's health was my major concern. There was no way really of knowing how long he would live but I had to give him every chance to survive and live for as long and as happily as he could. Frank's older sister June had been in Adelaide for ten years with her husband Bill and their twin sons. The fact that June was a nursing sister was a comforting thought. I wouldn't be the only one able to take care of him in an emergency. She and Bill were happy to put us up in Adelaide until we got settled, so we sold the two houses at Dunbogan, put our furniture on the train and motored south.

Olive and the family settled in with June and Bill and immediately began to look for a home. She transferred her membership to the South Australian branch of the Australian American Ex-Services Association and was looking forward to Anzac Day and meeting up with several American GIs who had migrated to Adelaide. Olive got on very well with June, with whom she had much in common. She had recently retired from nursing and her reminiscences of service in India during the war were always interesting. Her husband Bill, a former lieutenant colonel in the British army, was often taken aback by Olive's sense of humour and typical Australian ways. When she roared laughing at the American TV show M*A*S*H he would ask, 'Ollie, the Americans wouldn't really carry on like that in an army hospital, would they?' It delighted her to be able to say, 'Yes, of course they would, and so did us Aussies!'

The family had only been in Adelaide for about six weeks when Frank had a fourth heart attack and was again rushed into intensive care. It was Easter Saturday, 1980, and Olive and June sat with him for 24 hours. Again he recovered. She knew he was living on borrowed time but saw no sense in being negative so continued with her plans to buy a house. They found a three-bedroom cottage in the seaside suburb of Christies Beach, on the Fleurieu Peninsula, 20 kilometres south of the city centre. It was reasonably priced so they bought it without delay.

All three took an immediate liking to the area. Once again they were near the water and Frank and Steven went fishing regularly. Olive attended the Anzac Day march and was impressed when, unlike in Sydney, her contingent marched immediately behind the Australian troops. There were about 40 Americans who had served in Australia during the Second World War. She determined never to miss the march.

Frank again set up his ham radio station, partitioning off half of the large garage to create his radio shack with the very best of equipment. He had numerous contacts around the world. Radio communication served the purpose of entertaining him without physical exertion and also allowed him relaxation, the only answer to the stress that was his worst enemy. That same year Olive's father died in Sydney. Though she had been very close to her father as a youngster they had drifted apart and she had become much closer to her mother as the years passed. As he was a strong unionist she was prepared to have the Waterside Workers' Union look after his funeral arrangements.

Olive found just one drawback to living at Christies Beach. There was no sheltered workshop in which to enrol Steven. In fact the only local facility for the intellectually handicapped was an enclave at Christies East Public School where remedial teachers ran classes for young children. Adelaide's facilities for handicapped people were most inadequate. Olive found only two groups acting on behalf of disabled people, Bedford Industries Rehabilitation Association and the Phoenix Society, neither of which provided any opportunities in the Christies Beach area.

Bedford Industries, which rehabilitated and trained people from fifteen years to 65 for employment and conducted an activity therapy centre, employed disabled workers at their Crown Hotel in Victor Harbor as kitchen staff and housemaids. Unfortunately their waiting list was so long it took months to arrange an interview because the number of jobs available was far less than the number of people who required them.

Phoenix employed people in a large factory doing routine tasks like sewing buttons onto uniforms, packing airline food into plastic containers and so on. The girls working on the machines were treated very harshly; if they broke a needle its replacement cost was taken from their meagre pay. Both agencies found it easier to employ those with physical rather than intellectual disabilities. A person in a wheelchair with an IQ of 100 was given preference over an able-bodied person with an IQ of 70.

Olive was pleased when Steven was able to find regular work on a voluntary basis at the Baptist church opportunity shop, but was concerned for his future. Disappointed as she was with the situation, she knew there were much worse alternatives. There were two institutions, Minda and Strathmont, in which handicapped people with no family support were incarcerated. She realised that if something untoward happened to her then Steven would probably be locked away forever. She was dismayed and very angry at the thought that this could happen after all she had done and the progress he had made.

Olive set about correcting the situation just as she had done in Sydney 25 years earlier, setting up an action group in Christies Beach. She knew there must be many parents in the same situation as her own. Consequently she got in touch with the local papers appealing for help. The following article appeared in the *Southern Times* on 29 April 1981:

> A local parent of an intellectually handicapped adult has called for a sheltered workshop in the South. Mrs Olive Weston, a committee member of the Intellectually Retarded Services Christies Beach Parents Action Group, said the nearest sheltered workshop was Bedford Industries at Panorama.
>
> 'There is a real need as there is no such thing as an activity centre or sheltered workshop in the southern districts,' said Mrs Weston. 'Bedford Industries is unable to cope with the demand and has a long waiting list. We waited six months to get an appointment at Bedford but even after that nothing could be done because of the long waiting list. It is up to us as responsible parents to get together and institute such a place here in the south, preferably in the Christies Beach–Port Noarlunga area.'
>
> Mrs Weston said a local sheltered workshop would give handicapped people some independence and help them lead creative and productive lives.
>
> Mrs Weston would like to contact families with handicapped adults including those of families already placed

at Bedford, Phoenix or Minda. She would also like to hear from local church groups or other organisations interested in helping to set up a local sheltered workshop.

Less than a fortnight later *The News* also published an interview with Olive during which she again described the situation as hopeless: 'These people are so isolated. No one wants them as friends. They need activity centres or sheltered workshops. Space is available at Seawinds, a centre for totally dependent children, to organise an activity centre which could eventually lead to a sheltered workshop.' Again Olive appealed for people to volunteer their time in providing activities at the proposed centre. The reaction was exactly what Olive had anticipated. No fewer than 50 parents were soon in touch with her as well as others willing to help. She felt a sense of déjà vu when she recalled similar circumstances back in Marrickville 25 years earlier. There would be the same long road ahead, but, having travelled it once, she was prepared to travel it again, knowing that with enough persistence changes could be made. As Frank passed his time in the radio shack and Steven served in the opportunity shop, Olive organised her troops.

The first small workshop was established at the back of the Baptist church in which half a dozen intellectually handicapped adults were taught a variety of skills. Simple wooden toys were manufactured and sold at public markets. With the returns a small compactor was purchased at a cost of $30. Newspapers were collected and soaked in soapy water then compacted into solid cubes that made excellent fuel for combustion stoves. When huge stacks of paper were donated a paper shredder was bought to expedite manufacture. Many people in the area had apricot trees and they were happy to have people from the workshop collect the fruit to take back to the church where they were sun dried and sold. A small nursery was set up; different cuttings were potted and nurtured until they were ready to be sold. Soon government cars were washed in an area behind the church. The workshop, small though it was, became self-sufficient and those attending were given lessons in numeracy and literacy as well.

Just two years after their arrival in Adelaide from Dunbogan, Frank had his fifth and final heart attack. February 13, 1982, was a day Olive will remember forever:

I was in the kitchen and Frank was in the bedroom. He came crawling to me saying, 'Ollie, I'm in trouble. Please get me to the doctor.' With considerable difficulty I got him to the car and into the passenger's seat. The surgery was less than two blocks away, which was one of the features that had made the house attractive to me, but he collapsed and went into a coma. He was dead before we got there. Frank was 63 and we'd been married almost 30 years.

We'd had differences of opinion as any couple would during that time but he'd never once raised his voice to me, or Steven. He was always perfectly mannered no matter what the circumstances. Even if he'd drunk one too many glasses of Scotch he was as polite as he was when cold sober. He was the English gentleman to his last breath, which I watched him take.

He was interesting and intelligent but also a very romantic and passionate man. There was a saying in England that marriage was something of a lottery and that it was easy for a young bride to get a dud, meaning an inexperienced man who proved unable to satisfy a woman's needs. There were a lot of duds. Nothing was further from the truth in Frank's case. At 33 he was a man of the world and I was a virgin bride. He was my husband and my teacher, the only lover I would ever have and I was a very willing pupil. There was no 'lie back and think of England' with Frank. I was never subservient to him in any way, not that he would have expected it. My satisfaction was as important to him as his own. He never lost that desire to surprise or please me. My pleasure was as important as his. He bought jewellery and flowers every birthday and every anniversary. I remember on our twentieth wedding anniversary an enormous bunch of flowers arrived at Joe Palisi's repair shop with a beautiful card. It brought tears to my eyes even then.

The people from Steven's Baptist church rallied around me wonderfully, making all the arrangements for his funeral and the cremation. June, Bill and the twins came to his funeral. At least he had family to see him off. Steven and I were in the mourning coach and when they took Frank's body away to be cremated we went back home for a quiet wake. Steven looked at the house, turned to me, half crying, and said, 'Mum, I have to be the man of the house now.' In the circumstance I suppose it was a natural thing to say but nevertheless it sounded quite strange. It was a very odd expression for Steven to use. If I could have waved a magic wand I would have taken us back to Dunbogan. Still, it was no good looking back.

Frank's wishes were that his ashes be scattered in the sea at Noarlunga where he and Steven used to fish off the jetty. One night Steven and I went down with June and Bill, did as he wished and that was that. I sold the equipment from the radio shack with the help of some friends who knew a bit about it. It was apparently very good and realised over $5000. June and the twins, Eric and Bill junior, were a wonderful comfort to me in this very lonely time and I got to regard the boys almost as my own. They were delightful kids and gave me a lot of attention and time even though they were teenagers with their own friends and interests. I guess they took the place of the twins I had been denied in Sydney all those years earlier.

Soon after Frank's death Olive met Major Vivienne Holmes, former personal aide to General Sir William Slim, commander of the British forces during the Burma campaign. Vivienne's family, like Frank's, had lived in India and Vivienne, who had gone to school with June, was about to visit from Perth when Frank passed away. She, Olive and June had much to talk about. Vivienne Holmes, a few years older than Olive, was the secretary of the Burma Star Association. It was a position she would hold for over 20 years. Olive was well aware of Vivienne's wonderful service record and was thrilled with her friendship, one that would develop steadily.

With Frank gone Olive now threw all her efforts into the battle on behalf of the disabled. With a committed group around her she used all her experience to attract more public attention to their plight. The press were keen to help, publicising meetings and running stories and pictures of Olive and Steven. Bedford Industries had become interested with the first appeal Olive had made some months earlier and now proposed assistance with the project. A meeting, held in the Baptist Centre at Christies Beach, brought the following local newspaper report:

A most successful public meeting was held on March 29, 1982, by the foundation committee of the proposed Southern Region Branch of Bedford Industries.

More than 160 people attended the meeting, representing community and welfare service agencies, organisations involved with the care of disabled people, parents of and people with disabilities, members of the community and politicians.

Strong support for the venture was expressed. Information presented at the meeting showed that, of 153 850 people within the 15–65 age group in the Central Southern region, about

7 per cent, or 10 800 people have some form of disability. This is a conservative estimate because there is no complete register of people with disabilities.

Meeting chairman, Grant Chapman MP, was asked to seek federal support as there was strong public support for the development of a national register of birth defects.

An interim committee was formed to develop a two-year program with services for the disabled through a community based branch of Bedford Industries in the Fleurieu Peninsula. Mr Shane Freeman has been elected chairman of the committee. Mr Freeman is the personnel officer at the Adelaide Oil Refinery at Port Stanvac.

A Bedford Industries spokesman said it was evident a great need existed for services to the disabled throughout the Fleurieu Peninsula.

'There has been strong interest and support for the development of such services,' he said, 'for services to be developed satisfactorily there must be continuing strong support from the local community in all its aspects. Innovative and flexible programs will be developed which will be a new approach to the training and rehabilitation of disabled persons in Australia. It is an exciting and challenging concept which is matched by strong local support.'

Olive was very pleased with the meeting and the press coverage, which continued for some time. Publicity could only help to keep the ball rolling and she saw it as important to have strong commitment from Bedford stated publicly:

We called ourselves PODs, Parents of Disabled. Our first task was to clearly define our objectives. In essence they were to provide opportunities for the older ones to work in a sheltered environment as well as to help in caring for them at home and to assist youngsters with a chance to be educated so that they could achieve their true potential, whatever that potential was. Our major obstacles would be the general public's lack of knowledge and apprehension about such people, along with the task of convincing those with the public purse strings that the situation should be addressed. I told them what we had been able to achieve back in Steven's childhood and it gave them great heart.

We agreed it was essential to define the people we were talking about. They were called mentally ill, mentally retarded, mentally handicapped, mentally impaired, subnormal and so on. Once the word 'mental' was used the public had the misconception that they were, in some way, mad and possibly dangerous. This was quite inaccurate. They had much more to fear from the public than the public had from them. They were merely of lesser intellect than normal. All were capable of performing certain simple tasks and were, in the main, very happy and friendly. Nothing made them happier than to be able to contribute to society. After much debate they were categorised, with complete accuracy, as being intellectually disadvantaged. This is the term by which they are now officially recognised.

Obviously we needed immediate funds so I approached various government departments but found the same problems with red tape and apathetic public servants as I had done in Sydney. After some weeks of fruitless negotiations my committee agreed we should put on a couple of demonstrations in an attempt to rally public support. The first one we called RAID, Rights of Assistance to the Intellectually Disadvantaged. Three hundred of us protested at noon on the steps of parliament house, in September 1982, about the lack of support and facilities for people with intellectual disadvantages. We handed out hundreds of pamphlets explaining the difficulties faced by these people.

RAID

(Rights of Assistance to the Intellectually Disadvantaged)

DID YOU KNOW THAT ...

There are about 13 000 intellectually disadvantaged people living in South Australia.

Approximately 1500 of these people live in institutions, however institutions absorb 90% of the budget available for the intellectually disadvantaged in South Australia (About $16 000 000).

The needs of the 11 500 intellectually disadvantaged people living at home are expected to be met from an allocation of only $500 000 per year.

CAMPAIGN RAID ASKS ...

That more money be given to develop resources in the community without detriment to those living in institutions.

That all intellectually disadvantaged people be given the right to work and receive decent wages.

That access to the public school system be improved.

That home and community-based support services be increased.

That a range of community accommodation options be established to meet the needs of the intellectually disadvantaged.

Campaign RAID is not a revolt, nor is it a government bashing exercise, it is a means of bringing before the public and the relevant government departments our needs, some of them urgent, all of them necessary.

RAID NEEDS YOUR SUPPORT!

The demonstration was well organised, well received and very well publicised. The United Nations had declared 1982 the Year of the Disabled, so the media was 'ready to go'. The second event involved a large number of intellectually and physically disadvantaged people in a march up Adelaide's main thoroughfare, King William Street, to Victoria Square. Again there was plenty of publicity and PODs sensed momentum was gathering.

Olive was now invited onto several committees. Her experience and willingness to confront tough issues and to deal with eminent people was something of a revelation. She was offered a position on the board at Bedford and was appointed the southern representative of IDSC, the Intellectually Disadvantaged Services Council. These were honorary positions, an arrangement that suited her. Frank had always advised Olive never to take any remuneration for her work in such situations. His reasoning was that she was always outspoken and she must not put herself in a position where she felt restricted in voicing her opinions. Olive took her position on the Bedford board in a very positive frame of mind but resigned after some months because she was continually at odds with the way people were accepted into their workshops. Her particular interest was the intellectually disadvantaged, Bedford's was not.

The Bedford board was keen to sell the Crown Hotel, which it operated in conjunction with the state government, to obtain money to build larger workshops. When the hotel was sold the money from the sale sat for almost two years while the government approved its use. Meanwhile, in association with Bedford, PODs set up a small sheltered workshop in an existing building at Christies Beach, employing a dozen people. It was quite a breakthrough for the southern area. Olive had become a key figure in negotiating for the release of the money raised by the sale of the Crown Hotel.

When treasury eventually freed the money, Bedford immediately sent Olive the following letter, dated 13 December 1983.

Dear Mrs Weston,

As you may be aware, an evaluation of the services provided by Bedford Industries from its Fleurieu Centre Branch was carried out during September to November this year. The evaluation study was conducted by Elizabeth Bleby, M.A. (Social Admin) on behalf of the department of social securities, the Fleurieu Centre Committee and Bedford Industries.

Following consideration of the recommendations of the report, and having regard to the numbers of people at present seeking service, it has been decided that the following action should now be taken.

a) Close the Centre at 98 Beach Road, Christies Beach, with effect from 22nd December 1983.

b) Offer placement to people now attending the Fleurieu centre at either the Katuni or Panorama locations of Bedford Industries according to interests and capabilities and, also, extend this offer to any people on the waiting list.

c) In the immediate future, continue to provide a service to the region from Clapham, Panorama and Edwardstown.

d) Work with community groups and other agencies for the development of suitable services within the region as demand and resources permit.

e) Establish a working party to co-ordinate activities related to the development of services comprising representatives from

P.O.D.s

I.D.S.C.

Bedford Industries

Christies East Special School.

In reaching the above decisions, emphasis was put on the need to continue work for the development of regional community based services. Bedford Industries is committed to this approach and will do whatever possible to achieve the establishment of services. In the immediate future however, it is clear that we must provide services from our existing locations, whilst we seek to identify business or manufacturing activities which can be based in the region of assessment, training and employment purposes. Whilst this relocation of services is regretted, we look forward to a continuous association with you.

Yours sincerely,

John A. Munchenberg.

Chief Executive.

I couldn't believe it. The closure of the workshop at Christies Beach was absolutely devastating. I felt I had been betrayed. Not once while I was using my influence to help free up the money from the Crown Hotel sale had there been any suggestion of closing the workshop. Now we were being given three days notice.

When I was composed enough I rang and asked them about 'their innovative and flexible programs and their exciting and challenging concepts'. How did they imagine closing the workshop was innovative and challenging? It was a waste of time. I saw to it that PODs had nothing more to do with the Bedford establishment. We would not let this setback stop us so we had no alternative but to go our own way, seeking to place our people in a variety of different work environments. We were concerned with caring for our people as well as getting them work. Looking after them outside of the workplace was also a major concern.

The tragic death of one of the PODs' committee, Jean Millgate, had a dramatic impact on the group. It focused their attention on the totally inadequate support for the disadvantaged in time of crisis. Jean's 26-year-old daughter, Toni, a sufferer of Down's syndrome, had been employed at the Christies Beach workshop. While friends and family rallied around her none was able to offer sufficient support to enable her to stay living in her family home. The existing human services were unable to act. None was even remotely organised enough to offer assistance that could help the woman in her own home. Even the two large institutions, Strathmont and Minda, poorly regarded options as they were, would not offer a placement as their books had been closed. After many formal and informal meetings, a family friend in Sydney discovered that a room was available in an enclave that housed six people at St Andrews Hospital, Lane Cove. With no other options available the lonely and distraught young woman was removed from her only friends at Christies Beach and her support network, built up over many years, was dissolved.

Her plight, with its pathetic and tragically unsatisfactory outcome, prompted PODs to concentrate their immediate efforts on correcting this situation. The need to become proactive was evident to all. They envisaged a service that did not take responsibility from the individual or their family and friends, but supplemented their roles in assisting the intellectually handicapped to remain living in their local community. PODs approached the IDSC, of which Olive was still a councillor, and the department of community services with the idea of creating a community living project. While their aims were generally clear enough, the knowledge and experience of the IDSC board was needed to ensure that the constitution for such a body was correctly written and legal requirements met. Confident that they were on the right track, Olive led the deputation to parliament. Overtures were made to the state government for funding to establish a service that would assist in supporting and sustaining people in their own homes in their local community. Initial reluctance to help was eventually followed by an offer. If the federal government agreed to grant financial help then the state government would do likewise. But there would be no money coming from the state without prior federal assistance:

We went to our local federal member for Kingston, Gordon Bilney, who turned out to be a wonderful fellow, very efficient and very helpful. He sent me copies of correspondence and press releases over quite a long period of time so we were always well informed. He then advised me of a plan to maximise our chances of federal assistance. It turned out to be simple and very effective.

Gordon Bilney organised an afternoon function and invited Tasmania's Senator Grimes, the minister for health, to attend from Canberra. I was also invited, taking with me a petition asking for financial assistance. He teed up the official photographer to take a shot of me handing the petition to Senator Grimes and then ensured that the senator's secretary put the petition in his briefcase. Senator Grimes, who I was told had a family member who was intellectually disadvantaged, also proved very sympathetic to our cause. We were very lucky to have those men involved. They worked really hard for us. The upshot was that we were eventually granted funding that the state government felt obliged to match, albeit with great reluctance. It wasn't a lot of money, about $40 000, but it was a start. Our committee was ecstatic. We had put in a lot of effort and it had paid off. Our community living project was underway.

Incorporated in January 1985, Community Living Project Inc. was almost entirely government funded as 'the mobile training team' with two permanent administration staff, four carers and a host of voluntary workers. Professional carers were subsequently hired on a part-time basis to help look after those disadvantaged people living with relatives. Serious problems still existed with those who could not be looked after at home. A major breakthrough came with agreement from the housing trust to buy two houses in Christie Downs, the next suburb to Christies Beach, which intellectually disadvantaged people could rent with payments made from their pensions and wages.

The immediate problem came from nearby homeowners, many of whom believed their properties would be devalued by having the intellectually disadvantaged as neighbours, and others who felt unsafe in their company. Educating them became an important issue. As usual Olive met this problem head on:

Another parent, Jill Wishart, and I went around and spoke personally to all neighbours within three streets of the houses. Some of the comments we got were quite disgusting but we persisted. There was nothing people could do about it but we did them the courtesy of telling them what was going on and that they had nothing to fear. Some listened, some didn't. We moved our people in and never had any problems. In time the neighbours took no notice. Their insecurities abated and in fact some became quite helpful.

Back in Port Macquarie Betty's husband Bill had died of a stroke and Betty became involved with a man named Bruno whom Olive had not yet met. They bought a block of land at Settlement Point in Port Macquarie which they sold soon after and Bruno travelled down to Yorke Peninsula in South Australia to buy another block. He then went back, returned with Betty and built a house on the property. Olive saw nothing of old Bill's charm or love in Bruno's association with Betty and became convinced he was simply using

Betty's pension to further his own ends. She again had her sister's interests to look after as well as Steven's. These she solved in typical fashion by making Bruno buy her out of the property and placing Betty in a retirement home on Yorke Peninsula. Olive visited Betty regularly, driving many hours to the peninsula to ensure she was looked after. This she would do for several years.

Though not even her closest friends were aware of it, Olive was reaching a crisis point. Since Frank's death she had thrown herself into her efforts with PODs, determined that her own personal tragedy would not consume her. In spite of this there were just too many memories of Frank in the home at Christies Beach. She saw him in every room. Suddenly she made a dramatic decision, deciding to sell up and return with Steven to her home town of Townsville. She sold the house, put the furniture in storage with the intention of shipping it north later, booked a sleeping car on the Ghan for her and Steven, and headed for Alice Springs. Her Datsun 120Y station wagon was on the train ready for the marathon drive from the Alice to Townsville.

Steven was a most unwilling passenger. He was very distraught at leaving his Baptist church friends whom he saw every day, assisting one of the social workers, making tea and running errands. But Olive had made up her mind. The 1500-kilometre train trip to the Alice took 24 hours and by the time the pair arrived Steven had come to accept his lot. Olive kept reassuring him he would love Townsville. On the station at Alice Springs they met a friend from the Baptist church who wished them good luck on their arduous journey. They had breakfast as the car was being unloaded then made sure it was full of fuel and water. Olive doubted there would be too many service stations before Tennant Creek, which lay 530 kilometres due north. Here they would turn east, travelling 665 kilometres to Mount Isa and eventually a further

885 kilometres to Townsville. In all they faced a journey of more than 2000 kilometres, much of it over dusty isolated roads. It would have been a daunting task for a professional rally car driver. Olive had ensured there was drinking water in the back of the wagon. It was just after eight o'clock and already obvious they faced a long hot day. As they left Alice Springs behind Steven sat silent, just staring straight ahead.

Hour after hour passed without a word from him. About three-quarters of the way to Tennant Creek Olive suddenly stopped the car:

I'd been driving about four hours and the only traffic we had seen were two road trains that had roared past us in the opposite direction. I looked at Steven, who was obviously very perturbed, and I suddenly thought, What in the bloody hell am I doing out here in the middle of nowhere? I realised if something had happened to me then Steven would not have had a clue what to do. He'd have been helpless. So I turned the car around there and then and headed back to Alice Springs. I'd been driving about seven hours by the time I got back. The fuel tank was showing empty. I was in tears, having panic attacks. I booked into the Casino Hotel and rang June in Adelaide and told her, between sobs, what had transpired and that I couldn't drive all that way. She said, 'I didn't think you could, Ollie, you come straight back here to Adelaide and stay with us until you get things sorted out. Put the car back on the Ghan and come back as soon as you feel well enough.'

The hotel organised a doctor who ordered me to rest and treated me with Serepax tablets. Steven kept fussing about, assuring me I'd be all right. He couldn't wait to get home to Adelaide. June rang me each day and we flew back to stay with her three days later. Steven was still terribly upset and kept saying, 'I don't want to leave Adelaide, Mum, I want to live here, this is where my friends are. Please don't leave

Adelaide, Mum.' So I shelved my plans to return to Townsville and that was that. June was wonderful. She knew I'd just reached a point where things had got too much for me. I went to a psychologist and had some counselling to get me past the panic attacks. It was during my counselling sessions that I went right back to my birth at the lighthouse in Townsville. It was the most extraordinary feeling. We stayed with June and Bill for several months until I felt perfectly well again.

I headed back to Christie Downs where I rented a house and Steven went back to his church. He came home one day and announced, 'Mum, I'm going to be a Baptist!' I said, 'All right, Steven, if that's what you want, so be it.' I fixed things up for him at the church and he went through with the ceremony and was officially sworn in to the Baptist faith. We were back in Adelaide for good, though a large part of my heart would always remain in Townsville. In fact I determined to spend the beautiful warm winter months in Townsville each year and that has turned out really well. When Adelaide gets cold Steven and I head north. The best of both worlds.

Chapter Eight

THE POLITICIAN

The Community Living Project, initiated in the early eighties, was proving to be an outstanding success. Though the struggle would never cease, all concerned could see steady progress being made. PODs continued to work closely with the professionals now running the project. As government funding and staff steadily increased, it provided opportunities for mildly disadvantaged people to experience independence as well as providing housing for some who had been incarcerated in unsuitable and inhospitable surroundings. They were experiencing dignity they had never known. Some preferred to live alone, others with partners or boarders, while many were still cared for in their family environment.

As people relocated they found themselves facing the normal problems of everyday living. There was occasional dissent between housemates, disagreements to sort out, emotional and practical problems to overcome. Carers kept a keen eye on their charges, allowing them enough rein to express themselves, but always ensuring their wellbeing and seeing that disagreements did not get out of hand. They were assisted in keeping a weekly budget, organising personal transport and shopping for essential household items. The plan proved a catalyst for other agencies as the department of mental health soon followed suit and were able to procure houses from the housing trust as well.

When Steven returned from June's place to Christie Downs he moved in, with three others, to the first home purchased by the trust. It was his first time living away from Olive since his boarding school days at Kendal Grange and, as such, constituted a major change to his life. It was an exciting challenge for him, one that caused some nervousness. Over the next few years his housemates moved and were replaced by others. One married and moved out with his wife, another who worked for Phoenix was able to get a unit of his own and the third, a girl who gained employment at the Community Living office, was also able to move into her own unit. Over this period, Steven worked for several different employers doing a variety of jobs, dismantling photocopy machines, mowing lawns, gardening and making furniture. He was not too keen on the gardening but enjoyed the mechanical tasks and woodwork. Each week, under the watchful eye of his carer, he payed his rent, managed his own spending money, kept himself well groomed and played his part in keeping the house neat and tidy.

A TAFE cooking class proved a success. Steven found he had a flair for the kitchen and was soon able to prepare meals. He was particularly fond of making pasta dishes — spaghetti bolognaise was his tour de force — but sausages, curried or cooked with Chinese, Thai or chilli sauce, were also within his scope. Like any good chef he was not afraid to experiment and his clientele were generally happy with his efforts. He later did a course on mosaics and contributed to a large stone mosaic at the Christie Downs Community Centre. Steven saw Olive regularly and his carer each day. He retained his strong interest in the church and continually reminded friends that he was a Baptist.

Meanwhile Olive became friends with Kathy, a woman she had met through her sister-in-law June when she first moved to Adelaide. June had actually introduced Kathy by telephone when Frank was undergoing treatment for his heart problems in Port Macquarie. Kathy often rang, sometimes on June's behalf, to enquire about Frank's health. A spinster some few years younger than Olive, she had lived all her life with her mother, who was now in her nineties. She suffered severely from psoriasis, the worst Olive had ever seen, as well as arthritis and diabetes. Despite Kathy's wont to feel sorry for herself, Olive got on very well with her:

Kathy was covered from head to toe with psoriasis and was naturally very self-conscious because of it. She had worked for many years with the post master general's department as a telephonist. When the time came for her to cease working she bought a house with her retirement money. I was living alone so she asked me if I would look after the new house and tend to the garden while she looked after her mother in the family home. I agreed. The house was a real mess with four old pigeon coops in a backyard that had been ignored for ages. I hired some tradesmen to fix it up and planted a lovely garden that included a lot of roses. By the time they finished it was immaculate, a real showpiece. I actually won a prize for the rose garden.

When her mother died, just short of her century, Kathy sold the family home and the money was divided up between six children, none of whom ever seemed to have done anything for the old lady except Kathy. She came home to her new place and we shared the house for about eight years. She needed care because of her psoriasis and was pleased to have me as a housemate. I did the cooking, most of the housework and applied cream to her every day for all those years.

Late in 1988 Olive lost her sister-in-law June. A heavy smoker, she had succumbed to lung cancer. Her husband Bill had died two years earlier. June had been a very close friend who had always offered Olive and her family unqualified hospitality and given her strong personal support, particularly after Frank's death and then when she came back from her aborted trip to Townsville. May, her elder daughter, came out from England to attend and help organise her funeral with the twins, Eric and Bill junior, both of whom were employed by the Parks and Wildlife Organisation.

Just as May arrived at Olive's house the phone rang. Olive let her in, phone in hand. To her complete surprise the call was from government house in Canberra. Having spent almost 30 of her 62 years looking after disadvantaged people, she had been nominated for the Order of Australia Medal for her efforts. The caller had no idea who had nominated her but wished to verify that she would accept it. Though she had often been sceptical of such awards when granted to wealthy businessmen or professional sports people, all of whom seemed to Olive to have already profited by their success, she duly accepted. As soon as she hung up she explained to May what had happened and said, 'Your mother would have been so thrilled if she had been able to hear that.' To which May replied, 'Ollie, I'm sure she is listening.'

On Australia Day, 26 January 1989, Olive, dressed in a navy blue frock and accompanied by Steven and Kathy, went by bus to government house in Adelaide where she was presented with her

OAM by the state governor, General Donald Dunstan. She was one of only four South Australian women afforded the honour that year. A photograph of the presentation adorns her dining room wall. Olive invariably smiles when she looks at that photograph with the handsomely uniformed officer pinning a medal on her while she was 'thinking of all the rebels way back in my family'. She remarked to him that he too had a most impressive array of medals, words that apparently pleased him. Then followed a very pleasant reception, sipping champagne and mingling with others who had also been honoured. She continued to work tirelessly for the disadvantaged and was later honoured with life membership of the Community Living Project Inc., which said of her in an annual report:

> Olive Weston has been an unstinting advocate and supporter of the Community Living Project Inc. Olive was a key voice in the group of parents whose activism gave rise to the Project and has always made use of any opportunity to promote the needs of the people who have intellectual disabilities and their families. Olive's outstanding leadership around these issues was formally recognised on Australia Day in 1989 when she was awarded the Order of Australia Medal. Olive stands as an outstanding representative of families and has never backed away from a fight where she was convinced there was an injustice to be remedied. We are enormously grateful for your assistance and encouragement, Olive.

Olive was very pleased that attitudes were slowly changing in the community. Youngsters with minor intellectual problems, previously ignored and neglected, were being eased into the education system. Community Living Project Inc. continued to expand and was able to address specific services. Just three years after its commencement people were able to travel with staff support for weekend and extended holidays. Olive accompanied them on several occasions, including an Easter holiday weekend to Kangaroo Island:

We took a group of about eight to visit a farm and they had a breakfast of eggs they had collected that morning. It was lambing season and they saw some just a few hours old. The locals were very good to them, the bus driver showed them a possum that had been caught in a roof and was being returned to the wild. They were always excited to see animals close up. On another weekend we took them crabbing at Windang Island, north of Port Pirie. These holidays were always a huge thrill to them. Some of them had never ever flown.

Two years further on funding was approved to allow 'long-term individualised support' for a small group who had severe and multiple disabilities. In time there would be special services for the aged. Though the task of looking after those with disabilities was never ending and could never be considered adequate, the enormous progress made since those dreadful days of the early eighties gave Olive enormous satisfaction. She also continued a close involvement with the US Ex-Services Association working on committees that organised functions for Anzac Day, American Independence Day and Thanksgiving. She had also begun a project to obtain items for a proposed American Military Museum. At one stage she was on eleven committees and subcommittees.

With Steven managing well with his housemates and enjoying his newfound independence, Olive now felt no real concern leaving him alone. She and Kathy decided to travel. Despite a yearning to go overseas, Kathy had never been out of Australia. With Olive to accompany her she now had the confidence to do so. Before they left Olive decided to sell her trusty 1977 Datsun 120Y station wagon that had served her so well for seventeen years. Frank had purchased the car in Taree on the strength of Datsun's successes in the Southern Cross rallies. It had just 76 000 miles on the clock and sold to the first man who saw it for $2000, much the same price they had paid for it.

Olive and Kathy began with trips to Hong Kong and then Fiji, where they took a cruise to the outer islands to stay in a typical native bure. In 1995 they went to England, setting up base in Kent with June's daughter May, in her lovely Tudor home. From there they journeyed to Ireland to find the tiny village from which Kathy's ancestors had come, a village that now contained nothing but a small schoolhouse and a church. On they went through Belgium, France, Switzerland and Italy, returning regularly to Kent to enjoy May's hospitality.

The highlight for Kathy, a devout Catholic, was to see the Pope on his balcony in the Vatican. Olive, though also originally of the Catholic faith, was slightly less overawed. She took a number of videos of the trip. After visiting Trieste on the Adriatic Sea the pair went to Austria and Germany before returning once more to England. Kathy was also keen to see Greece so they sailed across the Adriatic to visit the famous islands and on to the border of Macedonia to witness monks living in the mountaintops. It was a wonderful trip lasting over two months. Kathy was a willing traveller and an interesting companion while Olive, as ever, was the organiser:

Going away with Kathy got me into touring mode. I met a lovely young woman from Glenelg who was the niece of a very wealthy Indian family, the Ashoks, who owned a string of luxury hotels in India. She offered to travel to India with me as my guide and interpreter. She had another friend coming with us who helped finance her trip by buying jewellery to be resold in Adelaide. Because of the stories that Frank and June had told me, I had always wanted to see the country. The journey gave me a connection with Frank and his childhood but irrespective of this it would still have been a wonderful experience.

Having decided to go I thought, Hang the expense; I'll make it a five-star trip. It was something I would do only once. We flew to Bombay and stayed in the diplomatic enclave of the beautiful Taj Mahal Hotel. On the very first morning I sat having a cool drink in the foyer when in walked three Arabian sheiks, dressed in traditional robes, followed, in single file, by about 20 women who were obviously their wives and concubines. The women were followed by about ten children. I was told they regularly came across from Saudi Arabia to get away from the heat to holiday in Bombay. God knows what it would have cost them. Anyway, they set the scene for a very different kind of holiday.

We went on to Aurangabad to visit the Ellora and Ajanta Caves which were absolutely fabulous. They were thousands of years old. One featured ancient ornate carvings, the other rock paintings. A day or so later we were scheduled to fly to Udaipur to stay at the palace in the middle of Lake Pichhola. We left at eight in the morning for what was normally a two-hour trip but as it was Indian Independence Day, and because of a fear of Pakistani terrorists, all the timetables had been drastically altered. We flew over Udaipur right out to Jodhpur then sat in the plane for an hour surrounded by armed military personnel. Next we were flown to Jaipur and again we waited in the plane for an hour. Eventually at half past four that afternoon we arrived back at Udaipur. It was a bit nerve-wracking but it was worth it.

We had a week in Udaipur and I saw as many palaces as I could. Though we were tourists I was able to imagine the situation when

Frank was a boy and the maharajah and his family were looked after by twelve or fourteen servants. It was impossible to imagine such opulence. We then flew on to Jaipur, site of the famous pink palaces, and had dinner with Maharajah Jai Singh in his palace. He was a charming man. During dinner I noticed several men being very busy. Though I didn't speak to any of them I somehow found their manner slightly different. It came as quite a surprise when I found they were eunuchs. The hotel at Jaipur was air-conditioned and I used to turn it off and open a window. Each time I went out and returned the window would be shut and the air-conditioning running. When I told the chief porter I preferred the fresh, warm air he said, 'Oh no, Memsahib, you must never leave the window open, never.' Then he showed me several large monkeys by the tennis court and said, 'The monkeys come in and steal things and I get into much trouble, Memsahib.' At Jaipur I rode on an elephant up the mountain to Amber Fort. She was a lovely old thing about 80 years old.

Of course we had to see Agra and the Taj Mahal. Like everybody else I'd seen magazine photographs and television footage of the building but nothing can prepare you for its magnitude and magnificence. All the time we were staying in beautiful hotels arranged by my guide. We spent a day at Fatehur Sikri, a beautiful, perfectly preserved ghost town a half-hour's drive from Agra, which had been deserted for centuries. It had been built by the Emperor Akbar who invaded from Persia. The sense of history was amazing. I was sitting on a wall dressed in all white, contemplating just how different it was to anything in our culture, when I saw some mongooses become animated and assumed they had seen a snake. Suddenly a large party of teenage schoolgirls, who were on an excursion from Portuguese Goa, appeared. I don't know who they thought I was but one after the other they came up to me and stopped, clasping their hands in front of them in what was obviously a very polite greeting. I responded to each one in the same manner. I found later this greeting was called namaaste or namaskar.

From Agra we caught a special train to Delhi and then flew on to Srinagar in Kashmir to see the Shalimar gardens also built by Akbar in the fifteenth century. We hired a taxi that took us to Gulmarg, right on the border of Pakistan, which has the highest altitude golf club in the world. Because we were so close to the border there was a lot of military activity. Our party took ponies up into the Himalayas where we stayed in a luxurious houseboat at Dal Lake. It was absolutely fantastic. We trekked up into Tibet to Leh and Ladakh, but the rarefied atmosphere was too much for me and I got nosebleeds so we came back down.

We returned to Srinagar from Tibet and flew back to Delhi on a huge jumbo with surprisingly few passengers. We left about six-thirty in the morning and there would have been only about 40 people aboard. As we approached Delhi the captain thanked us for flying Air India and then said how pleased he was to have us on his first flight as captain. I wondered if it was common knowledge and whether the next flight might be better patronised.

It was one of the most wonderful months of my life even though it cost a good deal of money. Having my Indian-speaking friend with me made all the difference and it was just wonderful to see such different culture and also to go to the places where Frank had grown up. Ironically my two nephews, Eric and Bill, were backpacking through India at the same time so I told them, 'Don't you dare come looking for your aunty if you get into any bother. I'm going five-star and I'll be too busy living it up in luxury to help.'

For all her years in Adelaide Olive retained membership of the Australian American Ex-Services Association and her friendship with American servicemen whose ranks were slowly dwindling. She never missed the dawn service and Anzac Day marches and often attended special luncheons and dinners for visiting dignitaries as well as celebrations of important occasions from the Second World War. In 1995 she was invited by the association to take part in the fiftieth anniversary of the Allies' victory in the Pacific. Victory over Japan was now called Victory in the Pacific due to the political correctness of those whom Olive described as 'the gutless lot in Canberra'. She wondered what the victims of Buna and Gona, or the nurses who were slaughtered on Bangka Island, might think of the name change from VJ Day to VP Day. To Olive it would always be VJ Day. Do-gooders rewriting history for the sake of political correctness was one of her pet hates. She made her own way to Brisbane for the celebrations as service- and ex-servicemen and women came from all over Australia, America, England, New Zealand and Canada. A huge, enthusiastic crowd witnessed the ticker tape parade up Brisbane's main street:

It was a fantastic day. To see the heroes who had saved Australia given due recognition was wonderful. It's just too easy to take for granted what people had given their lives for. I couldn't believe the politicians had changed the name. I think it is insulting to those who died to be worrying about who might be offended. They were a brutal enemy who never showed remorse and who never admitted guilt. Their kids were never taught what had happened in World War II. When they eventually surrendered and the POWs were rescued in Sumatra, where so many had died of starvation in the camps, they found thousands of unopened Red Cross parcels with food that could have saved their lives. In contrast the bodies of the Japanese submariners who died in the midget subs when the *Kuttabul* was torpedoed in Sydney Harbour were cremated with full military honours and their ashes shipped back to their relatives. And we had to go along with a name change so as not to upset them!

Seven years later she would accept an invitation to celebrate the sixtieth anniversary of the Battle of the Coral Sea. Olive again paid her own way, this time to Townsville, to sail on the American battleship *Blue Ridge*, one of several visiting American warships, out into the Coral Sea where wreaths were thrown overboard. This time there was no cheering, no ticker tape parade but a very solemn and emotive ceremony. She was among guests entertained on board by Admiral Clements and his wife and was very moved by the occasion. She wondered how many young Australians knew just how close that battle had been fought to the Australian coast and how vital it was to the freedom they now enjoyed.

While in Townsville she took the opportunity to visit the Strand, the entire length of which was now meticulously landscaped with well-kept lawns and palm trees. On the far northern end, where the giant US landing barges had disgorged their cargo of trucks and heavy machinery in 1942, was the magnificent, large, rock pool named after the Rats of Tobruk. She stood on Kissing Point at the top of Jezzine Army Barracks and looked across towards Magnetic Island, imagining the 261 ships waiting to take MacArthur and his troops back to the Philippines. A monument removed from the original war cemetery at Belgian Gardens, dedicated to the American servicemen, now stood on top of Kissing Point.

In February 1997, just five months short of her 71st birthday, Olive required a triple bypass operation. It came as a complete surprise to her as she had not felt ill and her family had no history of heart problems. She had not had a solitary cigarette since her hypnotherapy session in Sydney 25 years earlier and regarded herself as a moderate drinker. Quality red wine from the McLaren Vale and two glasses of Scotch before bed were her only vices. She was not happy about the prospect and told her surgeon, 'You'd better make sure I come out of this, I've got a lot to do yet.' Her words were completely genuine. She was still vitally involved with the Community Living Project and she had much more in mind to ensure Steven's future. Not surprisingly she took the heart operation in her stride and recovered well, though slowly as one her age would expect.

During her convalescence in the peaceful surrounds of College Gardens Private Hospital, Olive had plenty of time to look back on her life. It was something she had seldom done. She knew that she had spent a great deal of her time caring for others but had never deliberately thought about how much. Now she did. There was Betty as a child and then again in later life when her parents were gone, the young American GIs, thousands of miles from their loved ones, Freddy at the Mater Hospital and the polio victims in Brisbane, even the Barnardo's Homes girl, the broken Englishwoman and the young boy returning home on her trip to England. Of course there was Steven, who had been with her for over 40 years, along with the countless disadvantaged people in Sydney and Adelaide. Then there was Frank, invalided for the last fourteen years of his life and more recently Kathy. She had never planned to live her life caring for or assuming responsibility for others. Being a fatalist she simply believed it was meant to be. She saw herself as nothing more or less than a humanitarian. Nevertheless she now decided she must put herself first for a while:

I thought I should take it easy and worry about my own health rather than anyone else's. I came home from the hospital after two months and found Kathy sitting there expecting me to cook for her. I knew Steven was living on his own so I rang and asked if he would like his mum to come home. He was very pleased at the thought so I told Kathy I'd be leaving. She wasn't happy but I'd made up my mind. I returned to the house at Christie Downs to be home with my big boy again.

Steven's section of the house was completely self-contained and he had become very independent. He set his alarm and prepared himself for work each day. He had tasks in the house he regarded as his own and was upset if I infringed on his responsibilities. Washing up was his domain, as was putting out the garbage and the dog. The cat stayed in. He sometimes cooked dinner and was quite adamant his cooking skills were superior to mine on certain dishes. I was happy to let him think so. His carer came in regularly to assist with certain things he could not handle.

The bypass operation had ended Olive's marching days so from then on she travelled by army jeep on Anzac Day. US veterans' numbers continued to diminish but some were still plugging on in typical military fashion. Their enthusiasm, thirst, and the ability to quench it, remained at a high level. On 1 September the same year as her operation, Olive received a phone call from John Sharkey in Perth, president of the Allied Armed Forces Trust:

I was amazed to be told I had been awarded the OOA, the Order of the Officer of Arms, and I would be getting a certificate authenticating my award together with verification that I had earned title to a plot of land on one of the Royal Estates in England. I had to make a one-off taxation payment of £40 sterling for the plot that would be handed down to my next of kin when I died. I'd never actually heard of it before. I'd seen the Sergeant of Arms carry the mace into the British parliament and discovered that though he could become a Master of Arms he could never aspire to being an Officer of Arms. I was assured that only five Australian men had received the honour and no women at all. Among other privileges listed on the citation was an entitlement to sit on a military court-martial, not that I saw any likelihood of that happening. The certificate actually refers to me as Lord of the Manor, substantiating the fact that women were not expected to receive it. It was strictly military and granted in recognition of almost 60 years continuous membership of the Allied Armed Forces Trust.

I saw this as a membership never to be relinquished. The president, Dick Chugg, and I had established the US Services War Memorial Museum in Port Adelaide. The authorities at the Military Vehicle Museum were good enough to give us an annex in their building into which we put uniforms, memorabilia and paraphernalia pertaining to American and Australian involvement in the world wars. We worked on that project for probably four years. Through a friend of mine in the military I was able to get a complete nurse's uniform from World War I that we displayed in the American section and a WAAF's uniform from World War II that went into the other section. Obviously this had a lot to do with the award but seeing it eventuate was a reward in itself. Still, I had to admit I was really thrilled to be recognised in this way. Frank would have loved it. I had four military medals I wore on parade but the OAM and the OOA meant much more to me. I was the only Australian woman to receive the OOA and one of only four South Australian women to receive the OAM in that year.

In a subsequent phone call Olive was advised that an American serviceman in Oregon was also to receive the OOA that year. John Sharkey, a previous recipient of the OOA, flew to London to pick up her certificate from Lord Barclay Beales, a member of the House of Lords who managed the Queen Mother's estates. Upon his arrival back in Perth he posted it on to her. She will never see the plot of land, it is symbolic, but she regards it as a great honour. She was the only Lady of the Manor. Steven had some difficulty understanding that he would one day be Lord of the Manor. He was far more interested in his local surroundings, his work at the furniture factory and an occasional light beer with Mum at the RSL or the local tavern.

If there was any suggestion of Olive slowing down a little it was soon to be dispelled. Early in 2000 she was approached to stand for state parliament on behalf of the newly formed United Australia Party. Brigadier Ellis from the Royal United Services Institute formed the party because of his frustration with the major parties, particularly the government, whom he believed had lost touch with the needs of the electorate. When Olive was approached at Keswick Barracks she asked, 'Why me?' The brigadier said, 'Olive, I've spoken to you about politics here in South Australia and I know many of our ideas are very much the same. I'm looking for people with enough nous and determination to form a party to give the average person an alternative to what we've been putting up with.' Here was another challenge:

We sat down to talk about it and I believed he was right in most of his assessments. The state government had been in power for a long time and was tired. We both felt money was being spent unwisely, wasted on unnecessary things and denied in other areas where it should have been spent. We agreed the only way to make our point was to get some new people elected into the lower house. We found plenty of people were interested and willing to stand. They all felt nobody was listening to the average person. The major parties were running around like chooks with their heads cut off screaming about law and order as usual. It's amazing how they become fanatical about law and order each election time. I stood for the seat of Wright and we stated our case as best we could on radio. There was a good deal of dissatisfaction with the government and we had 20 or 30 candidates but unfortunately none of us was elected. Just the same, I learned a lot.

When the federal elections came around the following year I was asked by several associates to stand as an independent. I was immediately tempted mainly, though not solely, because of my dislike of the GST. I'd seen the English version, the VAT, and I was appalled by it. I'd been warning friends for ages about the GST, which I regarded then, and still do, as a very unfair tax on the lower income earners and pensioners. I realised it would also have a very negative effect on agencies like our Community Living Project Inc. Commercial operations could pass on the cost of the GST but non-profit organisations couldn't do so. Even when the government was saying they wouldn't introduce it, I had no doubt they would try when they thought it was politically safe. I kept telling people, 'It's only a matter of time.' Then when it became part of government policy I told people how damaging it had been in England, New Zealand and Canada. It was a real concern to me.

Then I was absolutely incensed when they spent all that money sending every Tom, Dick and Harry to London with their wives at the taxpayers' expense to celebrate the Federation of Australia. I'd never seen a greater waste of money on pomp and ceremony. An estimated two million dollar junket was now costing more like three and a half million. They would have been staying at the best pubs in London. I thought of all the times we'd battled to get a few thousand dollars for the disadvantaged who needed it desperately. I also thought it was criminal how much money was spent by the government advertising their achievements in the months leading up to the election. Every time you turned on the TV there they were, spending our money, telling us what a great job they were doing. I was in my mid seventies and didn't need the angst but I thought, What the hell, Ollie, either do something about it or shut up.

So I stood on a platform of education, unemployment, particularly among the youth, and the disgraceful lack of funding for hospitals, which naturally was a hobbyhorse of mine. When the *Tampa* arrived with the 'children overboard' saga I believed people were falling for the greatest con job ever. Suddenly nothing else seemed to matter to anyone except the refugee problem. The press couldn't talk about anything else. You would have thought a boatload of refugees was the entire Japanese navy. This was classic politics. When you've got a problem in one area you find a diversion.

I told everyone to forget the very convenient refugee melodrama and worry about other issues and of course the GST. I did three separate interviews on the ABC in Adelaide. They must have seen me as interesting, they paid my cab fares. My lovely twin boys, Eric and Bill, helped me campaign for the seat of Kingston, driving me around all over the place for weeks prior to the election. We handed out pamphlets at different churches and I kept saying, 'Beware of the GST.' People were saying the tax bill would not get through anyway, it would be blocked in the senate, but how could you be sure? When I felt passionate about things I didn't see any sense in standing back hoping someone else would solve the problem.

Being an independent I got phone calls from other parties trying to get me to explain exactly why I was standing and where my preference votes would be directed. I always answered the same. I had a right to stand and I would advise on preferences when I was good and ready. I spoke to the Democrats, who were apparently going to block the GST in the senate but I had doubts that deals might be done later on. As it turned out I wasn't totally naive, was I? Despite a lot of asking, no one knew where I was directing preferences until we handed out our cards on polling day. In fact some never found out. Even months after the election, a journalist in Canberra rang me trying to find out about my preference votes.

At the same time Betty was dying in the nursing home. I didn't know if I was Arthur or Martha at that stage and had to get my solicitor to make Betty's funeral arrangements. Betty actually died on the day of the election, so I wasn't even able to have a drink with the friends who had helped me campaign. On the day there were something like 30 booths and we visited all of them. As it turned out I didn't get the four percent of votes needed to get my $450 bond back but my preference votes proved crucial. David Cox, the Labor candidate, also firmly against the GST, won by a few hundred votes so I was pleased I'd stood. I'd given it my best shot without engaging in any political gobbledegook or doing any deals with anybody. I knew I'd done my bit to try to stop the GST. You can't always win but you can always try.

The Community Living Project Inc. was now operating on an annual budget of almost a million dollars. It employed a chief executive officer, two full-time administrators, two full-time and two part-time coordinators and 33 support workers. These support workers, some employed full time, others on a part-time or casual basis, often worked with just one individual. Funding, predominantly from government, was complemented by donations from community members and businesses. The efforts of that dedicated bunch of parents wishing to create a worthwhile life and a secure future for their handicapped children had initiated and inspired a result even Olive could not have foreseen:

It is just marvellous how it has panned out. Everybody in the southern region has benefited. People who were simply abandoned now have support in all sorts of areas. We were very lucky to employ Ross Wormesley, who had had experience living with people in one of the first group houses in South Australia, and Jayne Barrett, virtually from the first day. Not all but many of our staff are parents or relatives of disabled children and they have tremendous empathy with the group. Many have actually lost children during the time of their involvement but have remained, working in paid or honorary capacities. Because of their own personal experiences they can relate to those with similar problems. This was not the case with Ross, our chief executive officer, but we sensed he too had the empathy needed and we were proven right.

Ross's recollections of those early days are still very clear:

> I guess there was a sense among all of us that we did not know exactly what we were getting ourselves into. In the case of the families involved in the PODs group, they had always seen themselves as wanting to support the service without having to run it themselves. I think they hoped the organisation would just happen. This was certainly not the case. Their input was needed more than ever. Being a support group is one thing, being a service provider is something else again. Their commitment could never be questioned but they now assumed different responsibilities. PODs actually sponsored the project for the first six months as the separate incorporations took shape. It was a new and complicated situation and leadership from people like Olive, Jill Wishart, Ray Brooks and others was very strong and absolutely invaluable. Their connections to the project have remained to this day.
>
> There are still not enough resources to allow us to address so much that still needs to be addressed. We face frustrations every day and probably always will. The political clout of the old established institutions is something understood only by those closely involved. They have no desire to relinquish this power.

There are too many vested interests to see many of them closed. Sadly, bureaucracy reacting to pressure from these vested interests has eroded some of the decisive early initiatives taken by Senator Grimes, who was an absolutely outstanding minister. Despite all the effort, institutionalising and incarcerating people who have substantial needs is still seen by some as an option. There would have to be far greater commitment to the problems of intellectually disadvantaged and physically handicapped people by all sorts of establishments, particularly government, to correct this situation. It is something that would take enormous political leadership.

Still, there is absolutely no doubt all the effort has been worthwhile. In many instances the lives of parents and their children have been greatly enriched. In some other instances we've actually saved lives. There are now quite a number of organisations across Australia that operate with a much stronger allegiance to the interests of handicapped people. Pioneers such as Olive must take great heart from what has been achieved.

Jayne Barrett says of the project:

I was employed in June 1984, the same month as Ross, and I guess the fact that we're both still here says something about how rewarding it has been. The size and shape of the operation has changed enormously in that time and some adjustments have been difficult but the underlying reasons for being here don't really change. To contemplate moving on to a different job would mean not only leaving the people we are working directly with, but also a whole network of parents and wonderful families who we've grown so close to. That would be very difficult and would cause great sadness.

With the southern region now expertly managed it might be thought that Olive would be happy to sit back and relax. Not yet. She still had a couple of goals to accomplish. The first concerned the recognition of some truly remarkable women who had played outstanding roles in the fight for the freedom enjoyed in the free world. The other was to do with Steven's future.

Chapter Nine

KAPUNDA

In the early months of 2000, in the quiet and historic township of Kapunda, a leisurely hour's drive north of Adelaide, a committee was formed to honour their most famous citizen. Kapunda was a most interesting town. An eight-metre high statue of a Cornish miner standing at the entry to the township is testimony to Kapunda's rich copper mining industry which began in the 1840s and generated enormous wealth for several decades. The richness of the ore, originally transported to Swansea in Wales for smelting, made Kapunda one of the most important towns in South Australia and contributed greatly to the state's development. Later Sir Sidney Kidman, owner of pastoral stations so vast that they were reported to have covered more land than the entire British Isles, ran his cattle empire from Kapunda. In recent years it had continued to prosper as a service town for the surrounding rural area, its population steady at around 2000. With its well-known history and many features preserved from the past, it has remained a favourite with tourists, as six hotels and several excellent bed-and-breakfasts confirm.

Despite the town's enormous significance during the state's early development, its most famous citizen was a modest military nurse, 'an ordinary person thrust into an extraordinary situation'— Sister Vivian Bullwinkel, to whom a plaque was to be dedicated in Kapunda's main street. Now 84 years old, Vivian, who had been living in Perth for many years, was the most celebrated and revered of all Australia's wartime nurses. She was the only survivor when 21 nursing comrades were massacred by the Japanese at Bangka Island as they attempted to evacuate from Singapore. Unarmed noncombatants who had survived the sinking of their rescue ship the *Vyner Brooke*, they had been captured, marched into the sea and machine-gunned in the back. Having miraculously survived, she later saw no option but to surrender and join other nurses to spend three and a half years as a prisoner-of-war in a series of wretched jungle camps. Her nursing career continued long after the war and it was for this as much as her remarkable courage in service that she was to be honoured.

On the Bullwinkel committee was Ron Humphries, father-in-law of Olive's nephew Bill. Ron suggested they could hardly find a more appropriate person to join the group than Olive. She was an ex-army nurse with many military contacts in Adelaide who knew Vivian and she had more experience on committees than could be imagined. He assured them she was just the person to vitalise the committee and had also been highly successful at raising government money. Olive was duly contacted and only too happy to contribute.

Though Olive had no significant personal association with Kapunda she knew country towns generally had great pride in their heritage and undertook her task with typical vigour. Here she met another committeeman, Charles Smythe, always referred to by his friends as Chas, an antique dealer with a very artistic sense and a desire to get on with things. She was immediately impressed by the attitude of this big, distinguished looking man whose pride in the township was so obvious.

Meanwhile she had been invited to the unveiling and dedication of what she considered to be a long overdue memorial in Canberra to the nurses who had served Australia in wartime. It annoyed her immensely that the memorial would be unveiled almost 100 years, and two World Wars, after the first recorded death of an Australian nurse at the Boer War. Nevertheless she was very pleased to attend. Among the World War II nurses there were Jean Ashton, Pat Darling, Wilma Young, Betty Bradwell and Vivian Bullwinkel. Also attending was Major Vivienne Holmes, with whom Olive had often spoken following her trip to Adelaide shortly after Frank's death. Here Olive had her first contact with Ita Buttrose:

Ita presided over the ceremony and did the job marvellously. It was a very grand occasion attended by the governor-general, Sir William Deane, the prime minister, the chief of the defence force and a host of top brass from all three services. A huge number of service and ex-service nurses had come from all over Australia with the World War II POW nurses having pride of place in the front row. Young volunteer nurses paraded in uniforms worn from the time of the Boer War until the present. Another 101 volunteers each carried a flag to honour those nurses who had given their lives in service. The ABC televised the event and there must have been a thousand people present. The most moving part for me was the laying of wreaths as the choir sang 'The Captive's Hymn', a lovely haunting hymn written by Margaret Dryburgh, a missionary who had been a POW at Palembang. It was a day to give long overdue, official recognition to the women of war. Even the catafalque party, marching out in slow time to guard the four corners of the stage, consisted of four servicewomen.

Ita Buttrose felt as Olive did about the length of time the veteran nurses had been forced to wait for such recognition:

> The government had spent years talking about it without getting anywhere. Margaret Read, who was president of the senate, rang me and asked would I become chairperson of the fundraising committee. I had no idea what the hell I was taking on but I didn't want a government job and didn't care what I said so I got on with it. In 1997 I became the Chairwoman of the Australian Service Nurses National Memorial Fund Committee. It was an extremely difficult job because, frankly, people just didn't want to know. Fortunately we had some wonderful women all over Australia running state committees and organising different fundraisers. We had a national button day on 15 August, VE Day. I was actually at the Cenotaph collecting from the diggers, as I recall. We badgered the federal government and the unions. In fact we badgered everybody.
>
> Within two years we had raised the two million dollars needed and had a national contest for design of the monument. It was appalling how long the World War II nurses had waited, so to see them there in the front row, wearing their medals, bursting with pride, was absolutely wonderful. It was a marvellous day for them. They did think they had been forgotten. They never suggested they'd acted with any special

bravery; the only claim they made at all was that but for them and other nurses who had passed on, a lot of the diggers would not have returned. The memorial recognises the efforts of all nurses but that contribution by the World War II nurses was extremely significant.

Following the opening of the memorial in Canberra, Ita and Olive spoke several times on the phone. When Olive came to Sydney's Sheraton on the Park Hotel to a military medical symposium she invited Ita to be her guest. Wilma Young and Pat Darling spoke with authority and pride of the now antiquated nursing methods used in the field and station hospitals in World War II. Hospitals that took several days to set up in those years were now established in a matter of hours. While Olive was recognised from the podium it took encouragement from Ita before she was inclined to speak about her own wartime experience among the table guests:

I'd learned a bit about her by now but she was very modest about her achievements. She was as quiet as a lamb until I dragged it out of her and then they were all fascinated by her story and asked her what General MacArthur was really like and so on. Those women were amazing, they didn't seem to think things were tough, they didn't complain, they just got on with things. I'm not sure they make these women anymore. They're just very special. Olive asked me to compere the ceremony for Vivian Bullwinkel in Kapunda and I got to know her and Chas Smythe really well through that. They both had enormous get up and go.

Upon her return to Adelaide, Olive travelled across to Perth to deliver Vivian's invitation personally. Both looked forward with tremendous enthusiasm to the event. It was one of Australia's saddest days when Vivian passed away in Perth's Hollywood Private Hospital on 3 July, just ten days before she was to come to Kapunda. Olive flew back to Perth to attend her funeral, then returned to speak on behalf of Vivian and the other World War II nurses when Ita Buttrose presided over a very moving occasion in Kapunda, made extremely sad because of Vivian's absence.

The unveiling of the memorial plaque by the state governor, Sir Eric Neal, took place on 13 July and ran with military precision. Olive had prepared her address which she altered after Vivian's death only to realise she had left it in the boot of the car in which she had been driven to the ceremony:

I'd been rushed off my feet in that very hectic week and I'd stayed up until eleven o'clock the previous night to make sure I'd do Vivian justice. As soon as the driver took off I realised what I had done so had to ad lib my tribute to her. When I explained this to the crowd they saw the humour of it. Ita was very kind explaining what a hectic week I'd had. Despite my small misadventure it was a lovely ceremony, which went off without a hitch. Tributes from the prime minister and the leader of the opposition were read to the crowd and all the speakers gave wonderful tributes to Vivian that would no doubt have embarrassed her enormously.

While in Kapunda, Olive was invited to see the War Memorial Gardens in Dutton Park, dedicated in 1918 to those who had lost their lives in the First World War. She was dismayed at its condition:

I was as embarrassed as they should have been to see how rundown it was. There wasn't a flower or a blade of grass to be seen by the large stone obelisk that paid tribute to the fallen. The path was a mixture of clay and red dust with the jagged roots of a tree that had been dug up lying opposite. A lonely looking native shrub sat five paces behind the monument and three palms, 20 metres apart, provided the only other pieces of greenery. What had obviously been an important feature of the town in 1918 had been sadly neglected. Directly across the road the cricket ground was green enough but this looked like a quarry. I decided that a memorial to the fallen in a place like Kapunda simply could not be left in this state.

With Charles Smythe, with whom I had become very firm friends, I immediately formed the Memorial Gardens Committee to restore and expand the site, and to plan an opening ceremony befitting the birthplace of such a wonderful woman as Vivian Bullwinkel. The following year, 2001, would see the centenary of federation as well as that of the Australian army, so it would be extremely appropriate to have this happen in that year. When Charles was made director of the Kapunda Festival we became determined to incorporate the opening of the gardens in the festival celebrations. I rang Reg McColl, an old friend who was a retired captain from the reserve army at Keswick Barracks. When I first joined the United Services Institute Reg was on the committee and later asked me to be a councillor with him. I served for two years and only resigned because I was snowed under with so many other committees at the time. He was very efficient with a great understanding of military matters so I knew he'd be perfectly suited to our committee at Kapunda. Reg agreed to be my vice chairman.

Our aim was not just to fix up what was there, but to make something very special. After several meetings we decided to create a path, dedicated to Vivian, which would lead from the front entrance to a beautiful fountain. The path would then split and go around the fountain with the left dedicated to Jean Ashton and the right to Nancy Wake. When they met, the path that led to a monument supporting the bust of an army nurse would be dedicated to all those nurses who had been lost in wartime. The coloured, concrete tile paths would be surrounded by lawns and gardens in which 101 roses would honour each nurse who had died in service from the Boer War until the end of the Second World War.

We couldn't have selected three more deserving recipients of the honour. After the war Vivian had continued her nursing, serving with various nursing and hospital authorities and the Red Cross for 50 years. No one did the things Vivian did. She was awarded the OAM, the MBE and the Florence Nightingale Medal. She was a marvellous woman who gave her whole life to humanitarian services. Jean Ashton was the senior officer in the prison camps in Sumatra, having also survived the sinking of the *Vyner Brooke*. She and Vivian had spent three and a half years together as prisoners of the Japanese. Her leadership and discipline, under the most hostile and humiliating conditions, were an inspiration, not only to her fellow nurses, but also to the civilian women in the camps. Nancy Wake, born in New Zealand and brought up in Australia, had returned to live in Port Macquarie after the war, which is where I met her. Her exploits while working with the French Resistance showed courage beyond belief. She was twice awarded the French Croix de Guerre and was the most highly decorated woman of the Second World War.

I was determined to get the job done and I really thought we should get substantial government and private assistance. We had meticulous plans drawn up with a realistic schedule that would enable us to finish the job in time for the celebration on 23 September 2001, twelve months hence. The estimated cost was $89 000. For this figure we would create a beautifully landscaped park with the four walks, a fountain with three tiers supported by swans and the brass bust of the army nurse. We also planned to add a plaque to the existing obelisk showing the names of all the men

239

from Kapunda who had lost their lives in World War I. Again I asked Ita to be our compere and of course she agreed. She had a wonderful sense of community and had been awarded the MBE because of all the voluntary work she did.

The Light Regional Council, with its headquarters in Kapunda, were fully behind the project and in early December the CEO provided a most supportive letter, a copy of which we were able to include in our appeals for money. It made particular mention of how proud they were 'to have Mrs Olive Weston OAM, OOA, JP, as chairperson and acknowledges her role on the committee as being a key patron in obtaining much-needed funding for this important project'.

The year 2001 was to be one of continuous celebrations. A century of federation was too good a chance to miss and official functions were held throughout the country for twelve months. The most lavish and expensive was the one that sent politicians, public servants and various 'dignitaries' to London. It was the extravagance of this event that annoyed me so much as to be a catalyst for my sortie into federal politics. But I felt very different about occasions to recognise people whose national efforts had been largely overlooked. I saw the dedication of the Kapunda Memorial Gardens was one such occasion.

Our first goal was to raise some money so I put a piece in the Adelaide press:

Calling all Ex-Servicemen and Good Samaritans

As this is the Centenary of Federation and the Centenary of the Australian Army, we few volunteer citizens of a small South Australian country town of Kapunda (the birthplace of Sister Vivian Bullwinkel) took up the challenge to re-establish the World War I War Memorial Gardens at Kapunda and at the same time to honour the 77 World War II nurses who gave their short lives for their country by paying the *Supreme Sacrifice* for freedom and democracy.

We have acquired a quote for $80 000 plus, for a fountain, honour rolls, plaque and bust of a nurse. We are looking for sponsorship and donations to establish these War Memorial Gardens to be opened by our own governor, Sir Eric Neal, on 23 September 2001. That is *if* we are able to raise the said monies to enable this to take place. All donations and grants will be recognised — donations of $2, $5 and $10+ will all add up. We want to show that these nurses did not die in vain so let's honour them and show that we care. We have one hundred and fifty thousand (150 000) Flanders Field poppy seeds as the highlight of this very important Memorial Gardens event.

For each $5 donated high school students will plant ten Flanders Field poppies and these have to be in by Anzac Day 2001 so that they will be blooming for the Centenary of Federation celebrations in September. All donations will be recognised with a certificate of appreciation.

Returned service veterans and others contributed around $2000, for which the committee was very appreciative. It was a start for our bank account. We also received a letter from Kapunda, addressed to 'Dear Lady Weston', which offered different but very important support:

Allow me to introduce myself. I am Daph Whitehead, Assistant Leader, Midland Region, Guides South Australia. You and I talked at Kapunda's Australia Day breakfast where we discussed the viability of putting up a plaque for the 'Women of the

Nation' on the Memorial Wall at Kapunda's War Memorial Gardens. Of course, I already knew you, having been present at the dedication of the Memorial to Sister Vivian Bullwinkel last year.

Now that's all the formalities taken care of, I can expand on the reason for this letter. Chas Smythe and I have had a number of conversations on how our Guides can contribute to the events yet to come in Kapunda and it was during one of these that, while listening to Chas give his reasons behind supporting this 'Wall of Remembrance' and wondering who was going to carry on the 'Spirit' of all you ladies who gave so much for Australia during the war, that I suddenly thought — the Guides could.

We could charge each and every one of our members with keeping this spirit alive in their hearts and in their communities, and in so doing, would help to achieve a similar united front as was evident during the war years.

It would put a new dimension into the making of our Promise as we pledge to *Serve God, Queen and Country* and give a tangible reason for participating in Anzac and Remembrance Day services, and best of all, it could be passed on to future generations.

I was thrilled to pieces. Having the Girl Guides to look after the gardens was a marvellous idea. We approached the state and federal governments for money. The local federal member was Neil Andrew, who was the speaker in the house of representatives. We realised his position as speaker of the house carried some weight so we had some optimism there. The local state member was Ivan Venning, who was also in government so we thought he too might find some joy in championing our cause. Neil Andrew immediately sent a letter expressing his pleasure at the prospect of the establishment of the gardens and endorsing our fundraising efforts. I told Charles Smythe we had every reason to be confident. We both soon had reason to worry that such confidence might be misplaced. Both Neil Andrew and Ivan Venning were very pleasant and offered a lot of encouragement but getting cash was a different matter. The state government, which had previously contributed $2000 to the original Bullwinkel project the previous year, was able to contribute absolutely nothing.

In May it was announced that the federal government had agreed to grant $25 000 to approximately 10 000 Australian POWs still alive from World War II. This was almost 60 years after they had been captured and they had been battling for compensation since the seventies, having discovered a treaty, signed in 1951, that precluded them from seeking any compensation from the Japanese. Mind you, at least this government had done it whereas a succession of previous ones had not. I rang Neil Andrew to ask if $75 000, the allocation for just three persons, could be made available from this money and explained my reason for asking.

Nurse Betty Jeffrey, who wrote that wonderful book *White Coolies* after serving as a prisoner-of-war in Sumatra, died three months before Vivian. Nurse Wilma Young, another survivor from the *Vyner Brooke* who had spent three and a half years as a POW also died as she was waiting to attend the celebration in Kapunda. She had been widowed for many years. Vivian's husband Frank had died eight months before Vivian. I suggested to Neil Andrew that their $75 000 would be appropriately spent on a memorial for the very women for whom the money had been earmarked.

There was a clause that said where a POW had died, the $25 000 would be deposited into their estates provided their spouses had been alive in February 2001. These three brave nurses were technically ineligible but I thought surely their entitlements need not go back into consolidated revenue and said so. The answer was yes they did.

When it became clear we were struggling for money the knockers came out of the woodwork. Chas began to get a lot of criticism, which I thought was most unfair. I was also bitterly disappointed that not one service club in the Kapunda district chose to assist in funding the project. It was obvious we would have to make some compromises in the plans for the gardens. Two gazebos on the perimeter of the park were omitted, hopefully to be added at a later date, and work on the outer gardens was curtailed. Nevertheless we were not about to give up.

The federal government, through Neil Andrew, found us $11 000 in the form of two different grants, and then on 11 September, another cheque for $2000 from the department of veterans' affairs' 'Their Service — Our Heritage' program. That was it! I thought it was pathetic, they thought it was very generous. I then read an article in which it was proposed that $6.4 million be spent on a memorial for the Australian troops in London. We were only ever looking for $89 000 and in fact just $25 000 would have covered our immediate debts.

Apart from the frustration of dealing with politicians, I made little progress dealing with the Kapunda Council. We locked horns on several occasions. I was amazed when council hired a consultancy firm adding additional cost without even discussing it with me. After all, I was the chairperson. Their consultants account contained meetings with people I hadn't even heard of. We were continually knocked back on our requests to use council machinery. It was just never available. People I spoke to who had dealt with other councils just could not believe it. We had to hire earth-moving machinery from private sources. Not once was our committee granted any favour with council equipment.

Still we pushed on. The financial shortfall put tremendous pressure on us but while some were inclined to pack it in, the three old hardheads, Charles, my deputy chairman Captain Reg McColl and I were determined to see the thing through. And, somehow, we did. We finished up a long way out of pocket but rather than have the whole thing fall to pieces we kept on finding ways to make progress while we fought to get further assistance. When the council eventually picked up a tab for roughly $5000, we had raised just on $21 000 and we had needed $89 000! By reducing our plans and with the help of some really talented tradesmen who worked voluntarily, we were finished with a couple of days to spare. The knockers went back into the woodwork and the backslappers came out. Still, the fact that it looked so wonderful and was dedicated to such worthy people was all that mattered in the end. We flew Nancy down from Port Macquarie, Major Vivienne Holmes from Perth and Ita from Sydney for the official opening.

Kapunda's six-day Centenary celebrations began on Tuesday and culminated in the opening of the memorial gardens on Sunday. Olive joined Nancy Wake and Charles Smythe in the official opening of the celebrations on Tuesday morning as well as the openings of art and photographic exhibitions that ran through the entire week. Each day Nancy signed copies of her recently published biography and Olive signed copies of Vivian Bullwinkel's biography on behalf of her dear friend.

In a hectic, exciting week, the likes of which Kapunda had not seen before, there were garden parties, concerts, sporting events, musical performances by local school groups including the Kaurna Plains indigenous choir, a luncheon attended by World War II nurses and a grand, formal ball. In Olive's words Nancy was 'at her incorrigible best. She danced until 2 am on the night of the ball.

Our only minor hiccup occurred when I put a bottle of gin other than Gilbeys in her fridge and had to sit through a lecture on the medicinal qualities of pure juniper berries, but otherwise we got on like a house on fire'.

Sunday 23 September brought a beautiful spring morning and the memorial gardens looked superb even though the flowers planted in the outer gardens were yet to bloom. There was a large crowd, many of them dressed to the hilt. Ex-servicemen, including a number of Olive's US marine friends, wore their uniforms and service medals. Some townspeople wore formal outfits from the Victorian era in readiness for participation in a parade after the dedication at the gardens. It was all very colourful with a number of locals holding brightly coloured parasols. Steven was there with his carer, Katie, looking most spick and span. The Australian flag flew over the monument with the veiled bust of an army nurse and the American flag was at half mast adjacent to it in memory of the terrorist victims in New York almost a fortnight earlier. The 32-piece Gawler Brass Band and the Tamaresque musical group entertained the crowd from nine-thirty. At a quarter to eleven the playing of the 25-piece 10/27th Royal Australian Regiment Band indicated the official function was about to begin.

At precisely 11 am a three-gun salute announced the arrival of the state governor and his wife, Sir Eric and Lady Neal, who headed an official party that included senior officers representing the three armed forces, Mayor Shanahan, the state member Ivan Venning and the federal member Neil Andrew. The town crier, in full regalia, led the party down the path ringing his bell and announcing the governor's arrival. The entourage was escorted by an armed guard consisting of servicemen just back from eight months' service in East Timor. Olive, in her US uniform, walked at the head of the party, beside the governor, as Charles Smythe accompanied Lady Neal. It was a feeling of tremendous relief for them to see the fruition of their efforts. Most of the people would have had no idea of the problems they had encountered. Ita Buttrose was at the dais, attired in a smart mauve suit, having previously warned the crowd not to be alarmed at the three-gun salute.

After the military band had played the regal salute followed by the national anthem and 'God Save the Queen', Ita introduced herself to the crowd and told them how delighted she was to be back in Kapunda. She was excellent as usual. In fact she was using a radio microphone that intermittently lost sound and each time she realised what had happened she paused and took up again exactly where the sound had cut out. No one missed a word. Ita quoted from the foreword in Rob Charlton's book *The History of Kapunda*: 'The history of all country towns is interesting because they represent the organic growth, to which all the activities of a district contribute. Some, like Kapunda, are of outstanding interest. A town's character is determined by the people who live in it and the buildings they leave behind them. Kapunda has produced a highly diversified selection of outstanding people.' She went on to say:

Rob Charlton's book was first published in 1971 and reprinted in 1990 but some things never change. Kapunda is still producing outstanding people and it is their combined effort and vision that has brought us all here today for the official opening and dedication of these war memorial gardens. When future historians look at the legacy that this particular group of people has left behind it will say much about the calibre of the citizens of Kapunda in 2001. So congratulations to Charles

Smythe, director of the Centenary of Federation committee and to Olive Weston, chairwoman of the memorial gardens committee, and to all the members of both committees and to everyone else who has played a part. Would you please give them a round of applause for the very long, at times quite difficult, effort. What we see today is just beautiful and I'm sure we can all use our imaginations and envisage how splendid the gardens will look in the years to come.

Ladies and gentlemen, the significance of today's event has, I think, been magnified by the recent terrorist attacks on the United States of America. What a sobering experience that has been for us all. I'm sure I'm not the only Australian who has been rethinking my priorities over the last ten days or so. It has also been a time, I think, when we are reminded of the sacrifices that freedom demands from ordinary men and women. As Kapunda's Vivian Bullwinkel said not long before she died, 'I would like people to appreciate that the lives, opportunities and freedom for our young were bought at a price.' As we have been so graphically reminded by the events in America, we must never take freedom for granted. The Kapunda War Memorial Gardens will be a constant, living reminder of that fact.

There are many special guests here with us today including the inspirational Nancy Wake, who has travelled from Port Macquarie. As a resistance fighter in France known as the White Mouse, she was the Allies' most decorated servicewoman of World War II and the Gestapo's most wanted person. Her bravery has been honoured and admired by nations around the world. As one of her colleagues, Henri Tardivat, once said, 'Nancy is the most feminine woman I know until the fighting starts, then she is like five men.' Kapunda honours you today, Nancy, and we are delighted to have you here with us.

Welcome also to Major Vivienne Holmes, Captain Jean Ashton, Captain Betty Bradwell and other World War II veterans, POWs, service nurses — and a big Kapunda welcome to the former United States marines who are here and to members of the Girl Guides and to everyone to whom these memorial gardens have special meanings. The gardens, of course, will honour all men and women who have served in all wars in which Australia has committed troops since the Boer War, but in particular it will honour Australia's war service nurses.

Ita then introduced army chaplain Reverend Katie Inches-Ogden from Keswick Barracks, who led the congregation in prayer as the memorial service began. The very moving dedication service ran just on an hour as hymns were sung, the American and French anthems played and Betty Bradwell read the 23rd Psalm. Wreaths were laid by the governor and members of the official party as well as people from the audience, followed by the playing of the 'Last Post' and 'Reveille' by a lone bugler. The governor then dedicated the walkways and monument to the nurses who had served Australia. During a short address in which he congratulated Charles Smythe, Olive and the committee on their efforts he said, 'There is now a focal point in this town which provides a fitting tribute to men and women who have made enormous contributions in times of war. These memorials pay particular tributes to all the nurses who have given their lives in wars over the past century from the Boer War to the Vietnam War. As this year is also the centenary of the army, these memorial gardens are particularly timely.'

Olive sat expressionless as always when on parade, but well satisfied at Sir Eric's words. One hundred and one rose bushes had been planted to honour every nurse who had died in service, from the Boer War to World War II, including 45 whose bodies were never found. Their names appeared on a plaque adjacent to the monument, as did the names of Vivian Bullwinkel, Jean Ashton and Nancy Wake by their dedicated paths. Towards the end of the ceremony Lady Neal inspected the Midland Girl Guides who had been left, along with the children of Kapunda High School, to care for the gardens in future years. Onlookers were invited to attend a barbecue in the gardens at the end of proceedings.

At noon Olive attended morning tea with the special guests in the marquee followed by the vice regal luncheon for which the state government paid. It was their one financial contribution. A grand parade featuring vintage cars, vehicles from the Port Adelaide Military Museum, floats and costumed parties from the Victorian and Colonial Dance Societies preceded special presentations to Nancy Wake and geneticist Dr Judy Ford, who had been recognised as one of the top fourteen innovative South Australian scientists of the century. By the end of the day Olive was very weary but happy that the festival, and in particular the memorial gardens ceremony, had gone without a hitch:

I'd been in Kapunda staying with Nancy at Pepper Trees Bed and Breakfast for the entire week. I was so exhausted I went home to Christie Downs and slept for two days. Still, I was happy things had gone so well. Our ceremony had gone off with military precision, thanks very much to Reg McColl's planning, and Vivian would have loved it. We still had things to sort out and I felt very let down by the lack of support we received, but there was no point crying over that. I would never do it again. I couldn't afford to, for a start. The plaques are worded so as to give credit to the people of Kapunda for the restoration but even this was very generous — sadly, we got little support there either, apart from our volunteers. Ironically, of the three who had carried the load when the going got really tough, only Chas was from Kapunda. But we had honoured three marvellous women and all those war service nurses as well, so it was worthwhile, even if we were left holding the can. A day after I got home a lovely handwritten letter arrived for me. It proved to be the only letter of thanks I received, which made it even more special.

> Dear Lady Olive,
>
> It is the morning after and the gardens are having a good soaking as the heavens opened up last night and rain has been tumbling down ever since. I trust that you arrived home safely and relaxed enough to have a good night's sleep.
>
> You are an amazing lady — you have done for Kapunda, in just a few months, what Kapunda couldn't do for itself in all the years it has had at its disposal. Thank you so much.
>
> As they watch over the gardens the Guide Leaders will ensure that they create in the girls an understanding, certainly of the sacrifice of the women who served our country so selflessly, but also of the strength, the courage, the determination, the love, patience and understanding, combined with a desire to be of service — this is the legacy that is theirs from the women who have gone before to live and fight for this nation. All of that and a deep thankfulness that it is so.
>
> I am enclosing a 'guardian angel' — even if I suspect that you are one yourself. Lady Olive, please wear it with my love, respect and admiration.
>
> Daph Whitehead

I pinned the guardian angel to my blouse immediately. I also received a letter from a representative of Monash University saying how much he had enjoyed the ceremony and enclosing a personal donation towards the upkeep of the gardens. My correspondence with Neil Andrew over Kapunda was far from finished. After the federal election I wrote asking if debts we had incurred could be paid. I didn't mince words with him nor did he with me. I explained that we were in the red to the tune of $25 000 after being rejected by the Centenary of Federation and the Year of the Volunteers Small Grants programs. I told him and Bruce Scott, minister for veterans' affairs, his government had spent money on far less worthy projects and offered to show him all receipts and enclosed our final balance sheets to show how frugal we had been. I finished by saying 'I do hope you enjoy the video of the occasion and realise what an enormous effort it took to be like JC and make the loaves and fishes go so far'.

Olive did not have to wait long for the reply, which began: 'Thank you for your letter and the accompanying photographs of the memorable opening day for the Memorial Gardens at Kapunda.' The pleasantries dispensed with, he made his point:

> Grateful as I am for all that you have done to make the Bullwinkle [sic] Memorial possible, I am just a bit annoyed at the continuing theme in your letter that suggests that the Commonwealth should transfer funds from other projects such as the War Memorial in London to meet the Kapunda debt. Frankly an extension of that theme would see me freeze the Social Security budget for a quarter of a second to free up $25 000 for the Kapunda debt. The unpalatable fact is that no Government sector has been as generous as the Federal Government in helping to fund the Bullwinkle [sic] Memorial Gardens.

Having criticised the decision to spend beyond their budget the minister went on to say:

> I will of course, lobby the Federal Government once again for additional resources, and take up your case with the incoming Minister for Veterans' Affairs, Hon. Dana Vale. I recognise all that was done voluntarily by your committee and especially by yourself was done with the noblest of intentions and that an appropriate and overdue memorial to a number of heroines has resulted. The Federal Government however has not failed to assist in this process. With grants of approximately $15 000 it has responded more realistically than any other group.
>
> Since the Kapunda Gardens are not the only memorial in Australia to Sister Bullwinkle [sic] and to nurses who courageously died, the Federal government does not have sole responsibility for meeting this funding shortfall.
>
> I will, without prejudice, take up this matter with the minister. Can I encourage you to continue to make strong representations to the State Executive of the RSL and to the state and local government authorities whose involvement in this Kapunda-based project should at least match that of the Federal Government.
>
> In many ways Olive, you and I are in the same boat. You cannot be held responsible for the unfunded outlays which I suspect occurred in spite of your caution and I cannot be held solely responsible (on behalf of the federal government) for the funding of a local memorial. The risk for both of us is that our willingness to help resolve this impasse will mean that we will be seen as accountable for the decisions (or indecisions) of others.
>
> Yours sincerely,
> Neil Andrew

Neil Andrew had great respect for Olive and her efforts. While he thought she should have been leaning on others as much as she had on him, he would never underestimate just how hard she and her colleagues had worked. Unfortunately Olive never did hear from the new minister, a fact that disappointed but did not surprise her. Just one year later, after thousands of Flanders Field poppies had been sown by the Guides and bloomed on Remembrance Day, 11 November 2002, local state member Ivan Venning was so impressed he wrote to the editor of the *Kapunda Leader*.

Dear Sir, whilst walking around Kapunda on Saturday morning I was very impressed with the War Memorial Gardens at Dutton Park. It looks an absolute picture with the red and white roses, neatly kept lawns, the memorial, the fountain flowing and the flag flying. I couldn't help but feel very proud of this wonderful memorial in our community. It was certainly at its best for Remembrance Day and isn't that what it's all about?

I would like to pay credit to the Caravan Park manager Mr Terry Modra and his willing offsider Mr Ron Smith (who was on the job tending the garden when I was there.) Also congratulations to Council for their input. I was very pleased to learn Council has donated a new fence which will now fully enclose this magnificent area.

I'd encourage anybody who is willing and has the spare time and skill to contact Terry at the Caravan Park and offer assistance in erecting it. It certainly is a fitting tribute to those who lost their lives in our wars and a further tribute to those who upgraded the Memorial to its present condition and established the wonderful garden and are caring for it.

Ivan Venning MP, JP
Member for Schubert

Ivan Venning wrote to Olive in mid November.

Dear Olive, I write further to my letter of 10 October 2002 regarding the Kapunda Memorial gardens. Enclosed find a copy of my letter to the editor, published in this week's *Leader* newspaper.

I understand you were concerned about who was going to look after these gardens. All I can say is somebody is, because it looks absolutely magnificent at the moment. Council has just donated the remainder of the fence which was being put up Thursday last week.

It is all go! It is sad that Chas is not around to see this. The community certainly appreciate it, because it is looking an absolute picture. I believe that Terry Modra from the Caravan Park and his offsider Ron Smith are the linchpins. I understand Council has made arrangements with Terry to keep an eye on the Garden.

It certainly looks a picture. I have taken several photographs and will send you one as soon as I have them printed off.

Yours sincerely,

Ivan Venning

Member for Schubert

Sadly, the War Memorial Gardens which had impressed Ivan Venning so much and which Sir Eric Neal had so aptly described at the official opening as 'a focal point which provides a fitting tribute to men and women who have made enormous contributions in times of war' was not even used for the Remembrance Day occasion. Instead a ceremony took place in the RSL Club! So much for the focal point. Olive's fears had been justified in just twelve months. Her intention had been to set up a committee called 'friends of women at war', one of whose duties would be to look after the gardens. After the struggle to have the gardens restored it was just too much to do. She could only hope the great significance of the gardens would not be forgotten as it had been in the past.

Chapter Ten

LAST CHORE?

The whole Kapunda crusade had taken a lot out of Olive physically, financially and, above all, emotionally. She was, to be blunt, glad it was over. Never one to look for credit, she nevertheless felt her efforts, along with those of Chas Smythe and Reg McColl, were largely unappreciated, though Ivan Venning assured her this was not the case. Her aim had not been to see so much pressure on a small group of willing workers but to see the load more evenly spread. One group who did appreciate the amazing transformation of the memorial gardens and the wonderful opening ceremony were the citizens of Terowie, a much smaller town than Kapunda, some 220 kilometres north of Adelaide. Now boasting approximately 200 people, it was once a thriving railway town with ten times the population.

Founded in 1877, Terowie had special significance for those who travelled interstate from Adelaide. From the turn of the century it was the terminus where the railway tracks changed from broad to narrow gauge so all passengers were forced to change trains. Large railway works and shunting yards developed around the terminus and spawned a thriving township. All freight, including vast shipments of ore from Broken Hill, was also transferred from one train to another. Of the 2000 living in Terowie at its peak, several hundred worked for the railways or associated industries. After 90 years of prosperity the town shrank when the wide gauge line from Adelaide was extended. Terowie lost its railway workers, along with the trade that came from passengers with time and money to spend, and gradually most of its population. Olive found it easy to relate to those hardy citizens who stayed and showed such pride in the town's history. Terowie's main street retained its nineteenth century charm with a row of heritage-listed buildings, most of which act as small museums to the tourist trade upon which the town now depends. The Arid Lands Botanical Gardens are kept in perfect condition by volunteers from the Terowie Citizens' Association. This is typical of the town's spirit.

It was also of significance to those with knowledge of World War II. The town became a staging area for troops travelling north from Adelaide. The football field and its surrounds housed American troops in transit to Alice Springs and Darwin. It was here at that same time that Douglas MacArthur, his wife Jean, four-year-old son Arthur and a group of his special staff stopped to change from their private three-carriage train that had brought them from Alice Springs on the narrow gauge Ghan tracks to another that would take them to Adelaide and on to his headquarters in Melbourne. The Broken Hill Express was at the adjacent station when MacArthur's entourage arrived. Reporters had driven up from Adelaide and American and Australian troops cheered his arrival. Here MacArthur gave his first, unscheduled Australian press conference, uttering the famous phrase he would often repeat. On the original railway platform stands a large obelisk with a brass plaque that reads: '"I came out of Bataan and I shall return." This historic message that echoed around the world was given on this spot by US General Douglas MacArthur at his first press interview in Australia, 20 March 1942.'

The Citizens' Association, in conjunction with the South Australian Tourist Board, had planned a celebration to honour the sixtieth anniversary of the famous general's stopover. The old Country Women's Association hall was used to display photographs of MacArthur's arrival. It was naturally to be a military occasion and in view of their efforts at Kapunda, Olive, Charles Smythe and Reg McColl were invited to help organise the event. Local historian Huon Gray, whose wife Marina first contacted Olive, had produced a stylish and authoritative booklet, *MacArthur from Bataan and Back*, telling of MacArthur's escape from Corregidor, his exploits in Australia and his subsequent triumphant return to Bataan. Included were press photos taken of MacArthur and his family on Terowie Station.

On a typically hot summer's day with the temperature in the high thirties, a stoic crowd battled the dust and flies to pay tribute to the man who had come to Australia to command the Allied armed forces. Many carried parasols to ward off the heat. So little had changed since his brief visit, MacArthur would almost certainly have recognised the town. The Gawler Brass Band was playing a medley of American pop tunes including 'Won't You Come Home Bill Bailey' as the five-car motorcade carrying the official party slowly made its way down the gravel road to the platform. Each car carried the American flag. The entourage that included the local member Barry Wakelin, officers representing the three armed forces and retired chaplain Roy Hillman took their places on the station as the band launched into a rollicking version of 'Hello My Good Time Gal'. Mary Fisher, a member of the Terowie Citizens' Association, welcomed the crowd to the function which she explained was part of Terowie's Year of the Outback celebrations. As well as the salute to MacArthur's arrival, another highlight of the two-day celebrations would be a tribute to one of Australia's film pioneers, John Paterson McGowan, a former Terowie citizen.

After apologies were read by Charles Smythe, including one from Douglas MacArthur's son Arthur, Marina Gray read a letter from the prime minister also regretting his inability to attend and commending the citizens of Terowie for marking such an important anniversary. Curtis Johnson, director of flight operations for Kistler Aerospace, was next to the podium to read a letter from Don Meyer, a member of the New York Stock Exchange, on behalf of the MacArthur Society, which remarked on the wonderful friendship and alliance that Australia and America had formed during World War II and which remained to this day. Curtis was suitably attired for a Year of the Outback function in a purple open-necked shirt and black wide-brimmed Stetson hat. His strong Texan accent gave no indication that he had spent the previous three years at the Woomera Rocket Range.

Chaplain Roy Hillman, Royal Navy retired, paid a tribute to the British armed forces and led the congregation in prayer. When Olive's turn came to speak she was introduced by Charles Smythe who referred to her service in the 12th Station Hospital in Townsville and her award of the OOA, mentioning that she was the only Australian woman so honoured, as well as the OAM for 50 years service to the intellectually disabled. She strode to the dais in deliberate fashion and spoke with admiration of her former commander Douglas MacArthur:

Very early in the life of Douglas MacArthur he developed a conviction that he was a child of destiny. This crystallised into an ambition to become one of the great soldiers of history: an ambition that was amply fulfilled. He became not only one of the greatest generals in modern times but also the most dramatic of American military leaders. Douglas MacArthur emerged from World War I as the youngest divisional commander in the US Army. You all know the history of how he came to be here in Terowie and his now famous speech.

When he did return to the Philippines in 1944 in the midst of a raging battle he said slowly and emotionally, 'People of the Philippines, I have returned. By the grace of the almighty God our forces stand again on Philippine soil. The hour of your redemption is here. Please rally to me.' This was Douglas MacArthur at his most dramatic, rhetorical and flamboyant — perhaps posing for history. But as a successful leader much criticism came to him for his theatrical streak and it was this kind of posturing that can be condoned only if it is accompanied by genius — and that MacArthur had.

In 1942 in Australia's gravest hour, enter MacArthur. Australia lacked trained troops and equipment but what was needed even more was a charismatic leader. Our prime minister, John Curtin, for all his virtues, was not that man. On 17 March 1942 this country got the man it needed in General Douglas MacArthur, who was then confirmed as the Allies Supreme Commander of the South West Pacific area. Upon his arrival in Canberra he told parliament, 'We shall win or we shall die — and it is to this end that I pledge you all the full resources of all the mighty power of my country and all the blood of my countrymen. My faith in our ultimate victory is invincible and I bring to you the unbreakable spirit of the free men's military code in support of our cause.'

Then once again at the formal surrender ceremony on board the US battleship *Missouri* in Tokyo Bay on 2 September 1945 in

MacArthur's own words, 'We are gathered here, representatives of the major warring powers, to conclude a solemn agreement whereby peace may be restored to both victors and vanquished — to raise to a higher dignity which alone will fix the sacred purpose which we are about to secure, committing all our peoples unreservedly to faithful compliance with obligations that are here for me to assume. It is my earnest hope and indeed the hope of all mankind that from this solemn occasion a better world shall emerge out of the blood and carnage of the past. A world founded on faith and understanding, a world dedicated to man and fulfilment of his most cherished wish, freedom, tolerance and justice.'

The Supreme Commander then invited the Japanese delegates to sign the instrument of surrender. When all representatives had finished signing MacArthur announced slowly, 'Let us pray that peace be now restored to the world and that God will preserve it always.'

And then again at his exit from the US army upon his retirement at Westpoint his final farewell speech was that 'old soldiers never die they just simply fade away'. And that was MacArthur at his finest.

It was Olive at her finest also, quoting her 'former boss' in a fashion entirely appropriate to the occasion. Olive's military background, though set long ago, was still obvious in her carriage and her words. Following Olive's oration Captain Reg McColl, whose daughter was on duty as a peacekeeper under the watchful eye of US troops in Timor, made welcome representatives of the armed forces and spoke of the lasting ties between Australia and America and the one million lives lost by America in the two world wars. He concluded with these words:

Despite the unforgivable and horrific events of September the eleventh there was a clear message in America's response.

Freedom must be upheld at all costs. Former American president Woodrow Wilson stated, 'America was established not to create wealth but to realise a vision — to realise and to discover and maintain liberty among men.' America's 'Star Spangled Banner' is a particularly moving national anthem in these troubled times, relating the symbolism of the nation's flag flying strongly to inspire courage in the fight for freedom.

At Reg McColl's invitation the crowd sang along as the band played the American anthem and then observed a minute's silence for the victims of the recent terrorist attacks and the million servicemen who died in both wars. The ceremony ended with the reading of a poem by a local World War II veteran entitled 'Who Are These Men?', written by a twelve-year-old girl as a tribute to fallen heroes, followed by the playing of the 'Last Post'.

The highlight of the afternoon was a tribute to the little known Australian film pioneer John P. McGowan, who was born in Terowie in 1880, the same year the railway reached the town. McGowan settled in Hollywood in 1912 working as an actor and director. As such he became the first Australian to direct feature films in Hollywood. Like the famous stuntman and actor 'Snowy' Baker, John McGowan lived out his life in Los Angeles where he died in 1952. A plaque in his honour was unveiled at Pioneer Park and that evening the Terowie Institute screened silent films directed by McGowan, including *Cold Nerve*, which starred Buffalo Bill Cody as well as footage from Douglas MacArthur's army career. Tourists from Adelaide joined the locals to fill the hall. An estimated 500 people visited Terowie for the two-day celebrations.

When Olive returned to Christie Downs she looked back on a weekend that gave her genuine satisfaction. She had been with her close friends Chas Smythe and Reg McColl, celebrating a significant occasion from an era that would never be repeated. She was happy in the company of people mindful of their past and grateful for the efforts of those who had gone before them. When she received a copy of the *Terowie Enterprise* there on the cover was a photograph of Barry Wakelin, Curtis Johnson, Chas Smythe and herself on the gravel station where MacArthur had stood 60 years ago. She read the paper with interest and some humour when a report on the Pioneer Gardens said, 'The two pumpkins looked good until some kids used them for balls.' Boys, no doubt. Well, unless they were tomboys.

The ceremonies in Canberra and Kapunda had brought Olive into contact with heroines from the war. She was able to count Nancy Wake, Jean Ashton, Betty Bradwell, Vivienne Holmes and the late Vivian Bullwinkel among her friends. She had no illusions about being a hero herself despite Chas Smythe invariably introducing her as such:

They really were heroes and I was delighted to be brought together with them and to be able to do something to recognise the contribution they had made. I saw my association with them as something that was just meant to happen. It was strange that it occurred so long after the war, which was what we had in common. They were heroes but I was simply a humanitarian. I knew I wouldn't be involved in anything like it again. Nancy went to England soon after to live in the penthouse of the Stafford Hotel in St James's Place, a top-class London hotel. How she afforded it was beyond us. She wrote to Chas and me asking if we could help her to come back to Australia but she eventually settled down. A second letter to Chas revealed she'd had a minor stroke which curtailed her from moving about and asking for help in organising all her assets into Barclays Bank.

She was worried her reserves were getting a bit low explaining, 'I'm too old to get into prostitution! So no help from that quarter.' At 90 years of age her sense of humour was still very much intact. She was still sipping her Gilbeys and giving orders. Little wonder the Nazis didn't rattle her. She must have been born with the constitution of an ox.

Steven was very contented making furniture. He built some lovely pieces for the house including cabinets for the TV and stereo as well as a penholder for my office. We were in Coles buying meat when there was a minute's silence called at eleven o'clock in memory of Alec Campbell, the last Anzac, who had died in Hobart. The dear old chap was 103 and the occasion got to me, not so much because of his age but because it closed a chapter in our history. It was very moving to have everybody stop their shopping and pause to remember. Steven saw me shedding a few tears. He put his arm around me and said, 'Don't cry Mum, don't worry, Mum.' I had to smile. After all these years he was looking after his mother. My one remaining challenge was to do with Steven's future.

Steven had lived in the brick housing trust home in Christie Downs since 1985, first with friends and then with Olive. During that time some of his intellectually disabled colleagues had been able to move into their own homes left to them by their parents. They were still looked after by carers from Community Living but it gave them a feeling of independence and dignity. Steven decided he too would like to become a homeowner. He had given Olive no indication and she was quite surprised when he said one night, 'Mum, I'd like to own this place.' She thought about it for some time before saying, 'All right, Steven, we'll see what we can do.'

She approached the housing trust through Community Living. This had not been done before and government departments are notoriously difficult with situations outside their normal procedures. Still, the more Olive thought about it the more determined she was to see it happen. Once she made up her mind it was all just a matter of time. After many months of negotiations, during which Community Living Inc. were extremely helpful, it was agreed that Steven would put in his life savings and buy a one-third share of the house, thereby reducing his rent considerably. The trust would retain two-thirds with the proviso that Steven could buy a greater share if and when he saved more money. The house would be used by other members of Community Living after his death, but in the meantime he was master of his own destiny. Steven was very pleased. He would be 'the landlord', as he told his mother, and would be secure in the home for the rest of his life.

While Olive was negotiating the sale at Christie Downs, Charles Smythe became very ill. He had been operated on for lung cancer soon after the memorial gardens had opened in Kapunda and the reports had been very positive. Now the cancer had reappeared. Olive took off for her regular three-month holiday in Townsville, staying at her favourite haunt, the Spanish Horseshoe Apartments, just a short walk from Jezzine military barracks at Kissing Point. Community Living was finalising the arrangements for the sale but Chas was in a bad way. For the first time Steven announced he did not wish to accompany his mother north, something she found a little surprising as he enjoyed holidays so much. The previous year he had won a jackpot at the RSL club and when Olive awoke she found he had already gone out. As it transpired he had taken himself off to the casino for a 'slap-up' breakfast.

Despite her concern about Chas, Olive enjoyed her break in Townsville, taking advantage of the superb winter weather and enjoying the company of the proprietor of the apartments, Marion Easterbrook. They frequently went to the RSL club, which had, to

Olive's pleasure, resisted the temptation to copy the bigger city clubs and retained its military decor and observance of the past. On this holiday, following a chance meeting with Gabrielle Kelly, the very charming wife of Jezzine barracks' commanding officer, Brigadier Mark Kelly, she was invited to the barracks for morning tea. Subsequently Gabrielle and her sister Bernadette took Olive to lunch and on a trip to the Black Hawk Museum. She appreciated the gesture enormously. Olive always felt comfortable in the company of gentle-mannered people who observed protocol.

While in Townsville Olive learned of the death of one of her few remaining US army friends, John Thorsten. John was an original 32nd Division man, a veteran of the Red Arrows' campaign in Buna, and his death reduced the number of remaining American GIs from 40, when she first moved to Adelaide, to just three. Reluctantly she realised the branch would soon have to be disbanded. Earlier that year they had been relegated to marching behind the Greek contingent on Anzac Day. It was the first time they had not been immediately behind the Australians. 'Maybe because they got the next Olympics,' Olive said derisively. She had not been back in Adelaide long when Charles Smythe also died. She was very upset at his passing:

I found Chas to be a wonderful man. While he was battling his illness he became embroiled in a controversy over some antiques he had bought from a well-known legal identity who had fallen foul of the law. The media got wind of it and because of this association Chas was persecuted by them. It was terrible and I'm sure it hastened his demise. It was most unjust that he died under these circumstances. I couldn't speak too highly of him. He was a thorough gentleman without whom we could never have finished the memorial gardens, and a wonderful support to me, not only at Kapunda, but at Terowie as well.

A visit from Vivienne Holmes cheered me up immensely. She brought her cousin over from Western Australia to stay for ten days. We kicked up our heels in the Barossa Valley and had a whale of a time. In December Captain Jean Ashton, who was almost 98, passed away in an Adelaide nursing home. I was driven to Kapunda next day to place flowers at the memorial gardens in her honour. She would have been thrilled at how magnificent they looked. Later on I attended her funeral, pleased that the grand old lady had a wonderful send-off and that we had been able to perpetuate her name and deeds in the gardens at Kapunda. They sang 'The Captive's Hymn' for her as they had done at the laying of wreaths during the opening ceremony of the Service Nurses War Memorial in Canberra. She was the last of the South Australian World War II POW nurses to go and might well be the last of the lot. Of the 65 nurses who left Singapore in 1942 only 24 ever made it back to Australia.

There are images from Olive's life that will never fade. Her carefree childhood days among the estuaries and rock pools in North Queensland, mangoes and mud crabs, the fascination of lighthouse holidays. Armstrong Paddock, drinking gin with the Angels of Bataan, GIs on stretchers, caked in mud and blood, arriving in their hundreds from Buna, Douglas MacArthur walking alone around the military compound munching on a head of lettuce, arguing aloud with Churchill and Roosevelt, the US navy chiefs, even with himself. The dapper English radio officer with the impeccable manners aboard the *Ormonde*, the hunting lodge in Wales under a foot of snow, the feeling of triumph that came with Steven's first word, the joy of disabled kids on a farmhouse holiday, the drama of the aborted trip to Tennant Creek. There were still other incidents too painful to recall, ones that she cannot bear to discuss that she will take to the grave.

But Olive was never one to dwell in the past. There was always too much to be done. Her journey was shaped by one thing above all else. A refusal to accept injustice: a desire to help the underdog. First shown in a natural instinct to mother orphaned animals it manifested itself in half a century of fighting for the rights of the disabled:

I have always fought against injustice to the vulnerable and the disadvantaged; those people who have been sinned against rather than have sinned. I simply couldn't tolerate the thought of one person discriminating against a lesser person. Of all the changes in my lifetime the one that pleases me most is the acceptance of the disabled and the improvements that have emerged for them. I've seen prejudice and fear give way to understanding and respect. It's taken a long time for the majority of the population to accept them instead of thinking of them as people who should be locked away out of sight. Early in my life there were situations where a handicapped person would live in a street and no one would even know. It was that bad. This new attitude has been achieved by the work of devoted people, most of whom were never paid. They were, in the main, brave parents who fought the system. And it took a lot of courage and effort, especially in those early days. Generally speaking, governments couldn't care less. As far as they were concerned if a parent had a handicapped child that was just bad luck, they just had to lock them up. They would never have instigated change without years of harassment. The intellectually and physically disadvantaged now have a dignity that once could only be dreamed about.

But I haven't just seen injustice towards the disabled. What of the young men who served their country in wartime and who have been ignored ever since? The volunteers, young Australian servicemen with a sense of duty and adventure, who were subjected to mustard gas and other experiments and who have suffered ever since without compensation. A succession of governments initially refused to admit their claims and then procrastinated and blocked moves to have them properly compensated for fear of opening a floodgate. By the time the authorities got around to admitting what had happened the victims were either dead or too old to worry. And the heroes from Z Force who attempted a second covert operation to blow up shipping in Singapore Harbour and who were abandoned by their rescue vessel. They were tortured and beheaded only weeks before the war ended and their loved ones were never officially notified of their executions. Injustice in wartime was not all suffered at the hands of the enemy.

I was appalled to read the other day that the RSL finally 'admitted' that the Japanese did not intend to invade Australia. No doubt the invasion money I have was just part of a cunning plot to fool us old-timers. Apart from the fact that I don't believe it, all the announcement achieves is to belittle the efforts of those who gave their lives in defending Australia, and to forgive the Japanese for atrocities they never acknowledged and therefore never apologised for. Like the Bangka Island massacre and the execution by sword of the missionaries at Gona. Not a day goes past without my thinking of them.

I'm pleased, though, that there have been a lot of young people in recent years who have become involved in the Anzac Day march and pilgrimage to Gallipoli. To see kids marching with their grandparents' medals is marvellous. There can never be adequate thanks given to those young people who sacrificed their lives to save Australia. Now that the Anzacs have all gone perhaps more emphasis will be placed on the battles close to home in the Second World War. Heroism there was just as great. I'd like to see all kids taught about the history of the two great wars. To take pride in what we have means to understand the sacrifices that made it possible.

One of my personal regrets had always been that our part of the Weston dynasty would end with Steven. It isn't something that has eaten away at me but I've always been proud of my ancestors; those adventurers and rebels who came to Australia in search of fortune. And yet in recent years I've found it more and more difficult to feel positive about our future. I know it's a common thing for aged people to become melancholy and to feel no longer relevant, but my concerns are based on the problems that face the young today. I know, by talking to those who fought to protect our freedom, that many look back and wonder was it all worth it. I constantly ask myself if the world has gone mad.

In 1942 when General Gordon Bennett came out of South East Asia he told the powers to be that it was common knowledge that the Asians were boasting that if they could not take us by force they would do so with drugs. I know many people were worried by his predictions but the hierarchy tended to poo poo his words, suggesting they were meant as a distraction from the embarrassment of the fall of Singapore and the controversial circumstances of his own escape. How prophetic have his words proven to be? Instead of wasting time with political correctness in schools, which is a load of 'codswallop,' every effort should be channelled into teaching our gullible youths to say no, no, no to drugs. If there is no demand there will be no sales. It's frightening to think what might be ahead of our kids being born now.

We came out of World War II euphoric that evil had been conquered. There was such a feeling of joy and relief that peace was to be restored. Now we look at a world that is so dysfunctional, it's as if we have lost all sense of proportion in many ways. On the one hand we have enormous wealth in some countries and thousands dying of hunger and malnutrition in others. There is hatred and mistrust between countries and religions and it's impossible to see an end to it. Australians have always been fortunate enough to avoid the sort of violence that others had become used to but that's no longer the case.

We just have to despair at man's inability to learn from the horrors of the past. Where once we knew who our enemies were, we now live in fear of terrorism, a result of hatred that we have no real idea how to combat. Despite the rhetoric you can't get surrender from terrorists. How can there be a conclusion? People just don't have peace and harmony. It seems that the likelihood of world peace gets further and further away. Jean Ashton said, 'We pray that all will decide in their hearts that we must have no more war, and work to that end.' And yet we so often work towards peace through violence.

Some of our attempts to create internal harmony seem laughable. We're so committed to so-called political correctness we have schools here in Adelaide banning Santa Claus and even Christmas decorations because it might upset the minority. What about the majority? After 200 years here in Australia and hundreds more beforehand, we Anglo-Saxons are being asked to hide our Christmas festivities in case it upsets the newcomers. What absolute humbug. Imagine the community being so confused that something as joyous as Christmas and Santa Claus is being apologised for.

I'm sure people generally are more mercenary than they have ever been. Obviously there has always been greed but it has become an epidemic. Too often a person is admired for wealth above all else. Wealth does not necessarily equate to worth. Company executives pay themselves huge amounts of money even if they do a poor job. Politicians vote themselves pay increases at will. Does that mean we should admire them? Is it any wonder people have become sceptics?

I read a poll in the *Reader's Digest* just the other day where 1400 readers were asked to rate 26 vocations in order of trust. The top four were ambulance officers, fire fighters, pilots and nurses. The bottom six contained lawyers, journalists and, in very last place, politicians. Is it any wonder? So often their promises mean nothing and their estimates mean nothing. The memorial to the Australian troops in London that was to cost 6.4 million is now out to ten million dollars. I'm waiting for a week to pass without one of them being accused of cheating on their tax or their travelling allowance or similar. I'm sure they didn't just poll the oldies. We're not the only ones who are disillusioned.

Still, there are a lot of wonderful, unselfish people in the world. People who want to make a difference but can't find a way. Maybe one day we will give them more credence. I live in hope that another John Flynn will emerge as a hero to us all. And that we might get back to the basic Christian concepts of the Ten Commandments. I always remember that little poem taught to me by the nuns at St Joseph's in Cairns. It is so simple and I believe it says what most people really wish for. It could so easily be followed by us all.

I shall pass this way but once
And what good I can do let me do it now
Because I will not pass this way again.

Olive is not planning to meet her Maker for quite a while yet. She has ideas of a unit in a retirement village in Noarlunga and more pressing, minor, but important issues with the housing trust over repairs to the hot water system and a proposed rise in Steven's rent. Her frustrations at continually having to negotiate recorded messages in order to get some kind of service has her longing for the days 'when people answered phones, not machines'. She is not alone in this regard. Nevertheless she has mastered the system well enough to have booked her annual holiday in 'paradise', where she and her good friend Marion Easterbrook will seek out the most generous poker machine in Townsville's RSL. She and Steven also plan a trip to look up some old friends in Dunbogan and Laurieton.

Still, whenever He calls she will be ready. There will be no fear, no trepidation. Olive Clare Weston is, and always has been, a humanitarian. The 'bloody Australian rebel', as Frank occasionally called her, is quietly confident she will be well received.

GLOSSARY

AAMWS	Australian Army Medical Women's Service
DCA	Department of Civil Aviation
IDSC	Intellectually Disadvantaged Services Council
MO	medical officer
NAORU	Northern Australian Observation Reconnaissance Unit
RAAF	Royal Australian Air Force
RAF	Royal Air Force (UK)
RPA	Royal Prince Alfred Hospital
VAD	Voluntary Aid Detachmen

INDEX